THE UNITY OF THE BIBLE

BOOKS BY H. H. ROWLEY
Published by The Westminster Press

The Unity of the Bible
The Re-discovery of the Old Testament

THE UNITY OF THE BIBLE

*W. T. Whitley Lectures delivered at Regent's Park
College, Oxford, and Rawdon College, near Leeds,
and Julius Brown Gay Lectures delivered at Southern
Baptist Seminary, Louisville, Kentucky*

BY

H. H. ROWLEY

LONDON
THE CAREY KINGSGATE PRESS LIMITED
6 SOUTHAMPTON ROW, W.C.1

First published 1953
Second impression 1955

MADE AND PRINTED IN GREAT BRITAIN BY
MORRISON AND GIBB LIMITED, LONDON AND EDINBURGH

CONTENTS

THIS VOLUME IS INSCRIBED TO THE
FACULTY AND STUDENTS OF
THE SOUTHERN BAPTIST THEOLOGICAL SEMINARY
LOUISVILLE, KENTUCKY
IN GRATEFUL MEMORY OF THE FELLOWSHIP
I ENJOYED IN THEIR MIDST
AND IN MANY OTHER PLACES IN
THE UNITED STATES AND CANADA
THROUGH THEIR GENEROUS INVITATION

———

The 'W. T. Whitley Lectureship' was founded in 1949 for the purpose of encouraging Baptist scholarship, primarily (though not exclusively) in Great Britain. The Lectures are so named in grateful appreciation of the outstanding services rendered by the Rev. Dr. William Thomas Whitley, M.A., F.R.Hist.S., to the cause of Christian learning and Baptist historical scholarship.

PREFACE

When I was honoured by the invitation to deliver the first series of W. T. Whitley Lectures in Regent's Park College and Rawdon College, I proposed to gather together material which I had published in a number of separate papers in widely scattered places and to show that it was all related to the theme of the unity of the Bible. There is no part of my course of lectures with which I have not dealt at some time or other, usually at greater length than has been possible here. In their collection, however, I think that something more is gained than the mere placing of them side by side. For each can now be examined in the light of the others and of the whole, and it is my hope that added cogency will be found.

The emphasis on the unity of the Bible is not new with me, for many scholars have in recent years stressed it no less than I. Not all that I have said figures in the work of others on this subject, however, and if I have contributed something to its study I shall have done as much as any man can hope to do. Scholarship, like many other things, is essentially team work and every man receives from his colleagues more than he can hope to give, and is satisfied if he can bring some contribution to the totality of truth.

For the delay in the publication of these lectures I would express my regret. They were delivered at Regent's Park College in January and February, 1951, and at Rawdon College in January, 1952. It was my hope that in the interval they would be prepared for the press. In the autumn of 1951, however, I went to Denmark and Sweden, and then to Canada and the United States to lecture at a number of institutions. The arrangements for these visits were made in the early summer, and involved me in the necessity of devoting the summer to tasks which had been planned for the autumn, with the consequent deferment of attention to these lectures. Moreover, the shortness of the time made it impossible for me to prepare further lectures for the American visit, and I repeated these six lectures at the Southern Baptist Seminary, Louisville, Ky., and some parts of them at the South-western Baptist Seminary at Fort Worth, Texas, and elsewhere. My American visit was sponsored primarily by the Louisville Seminary, which undertook all the arrangements, and which invited me to deliver the Julius Brown Gay Lectures at Louisville. For all the warm friendship I found in Louisville and at a score of other places in Canada and the United States I would express my enduring gratitude.

The text of the lectures as published is almost identical with the spoken word. The additional work for which they have been waiting will be found in the footnotes. These I have kept to a minimum, save that in the concluding chapter I have been compelled to deal with the current discussions, which are more numerous here than in any other part of my subject. It would have been easy to add largely to the notes throughout the book, as may be seen by reference to some of the separate articles I have devoted to the parts of the subject. It would also have been easy to develop my theme at greater length than time permitted me in the spoken lectures. The result would have been something different from the Whitley and Gay Lectures, and perhaps less welcome to the general reader.

For help in the preparation of my manuscript of these lectures I am, as so often, indebted to my daughter, Margaret. Of the extent of that debt the reader can have little idea without seeing my original pages of footnotes. To compile them is easier than to reduce them to order, and I acknowledge with gratitude her skill and patience.

H. H. ROWLEY

Manchester

January 1953.

ABBREVIATIONS

A.J.S.L.	*American Journal of Semitic Languages and Literatures.*
A.Th.R.	*Anglican Theological Review.*
A.V.	Authorized Version.
B.J.R.L.	*Bulletin of the John Rylands Library.*
B.Q.	*Baptist Quarterly.*
B.Z.A.W.	Beihefte zur *Zeitschrift für die alttestamentliche Wissenschaft.*
C.B.Q.	*Catholic Biblical Quarterly.*
Cent.B.	Century Bible, edited by W. F. Adeney.
D.B.	*A Dictionary of the Bible*, edited by J. Hastings and J. A Selbie.
E.B.	Études Bibliques.
E.B.	*Encyclopaedia Biblica*, edited by T. K. Cheyne and J. S. Black.
E.R.E.	*Encyclopaedia of Religion and Ethics*, ed. by J. Hastings.
E.T.	*The Expository Times.*
E.Th.L.	*Ephemerides Theologicae Lovanienses.*
E.Th.R.	*Études Théologiques et Religieuses.*
E.Tr.	English translation.
G.J.V.	*Geschichte des jüdischen Volkes.*
H.J.	*Hibbert Journal.*
H.K.	Hand Kommentar zum Alten Testament, edited by W. Nowack.
H.S.A.T.	*Die Heilige Schrift des Alten Testaments,* 3rd ed., edited by E. Kautzsch; 4th ed., edited by A. Bertholet.
H.S.A.Tes.	Die Heilige Schrift des Alten Testamentes, edited by F. Feldmann and H. Herkenne.
H.U.C.A.	*Hebrew Union College Annual.*
I.C.C.	The International Critical Commentary, edited by S. R. Driver, A. Plummer, and C. A. Briggs.
J.A.O.S.	*Journal of the American Oriental Society.*
J.B.L.	*Journal of Biblical Literature.*

Δ*

J.B.R. . . . . . *Journal of Bible and Religion.*

J.N.E.S. . . . *Journal of Near Eastern Studies.*

J.Q.R. . . . *Jewish Quarterly Review.*

J.R. . . . . *Journal of Religion.*

J.T.S. . . . . *Journal of Theological Studies.*

K.A.T. . . . Kommentar zum Alten Testament, edited by E. Sellin.

O.T.S. . . . *Oudtestamentische Studiën.*

P.G. . . . . *Patrologia Graeca,* ed. by J. P. Migne.

P.L. . . . . *Patrologia Latina,* ed. by J. P. Migne.

P.R.E. . . . J. J. Herzog's *Realencyclopädie für protestantische Theologie und Kirche,* 3rd ed., ed. by A. Hauck.

R.B. . . . . *Revue biblique.*

R.G.G. . . . *Die Religion in Geschichte und Gegenwart,* 1st ed., edited by F. M. Schiele and L. Zscharnack; 2nd ed., edited by H. Gunkel and L. Zscharnack.

R.H.P.R. . . . *Revue d'histoire et de philosophie religieuses.*

R.S.V. . . . Revised Standard Version.

R.V. . . . . Revised Version.

S.A.T. . . . Die Schriften des Alten Testaments in Auswahl.

S.B.O.T. . . . The Sacred Books of the Old Testament, ed. by P. Haupt.

S.B.U. . . . *Svenskt Bibliskt Uppslagsverk,* ed. by I. Engnell and A. Fridrichsen.

S.D.B. . . . *Supplément au Dictionnaire de la Bible,* ed. by L. Pirot and A. Robert.

S.E.Å. . . . *Svensk Exegetisk Årsbok.*

S.J.T. . . . . *Scottish Journal of Theology.*

Th.L.Z. . . . *Theologische Literaturzeitung.*

Th.W.B. . . . *Theologisches Wörterbuch zum Neuen Testament,* ed. by G. Kittel.

Th.Z. . . . . *Theologische Zeitschrift.*

T.S.K. . . . *Theologische Studien und Kritiken.*

W.C. . . . . Westminster Commentaries, edited by W. Lock and D. C. Simpson.

Z.A.W. . . . *Zeitschrift für die alttestamentliche Wissenschaft.*

Z.N.W. . . . *Zeitschrift für die neutestamentliche Wissenschaft.*

Z.Th.K. . . . *Zeitschrift für Theologie und Kirche.*

I

UNITY IN DIVERSITY

WHEN the writer began his theological studies it would have
seemed a hazardous thing to announce a course of lectures on the
Unity of the Bible. The emphasis then was predominantly on
the diversity of the Bible, and such a title as that of the present
work would have involved some suspicion that the author was
an out-of-date obscurantist. Within the Old Testament the
antithesis between the legal and the prophetic books, or between
priestly and prophetic religion, was over-emphasized, and many
cherished the prophetic books as of abiding significance, while
treating priestly religion as something unworthy of serious
attention. Religiously, the prophets were regarded as rebels
against the religion which crystallized into Judaism. The predic-
tive element in prophecy was minimized[1] and messianic prophecy
was largely explained away, while the prophets were thought of
as preachers of righteousness and moral reformers rather than as
men who in any sense pointed towards the Founder of
Christianity.

Within the New Testament a similar antithesis to that between
priests and prophets was found between the Gospels and Pauline
religion, and even within the Gospels the historical Jesus was set
over against the Jesus as portrayed by the Evangelists.[2] Some-

[1] Cf. R. H. Charles, *Daniel* (I.C.C.), 1929, p. xxvi: 'Prediction is not in any sense an
essential element of prophecy, though it may intervene as an accident—whether it be a
justifiable accident is another question.'

[2] Cf. C. H. Dodd, *The Present Task in New Testament Studies*, 1936, p. 31: 'The kind of
interpretation I have in mind will in one sense reverse the main direction in which New
Testament studies moved for a century. Our principal aim has hitherto been to discrimin-
ate as clearly as possible between various books and *strata*, so as to isolate for intensive
study the special problems connected with each separate part; for example the Pauline
Epistles, the Fourth Gospel, the Synoptic Gospels, and within these the Marcan *stratum*,
the "Q" *stratum*, and so forth. This process of analysis should now be balanced by a
movement in the opposite direction.' Cf. also A. M. Hunter, *The Unity of the New
Testament*, 1943, p. 11: 'The diversity of the New Testament documents has been so
emphasized as to become almost axiomatic; and the quest on which we are now started'
(*i.e.* for unity) 'may well appear a quest for the non-existent.'

times the essence of the Christian message was reduced to a few simple principles that had no relation to the historical events out of which the Christian religion was born.[1] The bonds between the two Testaments were thus broken, and Jesus was regarded less as the fulfilment of the hope of the Old Testament than as the setter aside of the Old Testament and its religion. The preacher was often at a loss to know what to do with the Old Testament, and too frequently he largely ignored it.[2] When later the writer became a missionary, he heard it seriously lamented that the Old Testament had ever been translated into Chinese, and even during his student days he was once sternly rebuked by a well-known minister because he proposed to waste his life by devoting it to so dead a subject as the Old Testament.

During the years of the writer's working life a very considerable change of climate has come over Biblical studies, and the positions just broadly outlined are not the ones characteristic of present day scholarship. Nevertheless, it must be said at the outset that we owe an immense debt to the scholars of those earlier days. There is diversity in the Bible, and with all the emphasis on the unity of the Bible which will be found in the present work, the diversity in which that unity is found must not be forgotten.[3] It is impossible to reduce all to a flat uniformity, and the effort

[1] A familiar example of this is Harnack's simplification: 'If, however, we take a general view of Jesus' teaching, we shall see that it may be grouped under three heads. They are each of such a nature as to contain the whole, and hence it can be exhibited in its entirety under any one of them.

'Firstly, the kingdom of God and its coming.
'Secondly, God the Father and the infinite value of the human soul.
'Thirdly, the higher righteousness and the commandment of love.'

Cf. What is Christianity? E. Tr. by T. B. Saunders, 3rd ed., 1912 reprint, p. 52. Cf. ibid., p. 65: 'The fact that the whole of Jesus' message may be reduced to these two heads —God as the Father, and the human soul so ennobled that it can and does unite with Him—shows us that the Gospel is in no wise a positive religion like the rest; that it contains no statutory or particularistic elements; that it is, therefore, religion itself.'

[2] Cf. W. D. Davies, J.B.R., xx, 1952, p. 234a: 'Few scholars in the early years of this century attempted closely to define the relation of the Old Testament to the New Testament and they often approached the New Testament not through the portal of the Old Testament, but through the somewhat alien classical disciplines.'

[3] Cf. F. C. Grant, An Introduction to New Testament Thought, 1950, p. 29: 'This Pauline statement of the doctrine of unity in diversity (1 Cor. xii. 4-6) ought to be inscribed as a motto over all our study of the New Testament.' We might go farther and say 'over all our study of the Bible'.

to make Old Testament and New Testament say the same thing is dishonouring to both Testaments. Without overstressing the difference between prophetic and priestly religion, diversity of emphasis may be recognized, and we can never go back on that recognition of the prophets as real men in human situations, which we owe to earlier scholars. Similarly in the New Testament, even though we draw our lines less sharply we may rightly recognize the individuality of the various writers. It is unnecessary to close our eyes to the diversity in order to insist on the unity, or to close our eyes to the unity in order to insist on the diversity.[1]

It is not without significance that during the present century there has been a growing sense of the fundamental unity of the Churches. The gibe of those who belong to no church that it will be time for them to take Christianity seriously when the Churches can agree as to what is Christianity and cease to present so many rival brands has less point than it once had. The Churches have learned to cooperate in ways once undreamed of, and have recognized that more important than all their differences are the things in which they are united. Nevertheless their diversity is no less real than it was, and shows little sign of being eliminated. This is not to say that equal validity belongs to their diversity, and any claim that it did would be resisted by the representatives of them all. It is but to say that while their diversity must be freely recognized, their underlying unity is of greater significance than the things on which they are divided.

In a somewhat similar way, the diversity of the Bible must be recognized fully and clearly, even though we see a more profoundly significant unity running through it all. Nor is it to be

---

[1] Cf. C. H. Dodd, op. cit., p. 32: 'The unity of the New Testament is original, underlying the diversity of the individual writings'; F. C. Grant, op. cit., pp. 45 f.: 'The most significant thing is, of course, not the variety in New Testament Theology, with each type to be studied in isolation, but the consistency, the unity, the unity in and through variety, the consentient testimony, what might almost be called the "catholicity" of the New Testament. . . . This is the result, not of later conformation or selection, . . . but of loyalty and fidelity to a common origin in the apostolic proclamation of the gospel, and of a participation in a common religious outlook rooted and nurtured in the Old Testament.'

supposed that in arguing for the unity the writer is claiming an equal value for all the varieties in which that unity is found. There are differences of emphasis as between law and prophets, and it is permissible to value the one above the other, even though rich common elements are found beneath their antitheses. There are some books of the Old Testament, such as Proverbs and Ecclesiastes and the Song of Songs, which on any showing fall below the spiritual heights of either law or prophets, without being deemed alien to the essential message of the Old Testament. In the same way differences between the Old Testament and the New, differences whose reality and importance may be recognized by Jew and Christian alike, can be discerned without excluding a bond of unity between the two Testaments which is of the utmost significance. In the New Testament, again, the very different atmosphere of the Gospels and the Epistles, or even of the Synoptic Gospels and the Fourth Gospel, may be frankly acknowledged, without accepting the conclusion that they were written by men who had irreconcilably different ideas about the Christian faith.[1]

So far as the Old Testament is concerned, it is important to observe that during the last thirty years there has been a growing interest in its theology. When the writer referred to this interest in a book published during the War,[2] an American reviewer observed: 'It may be true in North Wales that "there is a revived interest in the theology of the Old Testament as against the development of the religion of Israel", but this would scarcely describe the scholarly trend in this country.'[3] The reviewer was patently ignorant of what was happening in his own country, as well as of what was happening in the rest of the world. For in addition to articles in journals and books which testified of that

---

[1] Cf. C. H. Dodd, *The Bible To-day*, 1946, p. 2: 'Whatever may be the religious purport of the Bible, it is to be found in the whole range of the biblical presentation of life. . . . With all its variety there is after all a real unity in this literature.' Cf. also A. M. Hunter, *The Unity of the New Testament*, 1943, p. 7: 'There is a growing recognition of the essential unity of the New Testament and of the need for synthesis.'

[2] *The Relevance of the Bible*, 1941, p. 17.

[3] Cf. *The Christian Century*, October 25, 1944.

interest,[1] there were published in America within a few years of the appearance of the review two volumes devoted to the theology of both Testaments,[2] and a work devoted to Old Testament theology,[3] by writers of very different Protestant schools, and a translation into English of a German Roman Catholic work on the same subject.[4] In addition an important *Preface to Old Testament Theology* bore its evidence of American interest in the subject.[5] In the decade preceding the War three German works on Old Testament theology appeared,[6] two of which have gone into new editions since the War, while during the War the Roman Catholic work which has now been translated into English appeared in Germany.[7] This work has also been translated into Italian.[8] A further posthumous work by a Protestant scholar has been issued in Germany since the War.[9] A Dutch work on the theology of the Old Testament has

---

[1] Cf. J. Muilenburg, 'The Return to Old Testament Theology', in *Christianity and the Contemporary Scene*, ed. by R. C. Miller and H. H. Shires, 1943, pp. 30 ff.; J. D. Smart, 'The Death and Rebirth of Old Testament Theology', *J.R.*, xxiii, 1943, pp. 1 ff., 125 ff.; W. A. Irwin, 'The Reviving Theology of the Old Testament', *ibid.*, xxv, 1945, pp. 235 ff.; R. C. Dentan, 'The Nature and Function of Old Testament Theology', *J.B.R.*, xiv, 1946, pp. 16 ff.; O. J. Baab, 'Old Testament Theology: its Possibility and Methodology', in *The Study of the Bible Today and Tomorrow* (ed. by H. R. Willoughby), 1947, pp. 401 ff. Cf. C. T. Craig, 'Strangely, it is in the Old Testament that the fullest development of biblical theology has come during the present revival' (*J.B.L.*, lxii, 1943, p. 293).

[2] Millar Burrows, *An Outline of Biblical Theology*, 1946; G. Vos, *Biblical Theology: Old and New Testaments*, 1948.

[3] O. J. Baab, *The Theology of the Old Testament*, 1949.

[4] P. Heinisch, *Theology of the Old Testament*, E. Tr. by W. Heidt, 1950.

[5] R. C. Dentan, *Preface to Old Testament Theology*, 1950. In addition the following American books, while not formally devoted to the study of Old Testament theology, testify to the interest in the subject: W. F. Albright, *From the Stone Age to Christianity*, 1940; G. E. Wright, *The Challenge of Israel's Faith*, 1944; R. B. Y. Scott, *The Relevance of the Prophets*, 1944; W. A. Irwin, *The Old Testament, Keystone of Human Culture*, 1952.

[6] E. Sellin, *Theologie des Alten Testaments*, 1933; W. Eichrodt, *Theologie des Alten Testaments*, I, 1933, II, 1935, III, 1939; L. Köhler, *Theologie des Alten Testaments*, 1936. Cf. also J. J. Stamm, *Erlösen und Vergeben im Alten Testament*, 1940, S. Herner, *Sühne und Vergebung in Israel*, 1942, and W. Eichrodt, *Das Menschenverständnis des Alten Testaments*, 1944 (E. Tr. by K. and R. Gregor Smith, 1951); also C. Steuernagel, 'Alttestamentliche Theologie und alttestamentliche Religionsgeschichte', in *Vom Alten Testament* (Marti Festschrift), 1925, pp. 266–273; O. Eissfeldt, 'Israelitisch-jüdische Religionsgeschichte und alttestamentliche Theologie', *Z.A.W.*, xliii (N.F. ii), 1925, pp. 1–12; W. Eichrodt, 'Hat die alttestamentliche Theologie noch selbständige Bedeutung innerhalb der alttestamentlichen Wissenschaft?', *Z.A.W.*, xlvii (N.F. vi), 1929, pp. 83–91.

[7] P. Heinisch, *Theologie des Alten Testamentes*, 1940.

[8] P. Heinisch, *Teologia del Vecchio Testamento*, Italian Tr. by D. Pintonello, 1950.

[9] O. Procksch, *Theologie des Alten Testaments*, 1950.

now appeared,[1] and a French work is in course of pre-paration.[2] This list will sufficiently show that the writer had a more than insular interest in North Wales and its thought, and that there was, and is, a revived interest in this subject.[3] Singularly enough, no work bearing the title Old Testament Theology has been published in Great Britain in recent years, though many books and articles have testified of the interest it commands.[4] Principal H. Wheeler Robinson had pub-lished the Prolegomena to such a work before his death,[5] and had planned a full-scale treatment of it, but did not live to complete it.[6]

This interest in Old Testament theology testifies to the growing

---

[1] Th. C. Vriezen, *Hoofdlijnen der Theologie van het Oude Testament*, 1949.

[2] E. Jacob, *Théologie de l'Ancien Testament*, to be published by Delachaux and Niestlé in the series 'Manuels et Précis de Théologie'. Cf. also J. Guillet, *Thèmes Bibliques*, 1950, and earlier J. Guitton, *Le Développement des Idées dans l'Ancien Testament*, 1947, and A. Gelin, *Les Idées Maîtresses de l'Ancien Testament*, 1948. Also F. Michaeli, *Dieu à l'image de l'Homme*, 1950.

[3] It should be added that in an article reviewing Dentan's above-mentioned work, E. R. Lacheman challenged the value of this revived interest (*J.B.R.*, xix, 1951, pp. 71 ff.), and concluded: 'I cannot see what an Old Testament theology could do that a history of the religion of the Old Testament could not do much better' (p. 75a).

[4] H. Wheeler Robinson published a short sketch of 'The Theology of the Old Testa-ment' in *Record and Revelation*, 1938, pp. 303–348. There have been many books written in the field of Old Testament or Biblical theology, though not dealing formally and systematically with the subject, or monographs on individual doctrines, *e.g.*, W. J. Phythian-Adams, *The Call of Israel*, 1934, *The Fulness of Israel*, 1938, *The People and the Presence*, 1942; C. Ryder Smith, *The Bible Doctrine of Salvation*, 1941, *The Bible Doctrine of Man*, 1951; H. H. Rowley, *The Rediscovery of the Old Testament*, 1946, *The Biblical Doctrine of Election*, 1950; N. H. Snaith, *The Distinctive Ideas of the Old Testament*, 1944; H. Knight, *The Hebrew Prophetic Consciousness*, 1947 (Part 2 is devoted to Theology); C. R. North, *The Thought of the Old Testament*, 1946. Of recent articles in which the problems attaching to the treatment of the theology of the Old Testament are considered, the following may be noted: N. W. Porteous, 'Towards a Theology of the Old Testa-ment', *S.J.T.*, i, 1948, pp. 136 ff., 'Semantics and Old Testament Theology', *O.T.S.*, viii, 1950, pp. 1 ff.; C. R. North, 'Old Testament Theology and the History of Hebrew Religion', *S.J.T.*, ii, 1949, pp. 113 ff.; A. S. Herbert, 'Is there a Theology of the Old Testament?', *E.T.*, li, 1949–50, pp. 361 ff. For a survey of recent work in the field of Old Testament theology, cf. N. W. Porteous, 'Old Testament Theology', in *The Old Testa-ment and Modern Study* (ed. by H. H. Rowley), 1951, pp. 311 ff.

[5] *Inspiration and Revelation in the Old Testament*, 1946.

[6] A. R. Johnson is publishing a series of monographs which together will constitute his prolegomena to the study of Biblical Theology. Of these three have been issued: *The One and the Many in the Israelite Conception of God*, 1942; *The Cultic Prophet in Ancient Israel*, 1944; *The Vitality of the Individual in the Thought of Ancient Israel*, 1949. Some of the articles in the *Theologisches Wörterbuch zum Neuen Testament* (ed. by G. Kittel) have been published in an English translation made by J. R. Coates in the series 'Bible Key Words'

sense of the unity of the Old Testament.[1] So long as its parts
were set over against one another, and their diversity emphasized
to the neglect of their unity, it was out of the question to discuss
the theology of the Old Testament. The very term implies a
unity which was felt to be lacking. That a wider unity of the
Bible is being increasingly recognized is evidenced by the
demand for commentaries which offer a Christian interpretation
of the Old Testament. While there are obvious dangers in such
a demand, it is right that we should view the Old Testament in
terms of that to which it has led as well as of that out of which
it arose. The full significance of Magna Carta is not seen merely
in the study of the reign of King John, any more than the full
significance of the invention of the wheel is to be found in the
first primitive vehicle in which it was used. Ideas and inventions,
once launched, have a life of their own, which their creators
cannot foresee. Similarly the spiritual ideas which were given
to men through the leaders of Israel, and which were enshrined
in the Old Testament, had a life which extended into the New
Testament, as well as into post-Biblical Judaism.[2]

It will be perceived already that the kind of unity which the
writer sees in the Bible is a dynamic unity and not a static unity.
He recognizes development, and in particular development
from the Old Testament to the New. Yet, lest he be misunderstood, let it be said here, as he has often said elsewhere, that it is
not to be supposed that development was brought about by the
unfolding of the human spirit through the mere passage of time.

and all of these review the teaching of the Old Testament on these doctrines. The volumes
so far issued are *Love*, by G. Quell and E. Stauffer, 1949, *The Church*, by K. L. Schmidt,
1950, *Sin*, by G. Quell, G. Bertram, G. Stählin, and W. Grundmann, 1951, *Righteousness*,
by G. Quell and G. Schrenk, 1951, *Apostleship*, by K. H. Rengstorf, 1952, and *Gnosis*,
by R. Bultmann, 1952.

[1] Cf. H. H. Rowley, 'The Unity of the Old Testament', *B.J.R.L.*, xxix, 1945–46,
pp. 326–358, and separately. Cf. also the chapter 'The Unity of the Bible', in *The Relevance
of the Bible*, pp. 77 ff., and Mary E. Lyman, 'The Unity of the Bible', *J.B.R.*, xiv, 1946,
pp. 5 ff.

[2] Cf. C. H. Dodd, *According to the Scriptures*, 1952, p. 131: 'It would not be true of any
literature which deserves to be called great, that its meaning is restricted to that which
was explicitly in the mind of the author when he wrote. On the contrary, it is a part of
what constitutes the quality of greatness in literature that it perpetuates itself by unfolding
ever new richness of unsuspected meaning as time goes on.'

There is no automatic spiritual growth of mankind, and the Bible nowhere tells the story of such a growth. It records how men of God, acting under a direction which they believed to be of God, mediated ideas and principles to men. It does not tell how men by the exercise of their minds wrested the secrets of life and the universe from a reluctant Unknown, but how God laid hold of them and revealed Himself through them. If there is any truth in this, then a unity of the Bible is to be expected. If God was revealing Himself, then there should be some unity about the revelation, since it was the same Being Who was being revealed. There is still room for diversity, since God was revealing Himself to men of limited spiritual capacity and could only reveal to each what he was capable of receiving.[1] There are branches of Higher Mathematics which no one could apprehend without a long and exacting process of preliminary teaching. Similarly, there are secrets of the spirit which could only be imparted to men in the measure of their spiritual capacity to receive them. Moreover, since God chose to reveal Himself not alone to men, but through them, He was limited by the medium that He chose. That is why the full revelation in human personality required the Incarnation. The variety of the levels of the various parts of the Bible is then not surprising, and it does not spring from any variation in God, but from the variety of the levels of the persons whom He used.

Here I may appear to be passing from the realm of the scientific study of the Bible into the realm of dogma. To study the Bible simply as a human story, and to treat of men's beliefs about God without asking what validity they have, is sometimes thought to be the scientific study of the Bible. This tacitly assumes that there was no validity in their beliefs, since if there was validity, and if men were genuinely moved by God, the story cannot be fully understood while ignoring the supremely important factors in it. Science seeks to trace results back to their causes, and causes

---

[1] Cf. J. W. C. Wand, *The Authority of the Scriptures*, 1949, p. 62: 'Inspiration does not put man's common faculties to sleep while God is left alone to speak, but it quickens these faculties beyond the point of genius.'

forward to their results, and any truly scientific study of the Bible must ask for all the facts of a situation, and not merely for a selection of them. If we merely study the message of the Bible in the light of the political and social circumstances out of which its books were born, we are just as guilty of a dogmatic approach as the theologian may be. For it is just as dogmatic to suppose that God is not a vital factor in human affairs as to suppose that He is.

We are sometimes challenged to prove that God exists, and that He is active in the world. It is supposed that the admission that this cannot be proved in the same sort of way as that whereby we can prove that the three angles of a triangle equal two right angles means that we are left with a groundless faith. It is forgotten that it can no more be proved in that sort of way that God does *not* exist and that He is *not* active in the world. If abstract logic and mathematical reasoning alone can be employed, and nothing short of rigid proof be accepted, we are inevitably left with an arid agnosticism. But it is quite irrational to limit ourselves to abstract reasoning of this kind. We are all familiar with the problem of the hare and the tortoise, in which we are faced with the fact that a hare that ran ten times as fast as a tortoise and that gave the tortoise a certain start would find that by the time it reached the tortoise's starting point the tortoise had advanced one tenth of the distance, and that however often it repeated this performance it would still find the tortoise a further one tenth ahead, leading to the conclusion, which experience would soon prove to be fallacious, that the hare could never overtake the tortoise. All that is really proved is that within the distance covered by the series

$$1 + \frac{1}{10} + \frac{1}{100} + \frac{1}{1000} \quad \cdots \cdots$$

the hare would not overtake the tortoise, and this means that within the time that the hare would take to cover $1\frac{1}{9}$ times the distance originally separating them it could not overtake the tortoise. Within the limits of this geometrical progression there could be no overtaking. The fallacy lies in first limiting ourselves to this progression and then drawing a conclusion that goes beyond its limits. A similar fallacy is to be seen in the conclusion that because the Being and activity of God cannot be proved by abstract reasoning, the belief in God is an unscientific dogma.

Science is by no means limited to abstract reasoning, and it works with a great number of hypotheses for which it can advance no absolute proof. Yet they are not groundless hypotheses. There are many lines of evidence that point towards them and make them reasonable hypotheses, but they are not subject to rigid demonstration. The scientist tests his hypotheses in every way he can, and the more they stand his tests the more faith he has in them, even though he continues to recognize that they are theories, which are not susceptible of absolute proof. He is too scientific to profess the sort of agnosticism about them which leads him to ignore them. He relies on them and uses them, and they enable him to make the advances which have revolutionized modern life.

It is just as scientific in our sphere for us to test in every way we can the faith that the activity of God in human experience and personality is recorded in the Bible, treating this not as a dogma which must be accepted without question but as a faith to be examined, and to ask whether it may be reasonably established, and not whether it can be rigidly proved. The scientific method must be appropriately applied to each separate discipline. But when it is applied, what survives may be trusted without disloyalty to the scientific spirit.

The Bible records that Moses was sent by God into Egypt to lead the Israelites out, and that in obedience to this commission Moses went to Egypt and promised the Israelites deliverance. That deliverance was effected, but not by the exercise of any power which Moses or the Israelites possessed. In the supreme moment it was effected by powers of Nature, which lie beyond human control. This story hangs together as a consistent whole. If Moses was genuinely commissioned and inspired by God, and the promise of deliverance came from God and if its fulfilment was effected by God, all would be intelligible. But as soon as we begin to discard any of these elements, we find ourselves in difficulties. If Moses was not really called by God, but merely fancied himself to be so called, we are left without any explanation of the fulfilment of his promises. If they arose from nothing deeper than his own wishes and dreams, there lay here no power to set in motion the forces of Nature for their fulfilment. If, on the other hand, we suppose that it was by a fortunate coincidence that the forces of Nature effected the deliverance, we are left without any explanation of the prior confidence of Moses and the promise of deliverance which he brought. To distribute the elements of the story amongst self-deception and chance is to offer no explanation; to find the hand of God in it is to find a simple and sufficient explanation.

We may avoid this, of course, by casting doubt on the historicity of the whole story. If we wish to be scientific, however, we must not be content with an irrational doubt that merely relieves us of what we do not find it convenient to accept. That is as unscientific as an unquestioning credulity. It is undoubted that the present form of the story is from a much later time than the age of Moses, and it is well known that tradition can influence the form of the story it transmits. We cannot rely on the details of a tradition which may have been handed down orally for a long time, even though we recognize that tradition often shows great tenacity in small as well as in great matters. For along with tenacity here there may be accretion there. All this is quite insufficient to cast doubt on the main outlines of the story, as they have been set out above. We may leave out of account all the frills of the story, which may or may not be accretions, and build only on the central elements of the tradition, which may on every ground be accepted as reliable. There is no serious reason to doubt that a body of Israelites was once in Egypt and later came forth. This event was too deeply stamped in the memory and tradition of Israel to be wholly groundless. There is no reason to doubt that Moses went into Egypt from the desert to bring them forth. No rational explanation of the creation of such a tradition can be offered, if it contained no truth. There is no reason to doubt that the deliverance of the Israelites was not effected by their own activity and power, but by forces beyond their control and beyond the control of Moses. No people would have invented the story that it and its leader were passive in the supreme moment of peril, if they were not. There is no reason to doubt that Moses promised deliverance in the name of Yahweh, and that after deliverance the people committed themselves to this God in a sacred covenant. If this is denied, we are left without any clue to much in the Old Testament that finds its simple explanation in terms of this. If all this story is denied any historicity, we have not only to explain how and why it came to be invented, but what was the true origin of that which is explained in this story, and why the true origin was wholly suppressed, leaving itself to be recreated out of nothing today. The way of the sceptic is much harder than the way of faith, and an unreasoning prejudice can lay no claim to be called scientific.

Nor are we in better case even if we dispose of the story of Moses by mere denial. There can be no reasonable doubt that the whole of the Old Testament was written before the birth of Jesus. Throughout the Old Testament we find that it looks beyond itself to a fulfilment that lay in the future. In remarkable ways we find in the New Testament the fulfilment of the anticipations of the Old, and at these we shall look later. If the anticipations rested on the activity of the Spirit of God in men, and the fulfilment represented the activity of God in history and experience, we have a sufficient explanation of all. But if we wish to reject this explanation, we are hard put to it to find another which is more scientific and more satisfying. If the anticipations had no basis but the false claim that men were the mouthpiece of God, their fulfilment becomes a problem. There could have been no power in such self-deception to influence future events. On the other hand, we cannot suppose that the anticipations were a reflection of the fulfilment in subsequently created stories, since the anticipations were quite certainly written down before the fulfilment took place.

Again, when we come to the New Testament, we find that Jesus believed that His life and death were of universal and enduring significance, and that in Him the fulfilment of many of the deepest hopes of the Old Testament was to be found. That His expectations have been realized in ways that would have seemed fantastic to any of his contemporaries who rejected His claims cannot be denied. Once more, if we find the activity of God in the Christ Who promised and in the historical fulfilment, we have a sufficient explanation of all. But if we reject this, we find ourselves in difficulties. If Jesus was deluded, there could be no power in His delusions to effect their own fulfilment. On the other hand we cannot explain the delusions by the fulfilment. We may try to turn the edge of this by attributing the relevant sayings to the evangelists, or to others than Jesus who composed them after His death. Yet by the time when the Gospels were written there was little in the historical position of the Church to justify these hopes, and their creation out of the womb of the Church's thought could still not explain the fulfilment that has been experienced.

In all of these, and in other cases that could be added to them, the single hypothesis that the finger of God is to be found in expectation and in fulfilment is adequate, whereas if this is denied no single explanation of all can be found, but a variety of unrelated suggestions must be made in the vain effort to account for each separate fragment of the whole, and none of the suggestions is really adequate for the work that is demanded of it. It is surely more in accordance with scientific method to adopt the one hypothesis that is sufficient. This is neither to accept it as dogma, irrationally received on authority from some other human source, nor to claim that it can be proved in a way that dispenses with faith.[1] Reason and faith are alike involved, just as reason and faith are both involved in the acceptance of scientific theory.

This long digression has been necessary to make it clear that

---

[1] Cf. the writer's Joseph Smith Lecture on *The Authority of the Bible*, 1950, where it is argued that the authority of the Bible is ultimately the authority of the God Who is behind the Bible, and Whose hand is revealed in correspondences which could not be mutually determined.

when the writer speaks of the dynamic unity of the Bible, he is not thinking in terms of a merely human development that leaves God out of account, nor yet falling back on traditional dogma that leaves reason out of account. It is sometimes suggested that the real issue is between humanism and faith, and it is forgotten that humanism is as much a faith as the Christian faith. The important question is which is the true faith, and that means which is most deeply grounded on evidence and sustained by reason.

By the use of the term dynamic unity it is clear that it is not proposed to argue that the whole of the Bible is on a flat level of inspiration and authority, and that all so completely presents the same message that texts can be culled indiscriminately from all parts of the Bible and made the rule of life.[1] Whatever definition of the inspiration of Scripture men may offer there is none who really holds this in practice. Not a little in the Old Testament is superseded in the New, and even where there is no explicit supersession Christians recognize that whatever is alien to the spirit of Christ and His revelation of God has no validity for them. In other words, Christ is for them the standard whereby the Old Testament must be judged as a revelation of the character and will of God. When Jesus said 'Ye have heard that it was said of old time . . . But I say unto you',[2] He declared that not everything in the Old Testament is of enduring authority for men.

There are some who would maintain that what is superseded in the Old Testament represents what was the authoritative will of God for men in the particular age and in the particular circumstances at the time when it was given, and who find God to be wholly responsible for every statement found in the Bible. That this is not satisfying is clear from the fact that conceptions of God which fall below the standards of the highest in the Old Testament are found in some passages, and it cannot be that the God Who revealed Himself deliberately gave men false ideas about Himself. Samuel believed that God delighted in wholesale and unprovoked

[1] Cf. the writer's *Relevance of the Bible*, pp. 21 ff.
[2] Matt. v. 21 f., 27 f., 33 f., 38 f., 43 f.

14

massacre,[1] and Micaiah that God could send forth a lying spirit to deceive men.[2] David believed that God could find pleasure in the hanging of Saul's descendants in Gibeah to atone for some crime of Saul's long years before,[3] though we are told elsewhere that it is contrary to the will of God for children to be put to death for their fathers' sins.[4] In the New Testament we read that no man hath seen God at any time.[5] Yet in the Old Testament we have many stories of men who saw God and talked with him as man to man.[6] In all such disagreements it is important first of all to remember that each passage must be read in the light of its own literary form, and a wooden literalism, that we should never bring to poetry, should not be brought to forms of literature that have not a little in common with poetry. It is important also to remember the human element in all of these situations.

The Divine inspiration came through the organ of men's personality. Though they were men who were consecrated to God and sensitive to His Spirit, they were nevertheless imperfect men, with false presuppositions and with limited outlook. While the revelation which was given through them was the revelation of God, it bore the marks of the persons through whom it came, and its imperfections derive from them and not from the source of the revelation. Nevertheless—and this is the important thing— there was revelation through them, and in so far as there was revelation of God there was something of enduring importance to men.

Whenever we approach the Bible, and especially the Old Testament, which covers so long a period of time, we must maintain a historical sense, and read everything first of all in the setting of its own age and then in the context of the whole unfolding revelation of which it forms a part. The unity is the unity of a process and a development. Within the unity of a

---

[1] I Sam. xv. 3. It is important to note that according to the chronology of I Kings vi. 1, the 'provocation' which Samuel alleged took place more than three hundred and fifty years earlier, and on the shortest possible chronology it would be not less than one hundred and fifty years earlier.

[2] I Kings xxii. 22.   [3] 2 Sam. xxi. 1–14.   [4] Deut. xxiv. 16.
[5] I John iv. 12.   [6] Cf. especially Gen. xviii.

man's personality there is growth and development. The ideas of his youth are not identical with the ideas of advancing age; yet neither are they wholly different and unrelated. A continuing thread runs through them, and though there may be modification there is not a continual new beginning. The moments are fleeting and the experience of today will be gone tomorrow. Yet not wholly. By memory the experience of the past is retained in some measure, and there is a deposit in the stuff of personality of the things through which a man has lived. Moreover, the effects of his will are seen in his personality. The things he has chosen to do have modified his character, and he may have grown better or worse, either continuously or by turns, through the years. The continuing thread that marks the unity of his personality may not be set in a straight line. The unity of the Bible is of this kind, though given in the experience of a people and not in a single life. The experience, character, and will of the persons who mark the successive moments of the process all left their mark on the process. For each moment was more than a moment; it belonged to the whole.

That this is not to eliminate God from the story, and to make it into the record of a merely human development, has already been said. In a man's individual experience God may have played a part, and the influences which have moulded him may not be resolvable simply into the effects of the human environment in which he has lived and the human influences he has felt, together with the deposits in character of the exercise of his will. Often he may have resisted the Divine influence, but sometimes he may have been susceptible to it and have experienced its moulding power. It is in a comparable way that divine and human elements may be found interwoven in the process of revelation recorded in the Bible. But here the continuing thread that gives unity to the record is the divine element. For in the Bible we do not have a record of the life and thought of Israel, and then of the Christian Church in its beginnings, but a record of Divine revelation. The unity is not the unity of the spirit of Israel and of the Church, but the unity of the Divine revelation given in the context of history and through the medium of human personality. It is because it is given in the context of that history that we must preserve a historical sense if we would understand it.

In some quarters there is a tendency to return to an allegorical interpretation of the Old Testament in an effort to rehabilitate the Old Testament for a generation that so largely ignores it.[1] It is pointed out that in the New Testament we sometimes find this kind of interpretation. Paul could speak of the Israelite crossing of the Red Sea as baptism.[2] In earlier ages Christian interpreters carried this kind of interpretation to great extremes,[3] and the parts of the Old Testament which are the least prepossessing have been transformed for readers by the simple process of ignoring their historical content and reading them as allegories of spiritual experience. The supreme example of this kind of interpretation has been provided by the Song of Songs.[4] Interpreters who felt that there would be something shocking in reading its sensuous figures in terms of human love, despite their oft-repeated profession that marriage is a Divine ordinance and that the union of a man and woman may be fittingly consecrated at the altar of God, have read it in terms of the things that interested them. The breasts of the bride, enclosing a sachet of myrrh,[5] have been understood to mean the Old and New Testaments

[1] The early Reformers firmly rejected allegorical exegesis. Luther declared roundly that 'allegories are empty speculations, and as it were the spume of Holy Scripture, (cf. *Werke*, Weimar edition, xlii, 1911, p. 173: *inanes speculationes et tanquam spumam sacrae scripturae*), and went so far as to describe allegory as a harlot, seductive to the idle (ibid., xlii, 1912, p. 688: *est enim allegoria tanquam formosa meretrix, quae ita blanditur hominibus, ut non possit non amari, praesertim ab hominibus ociosis, qui sunt sine tentatione*). He did, however, allow it a certain value as an ornament of exegesis (ibid., xlii, p. 173: *licet etiam allegoriis ceu ornamento et floribus quibusdam uti, quibus illustretur historia seu pinga tur*). Cf. G. Ebeling, 'Die Anfänge von Luthers Hermeneutik', *Z.Th.K.*, xlviii, 1951, pp. 172–230.

[2] 1 Cor. x. 2. C. H. Dodd, *The Old Testament in the New*, 1952, p. 5, gives some further familiar examples, but observes that what is surprising is that this method of exegesis is used so little in the New Testament.

[3] This method of exegesis was especially characteristic of the Alexandrian school, and particularly of Origen, of whom F. W. Farrar observes: 'His system rose in reality not from reverence for the Scriptures, but from a dislike to their plain sense which had at all costs to be set aside' (*History of Interpretation*, 1886, p. 191).

[4] Cf. the writer's essay 'The Interpretation of the Song of Songs', in *The Servant of the Lord and other Essays*, 1952, pp. 187 ff.   [5] Ct. i. 13.

with Christ in between,[1] or the breasts of the believer, between which the memory of Christ's Cross is cherished.[2] The spring enclosed and the fountain sealed[3] have been interpreted in terms of the Virgin Mary[4] or of the Church.[5] The sixty queens and eighty concubines[6] have been interpreted of the true Church and the sectarians,[7] and the injunction to take the little foxes that spoil the vineyards[8] has been held to warrant the persecution of heretics and schismatics.[9] This is to abandon a historical sense and to open the door to undisciplined fancy; and on such principles any text may be made to mean anything we please. Whatever may be said for it homiletically, it can claim no standing as exegesis.

It was once the writer's lot to listen to a sermon on the text: 'But my servant Caleb . . . because he hath followed me wholly',[10] in which the preacher explained that the Hebrew language is fond of metaphors, and the word 'wholly' is a picture of a ship with all sails set 'bellying to the wind'. The whole of the sermon was built on this picture, and the terms of the preacher's description came as a refrain at regular intervals. The good man did not know a word of Hebrew, and was unaware that the word 'wholly' has no separate equivalent in the text with which he was dealing. The Hebrew says simply 'because he hath filled up after me'. The preacher had doubtless found some commentary which said: 'The Hebrew idiom is "hath filled up", as a vessel', or something like this, and had misunderstood the meaning of the word 'vessel', and let his imgination do the rest. Whatever virtues the sermon had—and the hearers were loud in their praises—it had none as exegesis. With all the writer's sympathy for the demand for a Christian interpretation of the Old Testa-

---

[1] So Cyril of Alexandria (Migne, *P.G.*, lxix, 1864, col. 1281). Cf. Philo Carpasius (Migne, *P.G.*, xl, 1863, col. 56).

[2] So pseudo-Cassiodorus (Migne, *P.L.*, lxx, 1865, col. 1060).   [3] Ct. iv. 12.

[4] So Justus Urgellensis (Migne, *P.L.*, lxvii, 1865, col. 978).

[5] So pseudo-Cassiodorus (*loc. cit.*, col. 1078).   [6] Ct. vi. 8.

[7] So Bishop Wordsworth (*The Book of Proverbs, Ecclesiastes, and Song of Solomon*, in *The Holy Bible with Notes and Introductions*, IV, 3, 1868, p. 148).

[8] Ct. ii. 15.   [9] So J. Durham (*Clavis Cantici*, 1669, pp. 143 ff.).

[10] Num. xiv. 24. The preacher preferred 'wholly' to the 'fully' of A.V. and R.V., because he found this word elsewhere, in Num. xxxii. 12, Deut. i. 36.

ment, he can muster no sympathy for this. The foundation for all exegesis must lie in the understanding of the text as its author and its first hearers or readers understood it, governed by a historical sense and the effort to place ourselves in the setting out of which it came. We may then go on to consider the place of its message in the whole process of revelation contained in the Bible, and the enduring message for us which it may contain, to be reinterpreted in the context of our life and in the terms of our experience. The maintenance of a historical sense does not mean that we read the Bible merely as the history of ancient situations. It but means that we read it as the Word of God mediated in the context of that history, but transcending in its significance the history which provided its background and its occasion.

There are some who turn to typology, and who find in the Old Testament a prefiguring of the New.[1] This method of interpretation treats the essential meaning and purpose of the

[1] On recent trends in the interpretation of Scripture cf. J. Coppens, *Les Harmonies des deux Testaments*, revised ed., 1949, and *Vom christlichen Verständnis des Alten Testaments*, 1952, where a considerable literature is surveyed and an extensive bibliography is given. Cf. also L. Cerfaux, J. Coppens, and J. Gribomont, *Problèmes et Méthode d'exégèse théologique*, 1950; J. Coppens, *Un Nouvel Essai d'Herméneutique biblique*, 1952, and *Nouvelles Réflexions sur les divers Sens des Saintes Écritures*, 1952. On the typological interpretation of the Bible cf. J. Daniélou, *Sacramentum Futuri*, 1950 (on which cf. A. Bentzen's review in *Erasmus*, iv, 1951, cols. 213 ff.); F. Michaeli, 'La "Typologie" biblique', *Foi et Vie*, l, 1952, pp. 11 ff.; S. Amsler, 'Où en est la typologie de l'Ancien Testament', *E.Th.R.*, xxvii, 1952, pp. 75 ff.; G. von Rad, 'Typologische Auslegung des Alten Testaments', *Evangelische Theologie*, xii, 1952–53, pp. 17 ff. C. H. Dodd, *The Old Testament in the New*, 1952, pp. 5 ff., contrasts the New Testament use of the Old with that of Philo, and argues that in the New Testament, despite occasional resort to allegory, the history of the Old Testament is treated seriously. Cf. von Rad, *loc. cit.*, pp. 30 ff. Wilhelm Vischer goes beyond allegory and typology in reading the New Testament back into the Old. Cf. *Das Christuszeugnis des Alten Testaments*, i, 6th ed., 1943, ii, 1942 (the first volume has appeared in E. Tr. by A. B. Crabtree, *The Witness of the Old Testament to Christ*, 1949). N. W. Porteous, *The Old Testament and Modern Study*, ed. by H. H. Rowley, 1951, pp. 338 f., says: 'The New Testament meaning is read into the Old Testament passage and so Vischer knows beforehand what the latter must mean. . . . In his discussion of Jacob's wrestling with the mysterious opponent at the Jabbok, he states roundly with Luther: "Without the slightest contradiction this man was not an angel, but our Lord Jesus Christ, who is the eternal God and yet was to become a man whom the Jews would crucify." This is certainly very muddled theology. Generally speaking, Vischer's wholesale use of allegory implies that he is not taking history seriously and therefore not taking biblical revelation seriously.' From this summary it will be seen that the present writer's position is widely different from that of Vischer. It is therefore surprising that W. D. Davies, *J.B.R.*, xx, 1952, p. 234, should mention them together in a single sentence, and give his readers the impression that both justify the verdict of Pfeiffer: 'If this is a fair sample of the result of the biblical research of our time, we have truly reverted to the

Old Testament as a prefiguring of the experience of Christ or of the Church. It can think of the sacrificial ritual of the Law as designed to foreshadow the sacrifice of the Cross, and can ignore the background of Israelite and non-Israelite practice out of which the institution of sacrifice developed, and treat it simply as an anticipation of the sacrifice of Christ, to prepare for that event. Later we shall consider the patterns which recur in the Old and New Testaments and the relations between those patterns. In many ways the writer finds a correspondence between the Old Testament and the New, but that does not mean that he reads the Old in terms of the New, or imposes the patterns of the New upon the Old. Each Testament is to be read first and foremost in terms of itself and its own *Sitz im Leben*. Its institutions and its ideas are to be examined for themselves before they are related to one another, and attention is not to be devoted exclusively to the elements that can be so related. Nevertheless, just because there is a continuing thread there is a process that leads from one to the other, and because there is in both Testaments the revelation of the same God, it is not surprising that there should be recurring patterns. The character of God is seen in His revelation, and because His character is one its stamp is to be found in the diversity of the forms of the revelation.

Reference has been made to a unity within a process, and to the importance of considering the separate parts of the Bible both for

Middle Ages'. On Vischer's exegetical principles cf. F. Baumgärtel, *Verheissung*, 1952, pp. 91 ff. Baumgärtel recognizes that Vischer is on the right track (p. 92), but maintains that his use of typology is methodically untenable (p. 93). Elsewhere Baumgärtel observes that the New Testament use of typology is foreign to our thinking and unconvincing (p. 83). It is inadmissible to interpret the Old Testament as it was not meant to be understood, yet we may legitimately recognize that above and behind the Old Testament stands the God Whose promise therein finds its realization in Christ (p. 85). With this the present writer is in broad agreement. For an example of the interpretation of the Jacob story above referred to at the opposite pole to Vischer's, cf. C. C. McCown, *J.B.L.*, lxiii, 1944, p. 331 f.: 'The story can be regarded only as a piece of chauvinistic patriotism proving to the Israelite that eventually his nation would prevail over all others in spite of the dark night through which they had to suffer and the handicaps that beset them. A common myth motif, of the struggle between a man and a superhuman being is used to . . . point to Israel's future triumph.' On the *sensus plenior*, defended especially by J. Coppens, cf. R. Bierberg, *C.B.Q.*, x, 1948, pp. 182 ff. For a careful study of exegetical principles cf. L. H. Bleeker, *Hermeneutiek van het Oude Testament*, 1948 Cf. further B. J. Alfrink, *Over 'typologische' Exegese van het Oude Testament*, 1945.

themselves and as moments of the process. As an illustration of what is meant we may take the work of Moses. This is of supreme importance in the Old Testament record.[1] It has been already said that the writer does not regard Moses as a shadowy figure, of whose existence and work we cannot be very sure,[2] but that he regards him as a truly prophetic figure who was commissioned by God to lead Israel out of Egypt and who, after leading them out, took them to the sacred mount where they committed themselves to God in the terms of the Covenant. His work was achieved in the political and in the religious sphere, and both are important. His religious work did not consist in the formulating of certain ideas which arose in his own mind; it rested on his political work and was inextricably interwoven with it. To that we shall have occasion to return. Here it will suffice to observe that in the religious ideas which were mediated to Israel through Moses lay the seeds of almost all the creative ideas which are to be found in the Old Testament, to be carried forward into the New. This does not mean that the Pentateuch is to be approached with an uncritical mind, or that the ideas of later times are to be read back into the work of Moses. None of the main documents on which the Pentateuch rests can have been compiled until long after the time of Moses. The legal sections, in particular, come from much later hands, and while many of the usages which they embody are much older than the documents in which they are enshrined, there is little which we can with confidence ascribe to Moses. The Decalogue can, however, with reasonable confidence be ascribed to him,[3] and this is of far

[1] The writer has frequently dealt with this question. Cf. 'The Significance of Moses and his Work', *Religion in Education*, xi, 1943–44, pp. 63 ff.; *The Rediscovery of the Old Testament*, pp. 77 ff.; *From Joseph to Joshua*, 1950, pp. 155 ff. J. Muilenburg, *Christianity and the Contemporary Scene*, p. 34, refers to 'the increasing respect for the traditions centering about the figure of Moses'.

[2] E. Meyer questioned the historicity of Moses altogether. Cf. *Die Israeliten und ihre Nachbarstämme*, 1906, p. 451 n. So also G. Hölscher, *Geschichte der israelitischen und jüdischen Religion*, 1922, pp. 64 ff.

[3] Cf. the writer's 'Moses and the Decalogue', *B.J.R.L.*, xxxiv, 1951–52, pp. 81 ff. (French Tr., by M. Simon, *R.H.P.R.*, xxxii, 1952, pp. 7 ff.). J. P. Peters, *J.B.L.*, xx, 1901, p. 117, observes: 'Writers who have denied the Mosaic authorship of the Decalogue have, in point of fact, reduced Moses to a nonentity, and offered no explanation of the ethical impulse given by him.'

greater religious significance than all the details of priestly ritual. That there has been expansion of the Decalogue is clear from the comparison of its form in Exod. xx and that in Deut. v, where different expansions of some of the commands can be found. Leaving out the expansions, however, the Decalogue in its original form may be accepted as given to Israel by Moses. Here are the seeds of ethical monotheism, which is the supremely important feature of Old Testament religion.

It is true that many scholars have attributed the Decalogue to a time much later than that of Moses, and have ascribed the achievement of ethical monotheism to the eighth and seventh century prophets whose influence is thought to be reflected in the Decalogue.[1] It would carry us too far here to examine that view in detail and to show why the writer holds it to be unsound. The ethical note in religion was struck long before the eighth century prophets, and while it was developed by them in ways that need not be underestimated, they built on earlier foundations. The prophet who denounced the judicial murder of Naboth,[2] and the earlier prophet who rebuked the royal adulterer,[3] stood in the succession of ethical prophets before the eighth century dawned. But long before their time the seeds of ethical monotheism are to be found in the work of Moses, and it is because they are to be found in his work that the writer can credit him with the formulation of the Decalogue.

In recent years there is a tendency to credit Moses with monotheism. Scholars of eminence have argued that he was a full monotheist.[4] Others, however, have sharply denied this.[5] It will

---

[1] For references to a large number of writers who have followed this view, as well as to those who have maintained the Mosaic origin of the Decalogue, cf. *B.J.R.L.*, *loc. cit.*, pp. 81 f., and *R.H.P.R.*, *loc. cit.*, pp. 7 ff.

[2] 1 Kings xxi.

[3] 2 Sam. xii.

[4] Cf. W. F. Albright, *Archaeology of Palestine and the Bible*, 1932, pp. 163 ff., *From the Stone Age to Christianity*, 1940, pp. 196 ff. (cf. review by R. T. O'Callaghan, *Orientalia*, xx, 1951, pp. 216–36); Fleming James, *A.Th.R.*, xiv, 1932, pp. 130 ff.; G. E. Wright, *The Old Testament against its Environment*, 1950, pp. 29 ff.

[5] Cf. T. J. Meek, 'Primitive Monotheism and the Religion of Moses', in *University of Toronto Quarterly*, viii, 1939, pp. 180 ff., and 'Monotheism and the Religion of Israel', *J.B.L.*, lxi, 1942, pp. 21 ff.

be observed that here we are content to find in the work of Moses the seeds of monotheism, rather than full and explicitly formulated monotheism.[1] It cannot be established that he denied that any god but Yahweh existed, and it is doubtful if he ever considered the abstract notion of monotheism. On the other hand, it can be established that he did not suppose that any other god but Yahweh counted. Whether they existed or not was of scant importance, since they were negligible. This is not monotheism, but it is the seed of monotheism. Yahweh's deliverance of His people from Egypt is not represented as a contest between Yahweh and the gods of Egypt, but between Yahweh and Pharaoh. The gods of Egypt do not count as serious factors in the story. We are told that the Israelites did not worship God under the name Yahweh until Moses came to them in His name, but that Yahweh adopted them as His people and gathered the God they had hitherto worshipped into Himself.[2] If the view that Yahweh had hitherto been worshipped by other people is correct—and this is a common view, though not universally held by scholars[3]— then up to that time Yahweh and El Shaddai had been considered distinct, just as Yahweh and the gods of Egypt were distinct. But from now on El Shaddai had no

[1] Cf. the writer's article 'The Antiquity of Israelite Monotheism', *E.T.*, lxi, 1949–50, pp. 333 ff. Cf. also W. A. Irwin, *The Old Testament, Keystone of Human Culture*, 1952, p. 24: 'This belief'—*i.e.* Mosaic religion—'could lend itself to monotheistic evolution, as it actually did if this premise is correct; but it was yet some distance short of the concept of a single God of all men everywhere.' Cf. also G. W. Anderson, *The Old Testament and Modern Study*, ed. by H. H. Rowley, 1951, pp. 290 f., esp. p. 290: 'There is some danger of lapsing into mere logomachy in the debate about Mosaic monotheism; and it is well to remember both that the label matters less than the content of the packet, and also that it is inconvenient to have the same label for different things.'   [2] Cf. Exod. vi. 2 f.

[3] Amongst the scholars who reject this view are A. R. Gordon (*The Early Traditions of Genesis*, 1907, pp. 106 ff.), E. König (*Geschichte der alttestamentliche Religion*, 1912, pp. 162 ff.), P. Volz (*Mose und sein Werk*, 2nd ed., 1932, p. 59), W. J. Phythian-Adams (*The Call of Israel*, 1934, pp. 72 ff.), T. J. Meek (*Hebrew Origins*, 2nd ed., 1950, pp. 94 ff.), M. Buber (*Moses*, 1947, pp. 94 ff.), F. V. Winnett (*The Mosaic Tradition*, 1949, p. 69); while amongst those who accept it are K. Budde (*Religion of Israel to the Exile*, 1899, pp. 17 ff.), T. K. Cheyne (*E.B.*, iii, 1902, col. 3208), G. A. Barton (*A Sketch of Semitic Origins*, 1902, pp. 272 ff., and *Semitic and Hamitic Origins*, 1934, pp. 332 f.), H. Gressmann (*Mose und seine Zeit*, 1913, pp. 434 f., 447 ff.), J. Morgenstern (*H.U.C.A.*, iv, 1927, pp. 44 ff.), W. Vischer (*Jahwe der Gott Kains*, 1929), A. Lods (*Israel*, E. Tr., by S. H. Hooke, 1932, pp. 317 f., 320 ff.), Oesterley and Robinson (*Hebrew Religion*, 2nd ed., 1937, pp. 148 ff., 156), A. J. Wensinck ('De oorsprongen van het Jahwisme', in *Semietische Studiën uit de Nalatenschap van A. J. Wensinck*, 1941, pp. 23 ff.).

reality, save in so far as He was identified with Yahweh. In this there was incipient monotheism. With our monotheistic point of view we find nothing difficult here. If there is One God, and beside Him is no other, then all who truly worship God, by whatever name they call Him, worship this One God. Syncretism is a familiar phenomenon in the history of religion. For a variety of reasons people have identified two hitherto distinct deities, as Israel later too often identified Yahweh and Baal. In all syncretism there is a seed of monotheism, but most commonly it has been a seed that bore no fruit. In this syncretism of Yahweh and El Shaddai, however, there was a seed that did bear fruit, and this seems to be due to the fact that it was no ordinary syncretism. Here Yahweh claimed Israel for Himself, and established His claim by His deliverance of her. El Shaddai as distinct from Yahweh no more figured in the story than do the Egyptian gods. Either, then, El Shaddai must be gathered into Yahweh and identified with Him, or be treated as of no more significance than the Egyptian gods. This syncretism was different from the uneasy syncretism of Yahweh and Baal, which was always apt to break out into conflict in times of crisis, and which never abolished the undercurrent of feeling that Yahweh was not really Baal. Here, however, we never find any conflict between Yahweh and El Shaddai. For this syncretism was born of the mighty acts of Yahweh, and the initiative was with Him Who called Moses into His service. As against Him no gods counted, and He was free to choose for Himself what people He would. Nor was there any limit to His power. It could be exercised in Egypt or in Canaan no less than at His sacred mount, and all the powers of Nature were under His control. Though there is no reason to ascribe to Moses, or to Israel for long after his time, theoretical monotheism, there is here an implicit practical monotheism, or at least the seeds out of which it should spring. When the eighth century prophets moved steadily on towards theoretical, speculative monotheism, and when Deutero-Isaiah formulated it with pellucid clarity,[1]

[1] Isa. xlv. 22.

24

they were but continuing the work which was begun through Moses, and their work is not to be thought of without relation to his.[1]

If the seeds of monotheism are to be found in the work of Moses, no less is to be said for the seeds of ethical religion. By ethical religion is meant more than a religion which makes ethical demands on men. There are few religions which are not to some degree ethical in this sense. By ethical religion is meant a religion whose ethical demands spring no less from the character of God than from His words. Yahweh asks of men that they shall reflect His own character, so far as it can be reflected within the limitations of human life. His resentment of the harsh dealing of man to man and His compassion for the oppressed were manifested in His deliverance of Israel, so that when the prophets denounced harshness and oppression and called for compassion for the unfortunate they were calling men to reflect the character which was uniquely expressed in God's deliverance of His people. Moreover, the whole basis of the Covenant at the sacred mount was the achieved salvation of God calling for Israel's consecration to Him in gratitude. It therefore had an ethical basis, since gratitude is an ethical emotion. A religion which from God's side is grounded on His grace and from man's side is grounded on an ethical emotion has an ethical seed no less than a monotheistic seed at its heart. It is because of this that it is reasonable to credit Moses with the formulation of the Decalogue. It is so wholly consonant with the essence of his work.

In what has been said it is implied that Yahweh may have been worshipped under that name by others before the time of the Exodus, though not by the Israelites in Egypt. In Exod. vi we are told explicitly that the patriarchs had not worshipped God under this name,[2] but we are not told that no others had

[1] Cf. T. K. Cheyne, *Exp.*, 4th series, v, 1892, p. 109: 'My own historical sense emphatically requires that from the very beginning there should have been the germ of the advanced "ethical monotheism" of the prophets.' Also E. Sjöberg, *S.E.A.*, xiv, 1949, p. 11: 'Yahweh was already from the beginning of a type which made possible a development in the direction of prophetic monotheism.'

[2] Cf. Exod. vi. 2 f., and also verse 7: 'I will take you to me for a people, and I will be to you a God.'

worshipped God under it. In Exod. iii, in the story of the call of Moses, we are told that God revealed to Moses that it was Yahweh Who was commissioning him to go into Egypt.[1] We are not told that Yahweh had never hitherto been worshipped under this name. On the other hand, we are told in some passages of Scripture that He had been worshipped under this name long before. We are told that men began to worship God under this name in the days of Seth,[2] the son of Adam, and even before this His name is said to have been on the lips of Eve when she bore Cain.[3] Biblical support can therefore be claimed for the view that though the Israelites had not worshipped God in Egypt by that name, others had so worshipped Him.

That this does not reduce the work of Moses to the mere transfer of Israel's allegiance to a foreign God has been already indicated. A wholly new quality was brought into the religion. For what matters most is not the name of the God, but the character of the worship. In our worship today we rarely use the name Yahweh, or even its conventional form Jehovah.[4] Following the Jewish usage, and that of the Greek and Latin Bibles, we substitute 'The Lord' for it. It is when we look at the essence of the religion that we recognize that whether others had worshipped Yahweh before or not, the religion which was established through Moses had significantly new features. The incipient monotheism and the ethical quality of the religion sprang out of the way in which it was mediated to Israel. These were not transferred from some other religion. The character that God was seen to have was the character that was revealed in His mighty acts towards Israel. Moreover, the fundamental concept of the Divine election of Israel, with all the rich fruits that this concept was to bear, sprang out of the events of the Exodus and were no mere borrowing from another faith.

Here, once more, we find a thread that runs all through the Old Testament at least from the time of Moses, and that gives a

---

[1] Cf. Exod. iii. 13 ff.   [2] Gen. iv. 26.   [3] Gen. iv. 1.
[4] It is well known that this word is a hybrid, consisting of the vowels of 'Adonai and the consonants of the Divine Name, whose pronunciation cannot be certainly known, but which was probably pronounced Yahweh.

unity to its thought. The principle of election is carried back, indeed, far beyond Moses in the Bible. But here it takes a new, and richly significant, form. God chooses Israel in unmerited grace, and not because of her worth;[1] and having chosen her, He claims her for Himself by what He does for her. Through Moses she is made aware that such grace and such deliverance lay an obligation upon her which can only be fulfilled in the Covenant. It is a moral obligation, therefore, which she is free to accept or to reject, but in whose rejection she would shame herself. The obligation is to cherish the revelation of God which has been given to her in her experience and to make it the heritage of the generations that should follow, and also to give to God her unstinting loyalty and obedience. Mosaic religion was therefore a religion of Covenant grounded in the prior election and deliverance of God. But this means that if succeeding generations could be born into the Covenant, they could not be wholly in it unless they made it their own by their acceptance of its obligations. The heritage of the election was offered them in grace, but the grace renewed its claim, and the claim could only be accepted by loyalty. Here is the seed of an idea which runs all through the Old Testament, and whose significance is not yet exhausted. The prophets were insistent that repudiation of the obligations of the Covenant was tantamount to the repudiation of Israel's election, and that Israel's claim on God ceased when her loyalty failed. His grace might still continue, and continuing would renew its claim, but an Israel that was disloyal to Him forfeited all claim on Him.

These examples must suffice to illustrate the kind of unity to be found in the Bible, and particularly in the Old Testament. It is a unity which lies in great diversity, and though in the present work we shall be considering the unity, it is important to remember the diversity. Moreover, it is not a static unity, but the dynamic unity of a process. The seed of monotheism that lay in the work of Moses became the clearly formulated monotheism of Deutero-

---

[1] That the divine grace though free is not arbitrary, the present writer has argued in *The Biblical Doctrine of Election.*

Isaiah, who never tired of reiterating that beside Yahweh there is no other God.[1] And when the seed of monotheism developed it bore the fruit of universalism. If there was no God but Yahweh, all men should worship Him alone. Just as He had laid His hand on Israel in Egypt and claimed her for Himself, so He was now seen to claim all men for Himself. 'Look unto me and be ye saved, all the ends of the earth; for I am God and there is no other.'[2] The seeds of ethical religion that lay in the work of Moses grew into a strong tree in the work of the great prophets. It is commonly recognized that the prophets of Israel are without parallel in any other people or any other faith. But this uniqueness springs out of that other uniqueness of the work of Moses, whose work they but continued, and this sprang in turn from the grace of God, Who chose him and used him to announce and to interpret His own deeds, but Whose deeds were His own, and not performed by Moses. Again, the obligations of the Covenant were more clearly seen as the unity and the character of God became more manifest. That loyalty to the Covenant demanded the cherishing of the revelation of God and obedience to His will was seen at Sinai. But as the character of God became clearer, the nature of His demands became clearer, and when it was perceived that He Who had chosen Israel was alone God and was therefore to be worshipped by all men, it was seen that the election of Israel carried a missionary corollary. The prophet who was above all others the prophet of monotheism was also the prophet of universalism and of the mission of Israel. This did not mean that he had ceased to think of Israel as the chosen people. No prophet dwells so constantly on the thought of the Divine election of Israel, or is more deeply aware of the grace of God revealed in that election. He dwells upon the thought of God's choice and on all that God has done and will do for her, in order that he may bring home to her a deeper insight into the purpose of that election. The only God Who desired the worship

---

[1] Isa. xliii. 10 f., xliv. 6, 8, 24, xlv. 5 f., 18, 21 f.
[2] Isa. xlv. 22. R. Levy, *Deutero-Isaiah*, 1925, p. 195, calls this 'the grandest verse in the prophet's scroll'.

of all men, had chosen Israel in order that she might share with all the revelation that had been made to her. It was not for her alone, and her unique honour was not only to receive but to communicate, and in communicating to perfect the service whose obligation was entailed in the Covenant. 'I the Lord have called thee in righteousness . . . and will give thee for a covenant of the people, for a light of the Gentiles.' [1]

Diversity and unity must be perceived together in the Bible, and neither can be sacrificed to the other. [2] A historical sense is essential for all satisfying study of this Book, but along with that sense there must go a perception of the continuing thread that runs through all, and that makes this library also a Book. There must also be the perception that what gives to this Book its unity is something of enduring significance, which has meaning therefore for the contemporary world and for us. [3]

[1] Isa. xlii. 6. This is the familiar rendering of A.V. and R.V. The phrase rendered 'a covenant of the people' has been much discussed. In *The Missionary Message of the Old Testament*, p. 51, the writer rendered 'covenant of humanity', or universal covenant. This probably represents the essential meaning, though it is reached in various ways. R. Levy (*Deutero-Isaiah*, 1925, p. 147) bases it on the meaning of the cognate Arabic word '*āmm*=*general, universal*; C. C. Torrey (*Second Isaiah*, 1928, pp. 231, 327) argues that elsewhere in poetry a singular form stands for the plural, and hence we may render *peoples*; G. Quell (*Th.W.B.*, i, 1933, p. 34 n.) takes the word rendered *people* to mean *mankind* here, as sometimes elsewhere. L. Dennefeld, however, rejects this view, and maintains that Israel alone is in mind (*La Sainte Bible*, ed. by A. Clamer, vii, 1947, p. 158; cf. J. Ziegler, *Isaias*, 1948, p. 124).

[2] Cf. Mary E. Lyman, *J.B.R.*, xiv, 1946, pp. 11 f.: 'The view of the Bible which recognizes diversity and change and different levels of value, but which at the same time appreciates the real unities of religious thought and experience is the view which has hope for the future of our world.' Also J. Muilenburg, *Christianity and the Contemporary Scene*, p. 36: 'The task of the competent Old Testament student is to do justice to the elements of diversity and unity within the Old Testament.'

[3] Cf. a series of articles on the unity of the Bible in *Interpretation*, v, 1951: G. E. Wright, 'The Unity of the Bible', pp. 131 ff.; F. V. Filson, 'The Unity of the Old and the New Testaments', pp. 134 ff.; R. C. Dentan, 'The Unity of the Old Testament', pp. 153 ff.; P. E. Davies, 'Unity and Variety in the New Testament', pp. 174 ff.; R. M. Grant, 'The Place of the Old Testament in Early Christianity', pp. 186 ff.; J. S. Glen, 'Jesus Christ and the Unity of the Bible', pp. 259 ff.; N. F. Langford, 'Gospel and Duty', pp. 268 ff.; F. J. Denbeaux, 'The Biblical Hope', pp. 285 ff.; G. E. Wright, 'The Unity of the Bible', pp. 304 ff. Cf. also P. Lestringant, *Essai sur l'Unité de la Revelation biblique*, 1942.

II

THE LAW AND THE PROPHETS

IN the preceding chapter reference has been made to the sharp antithesis which was formerly found between the Pentateuch and the prophetic books of the Old Testament, or between prophetic and priestly religion. In the present chapter attention will be directed to the measure of unity that can be found here.[1] It must not be forgotten, however, that by unity identity of message and outlook is not meant. Diversity of viewpoint is to be found continually within the Bible, and it is in no way surprising that it should mark prophets and priests. If the measure of unity that marked their fundamental conception of religion is here examined, that does not mean that there was no difference of emphasis between them.

It would be easy to multiply quotations from scholars who have represented prophetic religion as the complete antithesis of priestly, and who have argued that the prophets rejected the whole institution of sacrifice and all the ritual of the Temple.[2] There are familiar passages which can be used impressively to build up their case. Amos asks: 'Did ye bring unto me sacrifices and offerings in the wilderness forty years, O house of Israel?'[3] and this rhetorical question is understood to expect the answer

[1] On this chapter cf. the writer's earlier discussion in 'The Unity of the Old Testament', *B.J.R.L.*, xxix, 1945–46, pp. 326 ff., and 'The Meaning of Sacrifice in the Old Testament', *ibid.*, xxxiii, 1950–51, pp. 74 ff. Cf. also A. C. Welch, *Prophet and Priest in Old Israel*, 1936; N. W. Porteous, 'Prophet and Priest in Israel', *E.T.*, lxii, 1950–51, pp. 4 ff.
[2] Cf. J. Wellhausen, *Prolegomena to the History of Israel*, E.Tr. by J. S. Black and A. Menzies, 1885, p. 423: 'If the Priestly Code makes the cultus the principal thing, that appears to amount to a systematic decline into the heathenism which the prophets incessantly combated and yet were unable to eradicate'; E. Kautzsch, in Hastings's *D.B.*, Extra Vol., 1904, p. 686b: 'No one has any right to depreciate the merit which belongs to the above-named prophets, of having discovered the ideal of true service of God in the worship of Him in spirit and in truth, without any outward ceremonies and performances'; J. A. Bewer, *The Literature of the Old Testament in its Historical Development*, 1922, p. 267: 'Religion was a matter of the cult. The earlier prophets had violently protested against such a conception of religion and rejected the entire cultic apparatus as contrary to the will of God'; I. G. Matthews, *The Religious Pilgrimage of Israel*, 1947, p. 128: 'These men had denounced ritual as of no avail, but now, if possible, they went farther, and made social ethics the essential, even the sole, requirement of Yahweh.'
[3] Amos v. 25.

'No', and to be a denial that the institution of sacrifice went back in Israel to the Mosaic period. Jeremiah says: 'I spake not unto your fathers, nor commanded them in the day that I brought them out of the land of Egypt, concerning burnt offerings or sacrifices'.[1] Here again, it is held, we have a flat denial that sacrifice really belonged to genuine Israelite religion. In support of this view some external evidence can now be adduced, for there is reason to believe that the Israelite sacrificial system had much in common with the Canaanite.[2] This has led to the view that it was fundamentally of Canaanite origin,[3] and therefore taken over by Israel after the entry into the Promised Land. That the Canaanites had sacrifices known by the same names as some of the Israelite sacrifices is undeniable, and evidence from Ras Shamra is now brought forward to reinforce the view to which reference has been made. No one can deny that Israelite sacrifice came out of a wider background of ritual practice,[4] but while it is probable that much of Israelite sacrificial ritual was modelled on Canaanite, we have no evidence that it was identical with it in form or meaning,[5] and no evidence that for Israel

[1] Jer. vii. 22.

[2] Cf. J. Pedersen, *Israel: its Life and Culture III–IV*, 1940, p. 299: 'The Israelite sacrifice does not differ much from that in common use among the Canaanite peoples, but to a certain extent it has acquired a special Israelitish character.'

[3] Cf. R. Dussaud, *Les Origines cananéennes du sacrifice israélite*, 1921, and the enlarged second edition, 1941, where an appendix offers additional support for this view based on the Ras Shamra texts, which had been discovered in the interval. Cf. also J. Pedersen, *op. cit.*, p. 317: 'Our knowledge of the Phoenician-Canaanite cult is now quite sufficient to warrant the conclusion that the greater part of the Israelitish sacrificial practices had been learnt from the Canaanites;' J. P. Hyatt, *Prophetic Religion*, 1947, p. 128: 'Modern discoveries and research have confirmed the belief that the Hebrew sacrificial system was largely of Canaanite origin. This has long been suspected on the basis of fragmentary evidence, and has been further proved by the discovery of cuneiform texts . . . at modern Ras Shamra.' It should be added that Dussaud recognizes that the sacrifice of Passover was observed by Israel in the nomadic period, before the Settlement in Canaan. Cf. *op. cit.*, p. 207.

[4] Cf. S. H. Hooke, *The Origins of Early Semitic Ritual*, 1938, pp. 63 ff. In *B.J.R.L.*, xxxiii, 1950–51, p. 81 n., the present writer has said: 'I am inclined . . . to hold that while Israelite sacrifice came from a background of ancient Semitic sacrifice, the institution would naturally be differently developed in different branches of the Semitic peoples, and that while Israel doubtless brought some sacrificial ritual with her when she entered Canaan, she borrowed much from the Canaanites for its development in the post-Settlement period.'

[5] Cf. J. Pedersen, *op. cit.*, p. 317: 'They could independently appropriate the entire sacrificial cult; but also create new forms and new viewpoints from it.'

sacrifice began after their entry into the land of Canaan.[1] For such a view we have no evidence but the texts of Amos and Jeremiah above quoted, and we must return to examine them later to see how far it is valid to base this view on them.

There are many other passages in the pre-exilic prophets which express strong condemnation of sacrifice and of other forms of religious observance. Amos says: 'I hate, I despise your feasts, and I will take no delight in your solemn assemblies. Yea, though ye offer me your burnt offerings and meal offerings, I will not accept them: neither will I regard the peace offerings of your fat beasts.'[2] His slightly younger contemporary, Hosea, says: 'I desire mercy, and not sacrifice; and the knowledge of God more than burnt offerings',[3] while later in the same century Isaiah asks, in a familiar passage which need not be quoted in full: 'To what purpose is the multitude of your sacrifices to me? saith the Lord: I am full of the burnt offerings of rams, and the fat of fed beasts; and I delight not in the blood of bullocks, or of lambs, or of he-goats'.[4] Here, however, we begin to have some misgiving, for Isaiah goes on to include in his condemnation the observance of new moons and sabbaths, and—most surprising of all—prayer. If Isaiah's condemnation of sacrifice is absolute, and he meant that in no circumstances did God ever want sacrifice, then his condemnation of prayer is equally absolute, and he must mean that in no circumstances does God ever want men to pray. If he did mean this, he stands in disagreement with Jeremiah, who explored the riches of prayer as few others did. But from Jeremiah is culled the saying; 'Your burnt offerings are not acceptable, nor your sacrifices pleasing unto me,'[5] and this prophet is ranged with Amos and Hosea by those who hold that these prophets entirely repudiated sacrifice. To these passages may be added the great passage which stands in the book of Micah,

---

[1] Cf. A. Lods, *Israel from its Beginnings to the Middle of the Eighth Century*, E. Tr. by S. H. Hooke, 1932, p. 281: 'The Israelite system of sacrifice, in its essentials, does not seem to have been either a Jahwistic innovation . . . nor a borrowing from the Canaanites, as Dussaud has recently maintained, nor a creation of the Jewish priests at the time of the exile. In the main it comes from the old pre-Mosaic Semitic stock of religious practices.'

[2] Amos v. 21 f.   [3] Hos. vi. 6.   [4] Isa. i. 11 ff.   [5] Jer. vi. 20.

but which is ascribed by many scholars to some other and unknown prophet in the reign of Manasseh.[1] For our present purpose it does not matter from whom it came, since it is only the attitude to sacrifice and the cultus which concerns us. It asks: 'Wherewith shall I come before the Lord, and bow myself before the high god? Shall I come before him with burnt offerings . . . Will the Lord be pleased with thousands of rams . . . He hath shewed thee, O man, what is good; and what doth the Lord require of thee, but to do justly, and to love mercy, and to walk humbly with thy God?'[2]

Here we have an impressive collection of passages which are held by many to repudiate sacrifice altogether, and to indicate an attitude irreconcilably opposed to that of priestly religion, as expressed in the Pentateuch, where sacrifice is enjoined and its ritual defined, and where it is credited with power to restore right relations with God. If this view is right, then within the Old Testament we have two fundamentally different conceptions of the very nature of religion set forth, each claiming to represent the will of God, and both canonized in the Scriptures of a single religion.

That such a view is not satisfactory is today felt by an increasing number of scholars, who do not feel forced to suppose that the legal and prophetic portions of the Old Testament were so completely at cross purposes.[3] Before we return to re-examine

[1] In the most recent commentary on Micah, A. George (*Michée, Sophonie, Nahum*, 1952, p. 12), who recognizes some later elements in the book, observes: 'One no longer refuses to attribute to Micah important fragments in v. 8–vii. 7', and further notes (p. 39) that the triple demand of vi. 8 corresponds to the teaching of the three eighth-century prophets who preceded Micah. In *The Growth of the Old Testament*, 19,8t5's pecahho present writer confessed that he 'is not inclined to pronounce for or a1.1ainsMi6, t authorship'. [2] Mic. vi. 6 ff.

[3] Cf. J. M. Powis Smith, *The Prophets and their Times*, 2nd ed., revised by W. A. Irwin, 1941, p. 62: 'It may hardly be supposed that Amos would have done away with sacrifice and ritual entirely if he could. . . . It was not ritual as such to which he objected, but rather the practice of ritual by people who believed that thereby they set in motion magical forces and insured for themselves well-being and happiness' (cf. 1st ed., 1925, p. 50). Cf. also W. O. E. Oesterley, *Sacrifices in Ancient Israel*, 1937, p. 208; H. Wheeler Robinson, *J.T.S.*, xliii, 1942, p. 137; J. E. Coleran, *Theological Studies*, v. 1944, pp. 437 f.; P. S. Minear, *Eyes of Faith*, 1946, p. 22; J. Paterson, *The Goodly Fellowship of the Prophets*, 1948, p. 27. Cf. E. Würthwein, *Th.L.Z.*, lxxii, 1947, cols. 143 ff. On the other hand, S. Herner still takes the opposite view, and holds that Amos repudiated sacrifice and the entire cultus. Cf. *Sühne und Vergebung in Israel*, 1942, pp. 30 f So, too, V. Maag, *Text, Wortschatz und Begriffswelt des Buches Amos*, 1951, pp. 225 f.

these passages, however, we may turn to some general considerations which may give us pause.

All of these passages stand in the pre-exilic prophets. As against this the attitude of the post-exilic prophets is admittedly in favour of sacrifice and all the observances of the cultus. The post-exilic prophets are therefore often sharply differentiated from the pre-exilic prophets, and classed with the priests as exponents of priestly religion. That there was a difference of message cannot be gainsaid, and it is to be understood, since they were addressing a different generation with different problems. Moreover, it cannot be gainsaid that the post-exilic prophets in general were men of lesser stature than the prophets of the eighth and seventh centuries. But it has to be noted that all the prophetic books in their present form, come from the post-exilic period. This does not mean, of course, that all of the materials which they contain were post-exilic creations. It means that the books, in their present form, were compiled in post-exilic days from older collections of materials.[1] So far as the twelve Minor Prophets are concerned, we should not think of them as twelve books, but as a single prophetic collection, which must have been gathered together in post-exilic days, since it embodies the oracles of post-exilic as well as pre-exilic prophets. The compiler of this collection, therefore, does not seem to have recognized any fundamental variance as to the very nature of religion between the pre-exilic and the post-exilic prophets. He may be presumed to have shared the post-exilic point of view, and he could not have felt that in preserving the oracles of Amos and Hosea, and of that prophet whose word is incorporated in the book of Micah, he was giving currency to a point of view which was anathema to himself. And since we have the two allegedly incompatible points of view within this single collection of The Twelve, we

[1] That a collection of Jeremiah's oracles was prepared during his lifetime is clear from Jer. xxxvi. 32, and it is commonly accepted as probable that this was one of the sources of our present book. It is similarly allowed by all scholars that many of the oracles preserved in the other prophetic books are genuine oracles of the prophets to whom they are ascribed, whether preserved orally or in writing, even though we have no explicit testimony as in the case of Jeremiah.

can hardly suppose that Isaiah and Jeremiah must have been compiled by circles that rejected post-exilic priestly religion and sought to preserve the words that exposed its hollowness. For here again we note that there is some similarity of shape about the compilation of Isaiah—First Isaiah—and Jeremiah, and to some extent also about the book of Ezekiel. There is no extract from the book of Kings in Ezekiel, because there was no relevant material there. In all these three books the oracles on foreign nations are gathered together, and in Isaiah and Jeremiah a historical extract from the book of Kings closes the collection. Since all three books are post-exilic in their compilation they may reasonably be credited to common circles.[1] And since Ezekiel is undoubtedly an exponent of priestly religion we find that once more the compilers do not seem to have been aware of the antithesis which modern writers have found. Yet if that antithesis were fundamental to the message of the pre-exilic prophets, this would be very odd.

Again, the formation of the Canon of the Old Testament was a post-exilic process.[2] That some parts of the Pentateuch come from the pre-exilic period is agreed by almost all, and so far as the book of Deuteronomy is concerned, its composition is attributed by most to the seventh century B.C., and its promulgation to the time of Josiah's reform.[3] This work greatly influenced the compilers of the books that are known in the Hebrew Canon as the Former Prophets—Joshua, Judges, Samuel and Kings—which could not have reached their present form, therefore, until the last generation before the Fall of Jerusalem. There are other parts of the Pentateuch which are attributed by most scholars to the post-exilic period, and with most support to the fifth century B.C. Since almost all of those who find the sharp antithesis between priests and prophets take this view, we shall do them no

---

[1] Cf. the writer's *Growth of the Old Testament*, p. 87: 'Most probably the four collections that comprise the Latter Prophets were compiled within a relatively short space of time by circles that were interested in pre-exilic and post-exilic prophets alike.'

[2] Cf. *ibid.*, pp. 169 ff.

[3] This is still the most generally accepted view, despite challenges on one side or the other. Cf. *Studies in Old Testament Prophecy* (T. H. Robinson Festschrift), 1950, pp. 156 ff., and C. R. North, in *The Old Testament and Modern Study*, pp. 48 ff.

injustice if we accept it here. This means that the Pentateuch could not have been completed until the fifth century B.C., at the earliest, and its acceptance as sacred must be placed even later. On the other hand it would seem that it must have been accepted as sacred before the Samaritan schism, since it is accepted by Samaritans no less than by the Jews. But since the other books of the Old Testament are not accepted as canonical by the Samaritans, it would appear that their acceptance as sacred was of later date. To this we may add that if the prophetic books were not compiled in their present form until post-exilic days, their reception into the sacred Canon must be assigned to the post-exilic age. Not merely the compilers of the prophetic books were unaware of any antithesis between the two sorts of prophets, therefore, but the people who accepted the Prophets alongside the Law in the sacred Canon could not have felt this antithesis. We ought therefore to make sure that it is not a modern antithesis which we are reading back into the texts.

The antithesis between prophet and priest has been much softened by recent study along quite different lines. Attention has been called to many passages in the Old Testament which mention priests and prophets together as cultic officials who stand side by side. This has led to the wide recognition of what are called cultic prophets in Israel, who occupied a defined place in the worship of the shrines.[1] This recognition raises many questions to which different answers are offered by different scholars. Some have tended to regard all the prophets as cultic officials, and to read the Old Testament in terms of what is known of Babylonian priestly classes.[2] Others have been more cautious, and have recognized that cultic and non-cultic prophets probably both

[1] Cf. S. Mowinckel, *Psalmenstudien III. Kultprophetie und prophetische Psalmen*, 1923; A. R. Johnson, *The Cultic Prophet in Ancient Israel*, 1944; A. Haldar, *Associations of Cult Prophets among the Ancient Semites*, 1945. On these studies cf. O. Eissfeldt, in *The Old Testament and Modern Study*, pp. 119 ff., H. H. Rowley, *The Servant of the Lord*, 1952, pp. 104 ff., and N. W. Porteous, *E.T.*, lxii, 1950–51, pp. 5 ff. A. C. Welch, *Prophet and Priest in Old Israel*, pp. 75 n., 130 f. n., recognized the existence of cultic prophets. Cf. also *Kings and Prophets of Israel*, 1952, p. 184.

[2] So especially Haldar, *op. cit.*

functioned in Israel.[1] Some of the books of the prophetic canon
have been treated as partly, or even wholly, liturgies prepared by
cultic prophets for use on particular occasions.[2] It is clear that we
must beware of any easy division between cultic prophets and
true prophets, that would identify the cultic prophets with the
opponents of the true prophets, and define the true prophets as
men who opposed the whole institution of the cultus. Had any
such simple line of division existed, it would have been easy for
anyone to apply the test and to know who was a false prophet.
Yet we find that no simple or satisfying tests could be laid down,
and when the book of Deuteronomy endeavours to lay down any
tests they are on quite different lines.[3] It is probable that the very
strength of the denunciation of the false prophets by the canonical
prophets is due to the fact that ordinary people had no means of
detecting their deceptions. It was in the realm of the spirit, rather
than in that of function, that the difference lay.[4] Both claimed to
be prophets in the same sense, and the difference between them
was in the measure of their reflection of the message of God in
their word. To say this is to say that sharp lines of division cannot
be drawn amongst the prophets. Some functioned in the shrines,
but some quite certainly did not, and the same prophet could
sometimes function in a shrine and sometimes not. All prophets
were probably cultic persons, though not all seem to have been
attached to particular shrines; but if some prophets were regarded
as cultic officials and sharp lines could not be drawn within the
prophetic groups, we must be cautious of converting any of the
prophetic groups into such root and branch opponents of the

[1] Cf. R. B. Y. Scott, *The Relevance of the Prophets*, p. 43: 'With the great prophets
such a connection with the cultus was exceptional; but that bodies of "official prophets"
continued down to the seventh century to be associated with the temple priesthood is
clear from Jer. xxvi. 8, 11, 16.'

[2] Cf. P. Humbert, 'Essai d'analyse de Nahoum i. 2–ii. 3', *Z.A.W.*, xliv, 1926, pp.
266 ff., 'Le Problème du livre de Nahoum', *R.H.P.R.*, xii, 1932, pp. 1 ff., *Problèmes
du livre d'Habacuc*, 1944; A. Haldar, *Studies in the Book of Nahum*, 1947. Cf. too I. Engnell,
'Joels bok', *S.B.U.*, i, 1948, cols. 1075 ff., and A. S. Kapelrud, *Joel Studies*, 1948. Kapelrud
holds that the book of Joel is in part composed in the *style* of a liturgy. So long ago as
1907 P. Haupt maintained that the first two chapters of Nahum were a liturgy, though
he placed the composition as late as the second century B.C. and held that they were
composed to celebrate the victory over Nicanor in 161 B.C. Cf. *J.B.L.*, xxvi, 1907, pp. 1 ff.

[3] Deut. xiii. 1 ff., xviii. 20 ff.   [4] Cf. *The Servant of the Lord*, pp. 127 f.

cultus that it would be hard to understand why they should bear a common name with that borne by officials of the cultus.

One further general consideration may also be noted. It has been said that the school that finds the antithesis has found in the book of Deuteronomy Josiah's Law-book, and has usually ascribed its composition to the seventh century B.C. It has found this book to rest on the teachings of the eighth century prophets, and all its noble exhortations to humanity and compassion have been traced to this source. Yet it is certain that the compilers of Deuteronomy did not repudiate the institution of sacrifice and regard the cultus as something inherently evil. No more than the post-exilic compilers of the prophetic books or the shapers of the Canon do they appear to have realized that the eighth century prophets were inflexibly opposed to sacrifice and the cultus. It is hard to think that they, who stood so near at least to Isaiah in time, were completely confused in their understanding of his message and that of his predecessors.

With so many considerations to suggest that neither in pre-exilic nor in post-exilic days was any such root and branch antagonism between the exponents of prophetic and priestly religion felt as modern writers have alleged, we may return to the passages already quoted, to see if they will bear another interpretation more consistent with probability. First we may note one other general consideration, arising from the study of these passages themselves. When Amos denounces sacrifice, he continues: 'But let judgement roll down as waters, and righteousness as a mighty stream'.[1] Isaiah ends his great passage by saying: 'Your hands are full of blood'.[2] Similarly Jeremiah prefaces his declaration that the sacrifices are not acceptable by saying that the people had not hearkened to the words of the Lord and had rejected His law.[3] If these prophets really meant that sacrifice was wrong in itself and under all circumstances, it was very inept of them to bring into direct connection with their denunciation what was really irrelevant to it. If sacrifice and sacred seasons and prayer were just as hateful to God whether men's hands were full

[1] Amos v. 24.   [2] Isa. i. 15.   [3] Jer. vi. 19.

of blood or whether they were not, and if God hated to see men in the Temple sharing the forms of worship whether they came to Him with sincerely obedient hearts or not, it would surely have been wiser for these prophets to have said so unmistakably, and not to have befogged the issue by so persistently bringing in these irrelevances.

The general message of all these passages is 'not sacrifice, but obedience'—and by obedience the prophets meant the reflection of the character of God in life and the finding of its source in holy fellowship with Him. Here we may observe that it is characteristic of Hebrew idiom to say 'not this but that', when the meaning is 'that is more important than this'. This characteristic has often been observed,[1] and we are not ordinarily troubled by it. When our Lord said that no one could be His disciple unless he hated his parents and all who were bound to him by natural ties,[2] He meant that loyalty to Him must take precedence over loyalty to one's kindred.[3] We do not for one moment suppose that He Who enjoined the love of enemies enjoined the hatred of friends. Though the terms used were ostensibly absolute, we recognize that the meaning was comparative.[4] It is therefore possible that the prophets were really saying that obedience was more important than sacrifice, and that for lack of obedience sacrifice was invalidated.[5] So far as Hosea is concerned, we find that the

---

[1] Cf. C. J. Cadoux, E.T., lii, 1940–41, pp. 378 f.; C. Lattey, J.T.S., xlii, 1941, pp. 158 ff.
[2] Lk. xiv. 26.   [3] The saying is interpreted in this sense in Matt. x. 37.
[4] C. J. Cadoux, E.T., lviii, 1946–47, pp. 44 f., claims that so far as Mic. vi. 6–8 is concerned, sacrifice is definitely excluded, because it is not specified in what he maintains to be the *exhaustive* demands of God. If this rigid literalism is followed, then we must conclude that every form of corporate worship is unacceptable to God, because it is not here specified. A similar literalistic reading of Jn. vi. 27 would forbid the Christian to work for his living, since work is not merely excluded by implication, but specifically prohibited. 'Work not for the meat which perisheth, but for the meat which abideth unto eternal life.' It is always wrong to approach the Bible in the spirit of a lawyer arguing the meaning of an Act of Parliament.
[5] Cf. H. Wheeler Robinson, *Redemption and Revelation*, 1942, p. 250: 'The prophets' criticism of contemporary sacrifices was not necessarily intended to do away with them altogether, but was more probably intended to check the abuse of them, by which they became the substitutes, instead of the accompaniments, expressions and encouragements, of true piety and right conduct.' Similarly W. P. Paterson, in Hastings's *D.B.*, iv, 1902, p. 335b: 'Those who regard the prophets as abolitionists make a mistake which is common in studying polemics—viz. of misconceiving an attack on abuses as an attack on the institution which they have infected.'

second part of his statement is translated in comparative terms by translators ancient and modern, who had no axe to grind,[1] but simply sought to give a natural rendering: 'I desire mercy, and not sacrifice; and the knowledge of God more than burnt offerings.'[2] The two halves of the verse are parallel, and it is improbable that in the first half sacrifice is absolutely condemned and in the second part comparatively. Both halves express the same thought that sacrifice is not the most important of the demands of God.[3] This thought we find elsewhere in the Bible in such a passage as: 'Behold, to obey is better than sacrifice, and to hearken than the fat of rams.'[4]

This still leaves the rhetorical question of Amos and the statement of Jeremiah, with which we began, unexplained. So far as Jeremiah is concerned, it is hard to think that his teaching as a whole favours the view that he opposed the entire institution of sacrifice. It is true that he could contemplate, and even announce, the destruction of the Temple;[5] but that was not because the Temple was evil in itself, but only because men had polluted it. What had been intended for the house of God had become a den of thieves,[6] to which men resorted for safety in the vain hope that the God Whose way they despised would be bound to give them protection here. Yet Jeremiah could say that if only men would return to God in sincerity and do His will, the destruction of the Temple might be avoided.[7] Clearly he was not against the Temple as such, but found that men who came to it invalidated their worship by the spirit in which they came.

Nor is it probable that Jeremiah denied, in the verse that has

[1] E. C. Maclaurin, *The Origin of the Hebrew Sacrificial System*, 1948, p. 29, renders: 'and the knowledge of God *without* burnt-offerings'. So also S. Herner, *Sühne und Vergebung in Israel*, 1942, p. 36. That the preposition might have this meaning is indubitable, but that it is not a natural rendering is clear from the fact that the Septuagint, Vulgate, Peshitta, and the standard versions in modern languages render by the comparative. The rendering *without* has been adopted only by the school of writers that was antecedently persuaded that the prophets rejected all sacrifice. A rendering which rests on a theory can offer no support to it. The alternative rendering is perfectly natural and does not rest on any theory about the prophets.

[2] Hos. vi. 8.

[3] Cf. A. C. Welch, *Kings and Prophets of Israel*, 1952, p. 183: 'What Hosea demanded was a closer union between the sacrifice and repentance.'

[4] 1 Sam. xv. 22.   [5] Jer. vii. 14, xxvi. 6.   [6] Jer. vii. 11.   [7] Jer. vii. 3.

been quoted, that sacrifices had any part in the religion of the Mosaic period. The oldest Pentateuchal sources, that long ante-dated the days of Jeremiah, had records of sacrifices in the days of Moses, and long before in the patriarchal period. Moreover, the story of the Exodus was inextricably associated with the Passover, and it is hard to believe that Jeremiah was unwilling to admit that the Passover lambs were slain. It is true that the Passover was unlike other sacrifices, but it was certainly regarded as a sacrifice. Sacrifices were, indeed, of many kinds.[1] Again, it is clear that Jeremiah held Samuel in high esteem, as a holy man whose prayers might be particularly effective, though insufficient to avert the disaster that was coming upon Judah.[2] There can be no doubt that Samuel offered sacrifices, and Jeremiah could scarcely be ignorant of the fact. Yet in spite of this, he held him in honour. It would therefore seem that Jeremiah's condemnation of sacrifice was not so absolute. We may now observe that here again, in this passage, we have a statement of the type 'not this but that', where the intention is to stress the importance of that as against this. 'I spake not unto your fathers . . . concerning burnt offerings or sacrifices: but this thing I commanded them, saying, Hearken unto my voice, and I will be your God, and ye shall be my people.[3] It was this that was represented as the important thing, to which sacrifice was secondary. In this there is nothing antithetical to what is stated in the Pentateuch. On the contrary, the words of Jeremiah are but an echo of what we read there. For there God is represented as saying to Moses: 'If ye will obey my voice indeed, and keep my covenant, then shall ye be a peculiar treasure unto me from among all peoples . . . and ye shall be unto me a kingdom of priests, and an holy nation.'[4] In this passage, which is more fundamental to the Covenant of Sinai than the subsequent sacrificial legislation, there is no mention of sacrifice. For obedience was the first demand of God in the Law no less than in the Prophets.

---

[1] Cf. H. H. Rowley, *B.J.R.L.*, xxxiii, 1950, pp. 83 ff. Also, for a fuller discussion, W. O. E. Oesterley, *Sacrifices in Ancient Israel*, 1937, pp. 75 ff.
[2] Jer. xv. 1.   [3] Jer. vii. 22 f.   [4] Exod. xix. 5.

We are left with the rhetorical question of Amos, which is held to imply a denial that any sacrifices were offered in the wilderness period. Yet if it does imply such a denial, it equally implies that everybody knew that no sacrifices were offered in that period, since the answer was left to the people to supply.[1] It would surely be surprising to suggest that this was well known, when all our surviving traditions from days long antedating the time of Amos tell of such sacrifices. If Amos wished to deny the truth of those traditions, he might have been expected to do so directly, and not by such a rhetorical question as he posed. It is now more than half a century since a different understanding of the text of Amos was proposed,[2] and one which seems to the present writer to be more probable, especially in view of all that has been here said. It was noted that the words 'sacrifices and offerings' stand in the emphatic position at the beginning of the sentence in Hebrew, and that the verb used for 'bring' is unusual in connection with sacrifices. The meaning was therefore held to be: 'Was it only flesh-sacrifices and meal-offerings that ye brought me in the wilderness?' where the expected answer would be the confession 'We brought more than this; we brought true worship of heart and righteousness'.[3]

Viewing all these passages together, the attitude of the pre-exilic prophets would appear to have been that sacrifice as an external act unrelated to the spirit had no value, and was positively

---

[1] V. Maag, *Text, Wortschatz und Begriffswelt des Buches Amos*, 1951, pp. 221 f., thinks Amos relies on a historical source which was in disagreement with J and E. This is most improbable. Maag agrees that such a source was without foundation in fact, and since both J and E are generally agreed to be older than the time of Amos, it is unlikely that the prophet could have referred allusively to a different tradition as though it were unchallengeable.

[2] Cf. D. B. Macdonald, 'Old Testament Notes. 2. Amos v. 25', *J.B.L.*, xviii, 1899, pp. 214 f.

[3] Oesterley, *op. cit.*, p. 195, proposes a less likely view. He holds that the meaning of the passage is 'Did not your forefathers offer me sacrifices which were acceptable because they were offered in faithfulness and sincerity?' and that the answer expected was 'Yes', where the implied rebuke is then 'Why, then, do you offer sacrifices which, on account of your sins and on account of your false ideas about your God Yahweh, are worthless and unacceptable?' Similarly H. Junker, *Theologie und Glaube*, 1935, pp. 686 ff., holds that the expected answer was 'Yes'. E. Würthwein, *Th.L.Z.*, lxii, 1947, col. 150, suggests that the verse is a gloss which entered the text.

dishonouring to God.[1] It was a vain effort to deceive Him, appearing to express a meaning by the act but not really charging the act with the meaning. It was by obedience that the real attitude of the heart was expressed, and if there had been some lapse for which pardon was sought by the sacrifice, then there must be some true repentance in the heart, or the sin would be clung to in the heart and God be mocked by the cry for pardon. The prophets we have been considering could see no sign of such repentance or obedience. Men whose lives were an offence to God were inflexibly determined to repeat on the morrow the things that were seen by the prophets to be an offence to Him. No cry for pardon was in the heart, however much it might be on the lips; no plea for fellowship could have reality, while the heart insisted on being far from God. The pre-exilic prophets denounced sacrifices which were hollow and ineffective; but there is no reason to suppose that they held that no other sacrifices could be offered by men whose hearts were right with God. Indeed it is implied by the whole purport of the declaration 'Your worship is inacceptable; your hands are full of blood' that if the hands were not full of blood the worship would be acceptable. It was not the act alone that mattered, but the act as charged with the spirit of the worshipper. It was in the Temple that Isaiah had his call,[2] and in the moment of that experience he felt his lips touched with a live coal from the altar and his whole being was purified by its touch. It cannot be that he thought it wrong to tread the Temple courts, or supposed the altar to be a thing evil in itself.

When now we turn to the Law, we find it just as hard to sustain the common antithesis from this side. The Law nowhere

---

[1] Cf. H. Wheeler Robinson, *J.T.S.*, xliii, 1942, p. 137: 'Our parallelism suggests that for the prophets everything depended on the spirit in which an act was performed. . . . Similarly, we may say that they condemned the *opus operatum* of sacrifice, so long as it was not lifted up into the spirit of true devotion to Yahweh, and true obedience to His moral requirements.' I. Epstein says the prophets were all concerned with voluntary sacrifices in these passages, and that it was only such sacrifices that were fraught with spiritual peril. Cf. 'Introduction to Seder Ḳodashim', p. xxvi, in H. Freedman, *Zebaḥim*, 1948. On the attitude of Amos to the cultus cf. A. Neher, *Amos*, 1950, pp. 87 ff.

[2] Isa. vi. 1.

teaches that so long as men offer the right sacrifices they can live how they please. The Decalogue, which stands in the Law, and which may reasonably be ascribed to Moses, is the earliest expression of ethical religion. The Covenant, whose establishment is recorded in the Law, called first and foremost for obedience. The principles of humanity so dear to the prophets are expressed with power in Deuteronomy, and there we read the great word which has been cherished by Jews in all ages, and which was declared by our Lord to be the first law of life for all men: 'Thou shalt love the Lord thy God'.[1] In the Code of Holiness we find that other word which is lifted to honour in the Gospel: 'Thou shalt love thy neighbour as thyself.'[2] There is nothing in any of this of which the greatest of the prophets might have been ashamed, and the post-exilic Judaism that attached so great a value to the Law need not be dismissed as unspiritual.

The Law prescribed sacrifices, but it prescribed more than sacrifices. Where sacrifice for sin was offered—and we should beware of supposing that all sacrifices were offered for sin—confession of sin was demanded, and restitution in so far as restitution could be made. 'And it shall be, when he shall be guilty in one of these things, that he shall confess that wherein he hath sinned; and he shall bring his forfeit unto the Lord for his sin which he hath sinned . . . and the priest shall make atonement for him as concerning his sin.'[3] Before the sacrifice could be effective, it must be the organ of his approach to God. Moreover, if he had sinned against his fellow-man, he was required to make amends to him against whom he had sinned, before he could get right with God. 'When a man or woman shall commit any sin that men commit . . . then shall they confess their sin which they have done; and he shall make restitution for his guilt in full, and add unto it the fifth part thereof, and give it unto him in respect of whom he hath been guilty.'[4] It was not alone the prophets who were concerned with

[1] Deut. vi. 4 f.   [2] Lev. xix. 18.
[3] Lev. v. 5 f.   [4] Num. v. 6 f.

44

the relation of man to man, and found here something that vitally affected the relation of man to God.

Similarly, when sacrifice was made for the sins of the community on the great Day of Atonement, an essential element in the ritual was the confession of the sin of the community by the High Priest as its representative.[1] There is no reason to suppose that this was intended to be a hollow formality. If the priest did not truly represent the spirit of the community in his confession, he could not truly represent it in his sacrifice, and the one was as meaningless as the other.[2]

Again, there is an important passage in the Law which says: 'The soul that doeth aught with a high hand . . . the same blasphemeth the Lord; and that soul shall be cut off from among his people.'[3] It is clear that sinning with a high hand meant something more than consciously sinning, since there is provision for the cleansing of sins which were certainly conscious, and it is probable that this meant deliberately sinning, sinning as the expression of the settled purpose of the heart, as distinct from lapsing into sin.[4] Such a sinner could not sincerely repent, and for him no sacrifice was valid. It was the sacrifices of such persons that the prophets declared useless, and in this they were at one with the Law.

It is here of interest to observe that in the book of Proverbs we find the same point of view. That book is commonly spoken of as representing a spirit of shrewd worldly-wisdom, and it is certain that we do not find here the religious profundity of either Law or Prophets. Nevertheless, here we find that a fundamentally religious outlook prevails. The fear of God is the beginning of wisdom,[5] and it is recognized that in the will of God is the only true well-being of man. And here we find the same attitude which we have seen to characterize both Law and Prophets.

[1] Lev. xvi. 21.
[2] Cf. T. W. Manson, *J.T.S.*,, xlvi 1945, p. 7: 'As Elbogen points out, the immense numbers of Jews who could not be present at the Temple service kept the fast, and made their confession in their synagogues. The confession became universal and individual in Israel.'
[3] Num. xv. 30.
[4] Cf. *B.J.R.L.*, xxxiii, 1950–51, p. 97.
[5] Prov. i. 7.

'The sacrifice of the wicked is an abomination: how much more when he bringeth it with a wicked mind.'[1] Or again: 'To do justice and judgement is more acceptable to the Lord than sacrifice.'[2] Surely there is a unity of view dominant in the Bible on this matter, even though there is a difference of emphasis and of the strength of passion put into the words. Nowhere is sacrifice presented save as secondary to obedience and to rightness of spirit. And later Judaism, with all its emphasis on the Law, always understood the Law in this sense, and rated but lightly the offering without the spirit that made it the organ of the offerer's approach to God.[3]

It has been already said that it is not our purpose to argue that there is no difference between the Law and the Prophets. Indeed, it has been insisted that the unity to be found in the Bible is a unity in diversity, and that differences must be recognized as well as an underlying unity. It is therefore unnecessary to minimize the difference between the Law and the Prophets in the interests of the unity which is maintained. For the Law is much concerned with involuntary acts and ritual uncleanness, where no ethical considerations were involved. In part these are a legacy from

[1] Prov. xxi. 27. Cf. xv. 8. The translation given in the text above follows A.V. and R.V. Some prefer R.V. marg.: 'When he bringeth it to atone for wickedness.'

[2] Prov. xxi. 3. Cf. Eccl. v. 1 (Heb. iv. 17): 'To draw nigh to hear is better than to give the sacrifice of fools.'

[3] Cf. Ecclus. xxxiv. 18 f. (xxxi. 21 ff.): 'The sacrifice of an unrighteous man is a mockery, and the oblations of the wicked are not acceptable. The Most High hath no pleasure in the offerings of the godless; nor is pacified for sins by the multitude of sacrifices' (rendering based in part on the Syriac text and in part following the rendering of Box and Oesterley, in Charles's *Apocrypha and Pseudepigrapha of the Old Testament*, i, 1913, p. 435; cf. *B.J.R.L.*, xxxiii, p. 102). Cf. also Mishnah, *Yoma*, viii. 9: 'If a man say, I will sin again and repent, he will be given no chance to repent. If he say, I will sin and the Day of Atonement will clear me, the Day of Atonement will effect no clearance'; Tosephta, *Yoma* v. 9 (ed. Zuckermandel, 1937, p. 190): 'Sin offering and guilt offering and death and the Day of Atonement all put together do not effect atonement without repentance'; T.B. *Berachoth* 23a (cf. A. Cohen, *The Babylonian Talmūd: Tractate Berākōt*, 1921, p. 150): 'Be not like fools who sin and make an offering without repenting'. To suggest that Judaism was concerned only with the act and not with the spirit is quite unfair. It did not condone deliberate sin, or think of sacrifice as a magical means of evading its consequences. In the Midrash, *Lev. Rabba* ii. 12 (cf. *Midrash Rabbah*, ed. by H. Freedman and M. Simon, iv, 1939, pp. 32 f.), we read: 'This is so that a man shall not say within himself, I will go and do things which are ugly and unseemly, and I will bring an ox, on which there is much flesh, and offer it on the altar, and lo! I shall be in favour with Him, and He will receive me as a penitent.'

primitive ideas, and in part they were intended to foster the sense of the exceeding greatness of God, Whose lightest word must be law to man, and the sense of the heinousness of moral evil, since even ritual uncleanness must be taken so seriously.[1] We find none of this in the prophets, and we see its perils when we come to the New Testament and observe the concern for the trivial which is there condemned.[2] Nor can we read some of the tractates of the Mishnah without realizing that the attitude condemned in the Gospels was well represented. There was a deep concern for the technical and the trivial which is poles asunder from anything that stands in the Prophets. That this was not the only side of Judaism, and especially of Pharisaism, must be freely recognized. For Christianity received a rich heritage from Judaism, without robbing Judaism of it; it continued to be the heritage of Judaism and to mark with its high spirit many of Judaism's leaders.

That Judaism is not to be condemned as hard and unspiritual, and set over against the prophets in the way that has been here repudiated, is further to be seen from the fact that the Psalter had its place in the worship of post-exilic Judaism. Many of the Psalms were probably of pre-exilic composition, but the compilation of the Psalter was quite certainly achieved in post-exilic days. There was a time when the composition of most of the psalms was ascribed to the late post-exilic period, but that mood has passed in the scholarly circles of today. Indeed, the present danger is rather on the other side, in the too ready assumption that almost all the psalms were early. It is wiser not to attempt the impossible task of dating the individual psalms, but to recognize that we have both early and late elements in the Psalter. We should be particularly cautious in the ascription of psalms to the Maccabaean period, to which large numbers of them were once

[1] Cf. the saying of Rabbi Judah the Prince: 'Be heedful of a light precept as of a weighty one' (*Pirqe Aboth* ii. 1).

[2] Cf. J. Klausner's observation on the Pharisees: 'The casuistry and immense theoretical care devoted to every one of the slightest religious ordinances left them open to the misconception that the ceremonial laws were the main principle and the ethical laws only secondary' (*Jesus of Nazareth*, E. Tr. by H. Danby, 2nd ed., p. 216).

ascribed. Nevertheless, we may reasonably find in the post-exilic compilation of the collection of the psalms, and in the employment of them in worship,[1] a signal evidence of interest in spiritual worship in that age. Post-exilic Judaism expressed its spirit as much here, and in the collection and veneration of the Prophets, as it did in its veneration of the Law. By all must it be judged, and not by one alone, and that one expression of its spirit seen in distorted perspective, without emphasis on its more spiritual elements.[2]

It is frequently observed that in the Psalter there are passages comparable with those passages in the Prophets at which we have looked, where sacrifice is depreciated. Once more we observe that they stand alongside other passages where sacrifice is clearly approved of, and it would seem that the collectors of the psalms were not aware of any flat contradiction. The passage most commonly appealed to is: 'Thou delightest not in sacrifice; else would I give it: Thou hast no delight in burnt offering. The sacrifices of God are a broken spirit: A broken and a contrite heart, O God, thou wilt not despise.'[3] Immediately after this we find that sacrifices are referred to with approval in this same psalm.[4] As it is probable that the last two verses of this psalm are a later addition, they cannot be appealed to for the view of the author of our verses.[5] It is to be noted, however, that the heading

[1] It is commonly held today that many of the psalms accompanied ritual acts, both completing the ritual and interpreting its significance. Cf. A. J. Wensinck, *Semietische Studiën uit de nalatenschap van A. J. Wensinck*, 1941, p. 57: 'My thesis is that, for the greater part, the Psalms are spoken rhythmic illustrations of the acts of worship; just as the musical part of the Catholic Mass is an illustration and a rhythmization of the ritual acts' (first published in 1919). Such a view of the cultic use of the Psalter has been maintained especially by S. Mowinckel, *Psalmenstudien*, 1921–24. Cf. also A. C. Welch, *Prophet and Priest in Old Israel*, pp. 131 ff.

[2] Cf. N. W. Porteous, *Interpretation*, iii, 1949, pp. 404 f.: 'It must never be forgotten that the clue to the meaning of what Israel did in her religious practice is to be found reflected in the Psalter. It is quite unlikely that these ancient Hebrew hymns which have inspired so much that is best in Christian worship should have originally, many of them, been composed to accompany a ritual which did not represent a genuine synthesis of the religious and the ethical. To suppose anything else is to suppose that the Psalms were fundamentally irrelevant in the ritual setting to which they originally belonged. In other words, the evidence of the Psalter must be allowed to qualify the evidence of the prophets.'

[3] Psa. li. 16 f. (Heb. 18 f.).   [4] Psa. li. 19 (Heb. 21).

[5] Some modern writers have defended the originality of these verses. So C. A. Briggs, *The Book of Psalms*, ii, 1909, p. 10; G. Widengren, *The Accadian and Hebrew Psalms of Lamentation as Religious Documents*, 1937, pp. 31 f. The alternative view, that they are an addition, seems more probable, however; since they seem to be quite unrelated to the

of the psalm associates it with David at the time of his adultery with Bathsheba and the consequent treatment of Uriah, that amounted to murder. Little reliance can be put on the headings of the psalms,[1] but it is possible that the author wrote it with David in mind, or was himself guilty of some similarly heinous sin, or composed the psalm for people who were guilty of grave sins and yet were penitent. While the heading has little authority as evidence of authorship, it has much evidence on the understanding of the psalm at the time when it was added. We may next observe that in David's situation, at the time indicated in the heading, no sacrifice was relevant, for no sacrifice was prescribed in the Law for adultery or murder.[2] There were many sins too heinous to be cleared by any sacrifice, for with all its insistence on sacrifice, the Law is far from suggesting that any ritual act can be relevant where grave sin is concerned. When the prophets declared that sacrifice was unavailing because men's hands were full of blood, they were not saying something which is contradicted in the Law, but were speaking in full harmony with the Law, which declared that for sins of blood death alone was adequate. They were implicitly defining sins of blood to include more than direct physical violence, but they were adding nothing new as to the heinousness of sins of blood. We sometimes find that there is pardon even for such grave sins, when the sinner

---

individual penitence which is the theme of the rest of the psalm. John Paterson, *The Praises of Israel*, 1950, p. 107, thinks it was perhaps due to the addition of these verses that the psalm was preserved at all. S. Daiches, in *Essays Presented to J. H. Hertz*, 1944, pp. 105 ff., maintained that the last two verses had no reference to animal sacrifice, but used the terms of animal sacrifice as figures for 'sacrifices of righteousness', which he interpreted to mean righteous living. This is highly improbable. C. Ryder Smith, *The Biblical Doctrine of Salvation*, 1941, p. 85, asks: 'Why did some one, after having read the Psalm, add them, and why did others accept the addition? Not, surely, just because he and they wanted to push ritual in somehow, but because they felt that, when the experience so poignantly described in the psalm was theirs, they could go on to use the sacrifices of the Temple sacramentally. They were men who, having cried out for "a clean heart" and "a right spirit", knew that the right use of ritual would help them to find it.'

[1] The Davidic authorship is maintained by B. D. Eerdmans, *The Hebrew Book of Psalms* (O.T.S., iv), 1947, pp. 274 ff.

[2] Cf. H. Herkenne, *Das Buch der Psalmen* (in H.S.A. Tes., ed. by F. Feldmann and H. Herkenne, V, 2), 1936, p. 191, and E. Pannier and H. Renard, *Les Psaumes* (in *La Sainte Bible*, ed. by A. Clamer, v), 1950, p. 303.

in true penitence humbles himself before God; but it is always a pardon granted by God in His grace to the penitent, and not achieved for him by any ritual act. Hence in such a situation as David's who did repent and who was pardoned,[1] but for whose sins the Law prescribed no remedy, the words of the psalm are in full accord with the Law, and whoever read the psalm in the light of its heading had no need to abandon the Law when he read these words. Even without the heading, it is certain that the psalm was written by one who was deeply conscious of some great sin, or written for the use of such,[2] and equally certain that for the greatest sins the Law prescribed no ritual remedy. It is quite unwarranted to lift these words out of their context, and then to infer that the writer held that sacrifice was in itself wholly alien to the will of God.[3]

The Law prescribed no sacrifices for the most serious of sins. Nevertheless, within its limited range, sacrifice was certainly

---

[1] Cf. 2 Sam xii. 13.

[2] Cf. *B.J.R.L.*, xxix, 1945–46, pp. 352 f., where the writer has observed: 'If a sin-offering were being offered, I can think of nothing more appropriate or more effective than Psalm li to make the worshipper realize that his offering was of less significance than the spirit in which he brought it, or to call forth from him that spirit of penitence which could make the cry of his offering the genuine cry of his heart, that his offering might be at once the organ of his approach to God, and of God's approach in grace to him.'

[3] There are other passages in the Psalter which have been held to repudiate sacrifice altogether. Psa. lxix. 30 f. (Heb. 31 f.) can scarcely be pressed to mean more than that God is better pleased with the soul's attitude than with any act of sacrifice. But this, as we have seen, is the attitude expressed again and again in the Old Testament, and is but a variation of the thought 'To obey is better than sacrifice'. Psa. xl. 6 ff. (Heb. 7 ff.), again, offers an example of the expression in apparently absolute terms of a relative meaning, such as has been noticed above. It declares, in effect, that God does not delight in sacrifice, but in humble submission to His will, and this, in accordance with that frequent use of the 'relative negative' in Hebrew, can be understood to mean that God does not delight in sacrifice so much as in obedience. Psa. l. 9 ff., once more, seems at first sight to be an uncompromising declaration that God is in no need of sacrifice and takes no delight in it. Yet in the same psalm we read: 'Gather my saints together unto me: those that have made a covenant with me by sacrifice' (verse 5), where sacrifice is approved when offered by men in the right spirit. Further, verses 14 and 25 of this psalm imply that sacrifice is not absolutely repudiated. On these passages cf. C. Lattey, *J.T.S.*, xlii, 1941, pp. 161 ff. G. R. Berry, *The Book of Psalms*, 1934, p. 87, observes of Psa. xl.: 'It is probably not an entire repudiation of sacrifice, but it assigns to it a subordinate position', while of Psa. l. he says: 'The psalm is a protest against some features of the use of sacrifices in the time of the writer. It is not written in entire opposition to them, but . . . it disapproves the excessive reliance on them which was common among the mass of the people.'

thought of as potent when offered rightly.[1] The pre-exilic prophets, who were preoccupied with men who did not offer rightly, say little of this; the Law, which emphasizes both the right technique and the right spirit, was much concerned with it. When sacrifice was the organ of the spirit, it was believed to be charged with power for its specific purpose. The offerer had to lay his hand on the head of the slaughtered animal, thus to identify himself in symbol with the animal, so that its death symbolized his death to the past, or to whatever stood between him and God, and his approach to God in thanksgiving or in plea.[2] A symbol that corresponds to no reality is completely meaningless. That is Deutero-Isaiah's condemnation of idols. They were symbols of unreality, since the only God would have none of them. So here, the offerer who laid his hand on the head of the animal while his heart was far from penitence and from the humble approach to God was performing a meaningless act, that was a symbol of nothing. In a profound sense he must come to God with his sacrifice if it were to have meaning. But when he did so come, it was believed by the framers of the Law that his sacrifice could be the organ of God's approach to him in cleansing and in fellowship. Everywhere it was seen that obedience and the submission of the heart to God are primary, and more important than the external act, so that the sacrifice by itself could do nothing for him. For in the thought of the Old Testament, while sacrifice was the organ of blessing, it was not its source. God, and God alone, was its source. If men made their sacrifices the organ of their approach to Him, He could make them also the organ of His approach to them in blessing.[3] Where sacrifices were pre-

[1] Cf. H. Wheeler Robinson, *J.T.S.*, xliii, 1942, p. 131: 'That the personal act of sacrifice was generally regarded as doing something, *i.e.* as "efficacious", hardly needs demonstration. This is implied, on the one hand, in the detailed attention given to sacrifice in the Old Testament. This would be meaningless unless sacrifice were meaningful, to a degree far beyond a figurative and merely declarative symbolism.'

[2] Lev. i. 4, iii. 2, 8, 13, etc. Cf. H. Wheeler Robinson, *loc. cit.*, p. 130: 'The natural meaning of the laying of hands on the sacrifice is the closer identification of the offerer with his offering.'

[3] H. Wheeler Robinson described the sacrifices as 'actualized approaches to God' (*Redemption and Revelation*, p. 251). It is this which distinguishes them from the magic with which many in Israel confused them. 'Magic constrains the unseen; religion means

scribed, it was thought to be important that they should be offered, since no obedience to God could be genuine if it ignored His commands. This is the complaint of the post-exilic prophets. No longer did they see the splendid sacrifices offered with every ritual precision by people who proudly despised the will of God in their daily lives. Instead they found men offering half-hearted sacrifices, bringing to God not of their best, but dishonouring Him by offering Him their worst. They still believed in sacrifice, and professed to honour and obey God. The hollowness of their profession was quite differently shown from the hollowness in the time of the pre-exilic prophets. Nevertheless it was a hollow profession, the half-heartedness of whose spirit was shown in the unworthiness of what they brought to the altar. The post-exilic prophets no more than their pre-exilic predecessors taught that sacrifice could be effective when it was not the organ of the spirit, for both penetrated behind the deed to the spirit that prompted it. Taken throughout, the Old Testament nowhere teaches that sacrifice is valid without relation to the spirit, and nowhere does it teach that sacrifice is of universal validity.

Reference has been made to the Passover, which has unique features amongst the sacrifices of Israel.[1] We find it combined with the feast of Unleavened Bread, but it is generally believed that originally these were two separate festivals,[2] and that Passover was observed before the entry into Canaan.[3] The feast of Unleavened Bread was an agricultural festival and it may have been observed by the Canaanites, and have been taken over from them

---

surrender to it', says Wheeler Robinson (*J.T.S.*, *loc. cit.*, p. 132). In magic everything depends on the correct technique; in religion everything depends on the spirit. If the sacrifices were actualized approaches to God, they were meaningless without that inner approach which they were intended to actualize.

[1] For studies of this festival and its ritual cf. G. B. Gray, 'Passover and Unleavened Bread: the Laws of J, E, and D', *J.T.S.*, xxxvii, 1936, pp. 241 ff.; N. H. Snaith, *The Jewish New Year Festival*, 1947, pp. 13 ff.; T. H. Gaster, *Passover: its History and Traditions*, 1949. Cf. also A. C. Welch, *Prophet and Priest in Old Israel*, pp. 87 ff.

[2] Cf. J. Pedersen, *Israel III–IV*, pp. 400 f.: 'The events of the spring festival warrant the presumption that it is a combination of two originally independent festivals, a pre-Canaanite pastoral feast which sanctified the firstborn, and a Canaanite peasant feast which sanctified the barley crops.' This has long been the common view of scholars.

[3] Cf. Pedersen, *ibid.*, p. 382: 'It is clear that the Passover was such a popular festival before the immigration.'

by the Israelites and associated with their own faith. So far as
the Passover is concerned, it is closely connected with the Exodus
from Egypt,[1] and it is almost certain that it was not borrowed
from the Canaanites, but was observed prior to the entry into
Canaan. Neither in form nor in significance must it be traced to
an alien source. There are, however, singularly few references to
the Passover in the Old Testament, and of these none is found in
the Psalter and only one in the prophetic Canon, where mention
is made in the book of Ezekiel.[2] Nevertheless, the references
that are found stand in both the earliest and the latest documents
of the Old Testament. We find them in the oldest strand of the
Pentateuch,[3] in the Code of Deuteronomy,[4] in the Priestly Code,[5]
in the Deuteronomic history,[6] and in the work of the Chronicler.[7]
It is known that in New Testament times this festival was
observed, and in later Judaism it continued to be observed, though
in a modified form after the destruction of the Temple. Its
observance in Egypt was a domestic one, but with the centraliza-
tion of worship in the Code of Deuteronomy it was transferred
to the place where the central shrine should exist, and we learn
that in the reign of Josiah it was kept in Jerusalem by a great
concourse of people.[8] In New Testament times large numbers
went up to Jerusalem. The feast continued to have a family
character, however, and this it never lost.

More important than the form, and than any change of form
which the festival underwent in its history, is the significance it
bore. We have little more than speculation to guide us in deter-
mining what its original significance may have been. Many
scholars believe that it was originally a nomadic festival, and that
the choice of a time and the keeping within doors indicate some
relation to moon worship and the guarding against evil influences

---

[1] Its observance doubtless goes back far behind the time of Moses and the Exodus,
and its original significance is a matter of conjecture. Cf. Gaster, *op. cit.*, pp. 16 ff. For
Israel after the Exodus its significance was connected with that event.

[2] Ezk. xlv. 21.   [3] Exod. xii. 21 ff., xxxiv. 25.

[4] Deut. xvi. 1 ff.

[5] Exod. xii. 11 ff., 43 ff.; Lev. xxiii. 5; Num. ix. 6 ff., xxviii. 16, xxxiii. 3.

[6] Josh. v. 10 f.; 2 Kings xxiii. 21 ff.   [7] 2 Chr. xxx. 1 ff., xxxv. 1 ff.; Ezr. vi. 19 f.

[8] 2 Kings xxiii. 21 ff., 2 Chron. xxv. 1 ff.

associated with the moon.[1] To the student of the Bible this is completely immaterial. How ancient the rite may be, and what significance it may have had at first, have no bearing on the study of the Bible.[2] The Israelites were bidden to celebrate it in order to remember their deliverance from Egypt and what that deliverance had meant to them as a people.[3] It was charged with a historical and more than historical meaning. No longer was it supposed to do anything for them, whatever apotropaic power it might once have been supposed to have. It could, however, do something in them. To men who made this festival the vehicle of their remembrance in thanksgiving of the mighty acts of God for their fathers and of the divine election of Israel in grace, it could be the vehicle of the renewal of the Covenant and of their loyalty to God.[4] Its significance depended on the spirit they brought to it. If there was no thought beyond that of the slaughter and the meal, it would be as devoid of religious significance as a Christmas dinner. If it was kept as it was meant to be kept, as a sacred memorial, it could but strengthen faith in God and stimulate the spirit of consecration to His service. Although this sacrifice is mentioned only in the Law, and in writers who favoured the observance of the cultus, it is significant that here once more we find the same principles apply, and emphasis is laid on the spirit of remembrance that men brought to the festival, and not merely on the ritual details.[5]

There is one important passage in the prophetic Canon,

[1] Cf. Oesterley and Robinson, *Hebrew Religion*, 2nd ed., 1937, pp. 129 ff.; W. J. Moulton, in Hastings's *D.B.*, iii, 1900, pp. 688 ff.; J. N. Schofield, *The Religious Background of the Bible*, 1944, pp. 70 f.

[2] Cf. A. C. Welch, *Prophet and Priest in Old Israel*, p. 93: 'Passover was a palimpsest, like the religion of which it formed a leading feature. In the background appeared the characteristics of a lower type of religion, which had undergone the transforming influence of a higher faith. The motives which effected this transformation were taken from the historic and redemptive character of Yahwism, and so were directly derived from the Mosaic reform.' [3] Exod. xiii. 3, Deut. xvi. 3.

[4] Cf. the Deuteronomic law of the firstfruits, which is similarly made the vehicle of the remembrance of the deliverance from Egypt and of self-surrender to God in gratitude (Deut. xxvi. 1 ff.).

[5] Cf. N. W. Porteous, *Interpretation*, iii, 1949, p. 414: 'We must not allow the denunciation of Israel's prophets, justifiable as they undoubtedly were, to blind us to the service which Israel's cult must have rendered in maintaining through the centuries the faith and obedience of many a pious Israelite.'

dealing with a sacrifice quite different from any mentioned in the Law, and of a potency transcending that of any animal sacrifice, where we find that the same principles that we have found in the Law still apply. This passage stands in Deutero-Isaiah, who is commonly held to be the most spiritual of the prophets. He it is who rises to full speculative monotheism and its corollary in universalism, and who emphasizes the election of Israel, together with the call to a world-wide mission which that election lays on her. It is well known that there are passages called the Servant Songs,[1] culminating in the great song which stands in Isa. lii. 13–liii. 12. In this song we read that the Servant is led as a lamb to the slaughter and is cut off from the land of the living. Yet he is no mere martyr. By most writers a series of four songs is found, of which the first tells of the Servant's mission and the gentleness and persistence with which it is undertaken; the second indicates the double nature of the mission, first to Israel itself and then to the whole world; while the third tells of the suffering in which his mission will involve him. 'I gave my back to the smiters, and my cheeks to them that plucked off the hair.'[2] It is only when we come to the fourth song, however, that we learn that his mission will involve him in death and that the suffering will be more than the consequence of the mission. For here it becomes apparent that it is the organ of the mission. The Servant's death is referred to as a guilt-offering, and it is said to be potent.[3] It is not merely that we have this particular technical term applied to him. The whole thought is sacrificial. It is said that he shall bear the sins of many, and that men will say, 'Surely he hath borne our

---

[1] These are most commonly delimited as Isa. xlii. 1–4, xlix. 1–6, l. 4–9, lii. 13–liii. 12. For some variations of this view cf. the writer's *The Servant of the Lord*, 1952, p. 6 n. While this work was in the press J. Lindblom published his important study, *The Servant Songs in Deutero-Isaiah*, 1952, in which he found the verses immediately following the first three to contain interpretative oracles, while in the case of the fourth he delimited the song proper as liii. 2–12. [2] Isa. l. 6.

[3] Isa. lii. 10. The rendering of R.V. is 'When thou shalt make his soul an offering for sin, he shall see his seed, he shall prolong his days'. It is agreed by all editors that the text is here not in its original state, and many reconstructions have been proposed. The suggestion of R. Levy, *Deutero-Isaiah*, 1925, pp. 266 f., is very simple, consisting merely in the different division of the consonants of the first two words, to yield *'emeth śām* instead of *im tāśîm*. The rendering would then be 'Truly he gave himself an offering for sin; he shall see his seed, he shall prolong his days'.

C

griefs and carried our sorrows . . . He was wounded for our transgressions, he was bruised for our iniquities: the chastisement of our peace was upon him; and with his stripes we are healed.'[1] Just as the death of a sacrificed animal may be potent in the service of the offerer when it is the organ of his approach to God, so the death of the Servant is potent, but only, be it observed, when men bring to that death the spirit which makes it the organ of their approach to God. They must recognize that his death is for them, and must confess their sins: 'All we like sheep have gone astray; we have turned everyone to his own way; and the Lord hath laid on him the iniquity of us all.'[2] Just as in the thought and teaching of the Law sacrifice must bear a two-way traffic or none, being the organ of men's approach to God before it could be the organ of God's approach in power to them, so here the death of the Servant is the organ of men's approach to God before it is the organ of their healing. Its potency is then expressed in the words: 'My righteous servant shall justify many.'[3] In this context this means something more than 'shall declare them to be in the right', or 'give a verdict in their favour'. It is well known that this verb often has such a forensic sense. But a just judge only gives a verdict in accordance with justice, and never declares the guilty innocent.[4] That God is a just Judge is the fundamental

[1] Isa. liii. 4 f.   [2] Isa. liii. 6.
[3] Isa. liii. 11. The difficulties of the text here do not affect the present use of this verse. The Septuagint version and the Dead Sea Scroll (DSIa) add the word 'light' after 'he shall see'. P. Volz suggests that the word 'righteous', which stands awkwardly in the text, is a dittograph, and that a misread abbreviation has given 'by his knowledge' instead of 'with the knowledge of the Lord' (cf. *Jesaia* II, 1932, pp. 170 ff.). The text would then read 'And after his travail of soul he shall see light, and be satisfied with the knowledge of the Lord. My servant shall justify many, for the sins he bore are theirs.' With this compare the largely similar reconstruction of J. Lindblom (*op. cit.*, p. 45 n.). Many other reconstructions of this text have been proposed. R. J. Tournay, *R.B.*, lix, 1952, pp. 501 f., transposes the word 'righteous' to the previous clause, to give 'the righteous one shall be satisfied with knowledge.' Some Hebrew MSS instead of 'by his knowledge' read 'by his misfortune', and this is followed by P. Humbert, *La Bible du Centenaire*, ii, 1947, p. 417. The word is then read with what follows: 'By his sufferings my servant shall justify many.' So also E. J. Kissane, *The Book of Isaiah*, ii, 1943, pp. 182, 190; P. Auvray and J. Steinmann, *Isaïe* (Jerusalem Bible), 1951, p. 208.
[4] Cf. G. Schrenk, in writing of the Pauline doctrine of justification: ' "Forensic" does not mean that the sinner is treated as if he were righteous, for God's sovereign judicial declaration produces an actual effect.' (E. Tr. by J. R. Coates, *Righteousness*, Bible Key Words, iv, 1951, p. 45, from *Th.W.B.*, ii, 1935, p. 207.)

teaching of the Bible, and none of the prophets would have questioned it. If, then, a verdict is given in favour of men who confess their guilt, it is because they have become transformed in the very quality of their being. They have become righteous by the cleansing of their whole personality. This is the miracle that Isaiah felt to be wrought within his own personality in the moment when the live coal touched his lips in the experience of his call. 'Lo, this hath touched thy lips; and thine iniquity is taken away, and thy sin purged.'[1] The man who a moment before felt that in the presence of the holy God sin could not exist, and that therefore he must perish with his sin, now felt that he was separated from his sin, so that it alone might perish and he might live. So here, in connection with the death of the Servant, when men are pronounced righteous, it is because they have become righteous with the righteousness of the Servant. They who identify themselves with him in his death find that he identifies himself with them in his righteousness. For it is made clear that the Servant suffers wholly for others, and not for himself also. 'He had done no violence, neither was any deceit in his mouth.'[2] Just as a sacrificed animal must be without physical blemish, he was without moral blemish, dying a death he did not deserve to die, that men who deserved to die might be transmuted into his own righteousness in the presence of God.

Moreover, the Servant yields himself willingly to death. Unlike the animals that are sacrificed, and that are taken without their own volition to the altar, the Servant gives himself. 'I gave my back to the smiters . . . I hid not my face from shame and spitting.'[3] Not his body alone, but his whole personality bore the two-way traffic that lifted men to God and brought them cleansing of spirit. And yet again, the efficacy of this sacrifice is wider than that of any contemplated in the Law. There were sacrifices that availed for individuals, and the sacrifice of the Day of Atonement could avail for all Israel, when individuals or nation validated the sacrifice by their approach to God with the offering. Here, in the death of the Servant, however, is a sacrifice that

[1] Isa. vi. 7.   [2] Isa. liii. 9.   [3] Isa. l. 6.

reaches beyond Israel to the wider world to which Israel is sent in her mission. It is men of the Gentiles who are filled with awe as they contemplate the sufferings of the Servant, and who by confession realize that he stands in their place and then find justification.

Here, then, is a sacrifice that transcends any in the Law. It is by far the deepest word on sacrifice contained in the Old Testament, and it stands in the prophetic Canon and in the most spiritual of the prophets. It does not speak of a sacrifice that merely *ex opere operato* achieves something independently of the spirit of the worshippers, and it is not therefore like the sacrifices that the pre-exilic prophets so freely condemned. It conforms to the pattern of sacrifice as conceived in the Law, in that it is the organ of the spirit of man before it becomes the organ of blessing unto him, yet its blessing is not achieved by the spirit he brings, but is achieved in and for him as the act of God, Who lays his iniquity on the Servant in the moment of his confession.

The identification of the Servant does not directly concern us here, since our primary interest is to consider whether prophets and lawgivers in Israel had fundamentally opposed ideas as to the essence of religion, and whether they had irreconcilably different views as to the meaning and the efficacy of sacrifice. It seems to be clear that only a superficial reading of the Old Testament can lead to such a view, and that the more we penetrate to the essence of its thought the greater the measure of unity we find here. Nevertheless it has been said above that it is permissible to find peril in the Law's excessive concern for involuntary acts and ritual offences, and to recognize that in the differing emphases of Law and Prophets there may be differing worth. In the preoccupation of the pre-exilic prophets with the reflection of the character of God in life lies their chief glory, and in the prophecy of the sacrifice of the Servant the prophetic Canon carries the profoundest word on sacrifice and its power which the Old Testament contains.

While the identification of the Servant is not of direct concern to us at the moment, it is of importance for our general theme, and we shall find that it provides one of the most important links that bind the two Testaments together. To discuss this question fully would require a disproportionate amount of space in the present work, and is the less necessary as the writer has discussed it elsewhere.[1] Few questions arising from the Old Testament have been more discussed, and on few has there been less agreement, even amongst recent writers. Traditionally the Servant has been identified with the Messiah in the Christian Church and with Israel by the Jews. Since the coming of critical scholarship the identification with Israel has been heavily favoured by non-Jewish scholars, and there is certainly much to be said in its favour. Nevertheless, this identification leaves so many problems unsolved that it cannot be wholly satisfying, and in particular it is difficult to carry it consistently through the fourth Song which has been discussed above. It is hard to avoid the feeling that in this Song the writer has an individual in mind, and to this scholarship has inclined increasingly during the last half century. At first it tried to find some individual who preceded the prophet, or who was his contemporary, and a long line of unsuccessful candidates has been brought forward. Then it tried to identify the Servant with the prophet himself, but this only led to fresh difficulties which all the shifts resorted to have failed to resolve. [2] Hence there is now

---

[1] Cf. *The Servant of the Lord*, pp. 3 ff. For a much fuller study of the history of interpretation, together with a discussion of all the problems attaching to these Songs, cf. C. R. North, *The Suffering Servant in Deutero-Isaiah*, 1948. In both, and especially in the latter, the reader will find references to much of the vast literature devoted to this question.

[2] A. Bentzen, *Introduction to the Old Testament*, 2nd ed., 1952, Appendix, pp. 25 f., takes the writer to task because he said (*The Servant of the Lord*, pp. 11 f.): 'If the prophet really believed that he was destined to set judgement in the earth, and to see the isles wait for his law, and that men would acknowledge that he was wounded for their transgressions and bruised for their iniquities, and that his death was a sin-offering for their sins, whereby they should find justification, he was only a misguided, self-opinionated dreamer, and not in any sense the mouthpiece of God.' Bentzen observes that 'He who according to Church Theology fulfilled the prophecy . . . had the same ideas of himself', and asks 'Was he, then "a misguided, self-opinionated dreamer, and not in any sense the mouthpiece of God"?' To this the writer would answer with a definite 'No', and would observe that the two cases are in no way parallel. If the prophet entertained such thoughts of himself they were demonstrably vain; if Jesus entertained them they were demonstrably justified. Many have made the confession in all countries and are still making it. There is surely all the difference in the world between a justified and an unjustified faith.

a turning back to the messianic interpretation, though with the recognition of some fluidity in the concept.

Recent discussion has moved in two directions. It has sought to trace the concept back to its roots and to trace it forward to the fulfilment the author contemplated. It is probable that it had roots in the cultus,[1] but quite improbable that the prophet thought simply of Israel or of any contemporary or earlier individual. In the present writer's judgement there is oscillation in the thought, such as Wheeler Robinson found to be characteristic of much Hebrew thought.[2] But whereas in this connection Dr. Robinson thought of oscillation between the prophet himself and Israel, it is more probable that it was oscillation between Israel, that was called to be the Servant of the Lord, and a future individual who should perfectly represent Israel and carry its mission to a unique degree in himself. Nevertheless, it was probably not a linear development from community to individual, but a real oscillation. The mission the Servant would exercise would still be the mission of Israel, and in so far as he should be the representative of Israel he would call all Israel to enter into the mission, so that he might be truly its representative. Just as the High Priest could not truly represent the people in his confession on the Day of Atonement unless his confession was echoed in their hearts, so the Servant could not represent Israel unless she entered into his mission and realized that it was hers. As we proceed with our study we shall find the utmost significance in the whole concept of the Servant, and it will provide not only a powerful link to bind the two Testaments together, but an important focal point of the unity of the Bible.

So far as the immediate issue of the present chapter is concerned, we perceive that while there is a difference of emphasis as between the Law and the Prophets, in both and elsewhere there is a recog-

---

[1] Cf. *The Servant of the Lord*, pp. 86 ff., and the literature mentioned there.

[2] Cf. 'The Hebrew Conception of Corporate Personality', in *Werden und Wesen des Alten Testaments*, ed. by J. Hempel (B.Z.A.W. No. 66), 1936, pp. 46 ff.; also *The People and the Book*, ed. by A. S. Peake, 1925, pp. 375 ff., and *The Psalmists*, ed. by D. C. Simpson, 1926, pp. 82 ff. On this characteristic of Hebrew thought cf. J. Pedersen, *Israel I–II*, 1926, pp. 275 ff.

nition that sacrifice and other ritual acts were meaningless unless they were charged with the spirit of the worshipper, when they became effective because charged with divine power. Neither Law nor Prophets regarded man as the source of his own enrichment, but as able only to fulfil the conditions whereby its source in God might be opened up to him. Moreover, both regarded the attitude of the heart and the bearing in life as more fundamental to true religion than ritual forms. For in both Law and Prophets ethical religion can be found. Nor can any contradiction of this be found in the other books of the Bible, in the totality of their teaching, while in the Psalter we have passages which express rich spiritual teaching though without hostility to the cultus. The modern view of the Psalter finds its roots in the cultus, and holds that many of the psalms were sung to the accompaniment of ritual acts, for their completion and interpretation. The Psalter therefore forms a bond between the Law and the Prophets, and not a few of its psalms are well calculated to call forth from the worshipper the spirit which was so essential to the valid performance of the ritual.[1] There is therefore a significant bond of unity running through all the diversity of the Old Testament.

[1] Cf. A. C. Welch, *Prophet and Priest in Old Israel*, pp. 131 ff.

III

GOD AND MAN

EVIDENCE of the unity of the Bible is to be found in its teachings about God and man. It would be easy, of course, to cull texts from the Bible which present views of God or of man which are repudiated elsewhere. One of the most familiar instances is the statement in 2 Sam. xxiv. 1 that the Lord moved David to number the people and then was angry with him for doing it, and the variation of this in 1 Chron. xxi. 1, where the instigator is changed from the Lord to Satan. It is probable that the theology of the Chronicler was offended by the earlier statement, and that this was why he changed it. Or again, there are passages which say that at death all men go to Sheol,[1] where they are isolated from God[2] and in a common misery,[3] and whence there is no return,[4] while other passages teach a doctrine of resurrection,[5] or look towards something richer than the dreary prospect of Sheol.[6] It is unnecessary to deny or to minimize such divergences within the Bible. Nevertheless, when we look at the Bible as a whole we find a substantial, and indeed a remarkable, unity

[1] Cf. Psa. xlix. 14 (Heb. 15).
[2] Cf. Psa. xxx. 9 (Heb. 10), lxxxviii. 10 ff. (Heb. 11 ff.), cxv. 17.
[3] Cf. Job. x. 21 ff., xiv. 22.
[4] Cf. Job. vii. 9, 2 Sam. xii. 23.
[5] Cf. Dan. xii. 2 f. Cf. also Isa. xxvi. 19, where, however, E. F. Sutcliffe maintains that the reference is to national resurrection as in Ezk. xxxvii. 1 ff. See *The Old Testament and the Future Life*, 1946, pp. 128 f. So also E. J. Kissane, *The Book of Isaiah*, i, 1941, p. 298.
[6] Cf. Psa. xlix. 15 (Heb. 16), lxxiii. 23 f. The interpretation of both these passages is disputed, and there is no agreement amongst scholars as to how far we may find here the thought of an Afterlife. It seems probable that the writers were at least reaching after a more satisfying faith, and the same is true of the author of Job xix. 25 ff. Here the meaning is undeniably obscure, and some editors emend the text to remove any possible reference to resurrection, while others emend it in the opposite sense, to make such a reference clearer. It seems wiser to recognize the ambiguity of the text as we have it, and to see the writer as one who came to the verge of a belief in a more worth-while Hereafter without securely grasping it. It should be noted, too, that in Psa. cxxxix. 8 we find the thought that even in Sheol isolation from God is not complete, though there the writer is thinking of the power of God as reaching to it rather than of His fellowship as being open to the dead there.

about its teaching. It has been already said that it is the unity of a growth, and that ideas that were incipient at first were more clearly developed later, while other ideas were outgrown and repudiated in the course of the development. Yet it is not the case that we start in the Old Testament with a wholly primitive idea of God, which is transformed out of all recognition by the end of the process of development, so that it is only the end of the process which has abiding value for men. Much is constant from the earliest documents of the Bible to the latest, though with a developing richness of meaning,[1] and the idea of God and man which is taken for granted in the New Testament is that which is characteristic of the Old Testament; and it has been already said that much goes back beyond the earliest documents to the time of Moses. Here some of these elements will be noted, though it is clearly impossible to present a complete Biblical Theology within the limits of our present study.

It is commonly observed that monotheism is found in the three religions which developed out of the religion of the Old Testament—Judaism, Christianity, and Islam. The seeds of this monotheism can be found, as has been said, in the work of Moses, and the incipient monotheism of the faith established in Israel by Moses became the clear and explicit monotheism of the prophets, which continued in the faith of the New Testament. This monotheism is not in any way menaced by the New Testament teaching on the Person of Christ. For if Christ is presented as God and Man, the God was not a distinct Being from Him our Lord called Father. Certainly monotheism can be said to be the characteristic teaching of the Bible. Though passages can be found in which the existence of other gods beside Yahweh is implied,[2] and though it is freely stated in the Bible that many in Israel worshipped other gods, it is nowhere taught that Israel may rightly worship them. The worship of one God, and one God only, was legitimate for Israel. 'Thou shalt have no other gods

[1] Cf. O. J. Baab, *The Theology of the Old Testament*, 1949, p. 231: 'While changing with the passage of time, yet . . . Hebrew religion through the centuries perpetuated itself as a distinctive way of life and belief.'
[2] Cf. Judges xi. 24; 1 Sam. xxvi. 19.

C*

beside me' is laid down for Israel in the Decalogue,[1] and though many scholars have ascribed this to a much later time than the days of Moses, there seems no reason to deny that it stood in the Ten Commandments as delivered to Israel by Moses.[2] In the teaching of the Old Testament other gods were thought at first to be negligible, or at best for other peoples, and then to be non-existent. 'Beside me there is no God.'[3]

It is further characteristic of the teaching of the Old Testament, and carried over into that of the New without question, that God is not to be represented by idols. There are, indeed, many references to Israelite idols, and so commended a person as Gideon is declared to have made an ephod, which was obviously some sort of image here.[4] Nevertheless, it remains true that idols nowhere belong to the true religion of the Old Testament. In the Decalogue the making of any graven image is prohibited,[5] while in the so-called Ritual Decalogue of Ex. xxxiv the making of molten images is forbidden.[6] It is impossible here to discuss the relation between these two Decalogues,[7] but it is not without significance that in both the making of images of Yahweh is prohibited. The fact that one uses one word for image and the other another is of no significance. For it would be fantastic to suppose that the one permitted a molten image but prohibited a graven image, while the other permitted a graven image but prohibited a molten. The Decalogue of Exod. xx is usually attributed to the E document of the Pentateuch, while that of

---

[1] Exod. xx. 3; Deut. v. 7. The Hebrew here is ambiguous, and the meaning could be 'in my presence' as in R.V., or 'beside me' as in R.V. margin. Since it is improbable that the reference was local, and even more improbable that a law which prohibited the worship of other gods in one place would have permitted it in another—such an idea reducing the first commandment to triviality—we may accept the rendering given above. ·Cf. J. C. Rylaarsdam, *The Interpreter's Bible*, i, 1952, p. 980: 'Yahweh is to be the only God Israel recognizes and worships. The theoretical question about the existence of other gods is not raised.' Cf. also Hos. xiii. 4.

[2] Cf. the writer's paper 'Moses and the Decalogue', *B.J.R.L.*, xxxiv, 1951–52, pp. 81 ff. (French Tr. *R.H.P.R.*, xxxii, 1952, pp. 7 ff.).

[3] Isa. xliv. 6.

[4] Judges viii. 27. On Gideon's ephod cf. *B.J.R.L.*, *loc. cit.*, pp. 102 f. n. (*R.H.P.R. loc. cit.*, pp. 26 f.).

[5] Exod. xx. 4; Deut. v. 8.

[6] Exod. xxxiv. 17.

[7] This is discussed in the above mentioned paper on 'Moses and the Decalogue'.

Exod. xxxiv is ascribed to the J document.[1] That the choice of
the term graven image in E was intended to allow a molten image
is excluded by the simple fact that the story of the Golden Calf [2]
is assigned to E, and it shows that by the authors of this document
molten images were no less strongly condemned than graven.
Moreover, we have no evidence that any image of Yahweh ever
stood in the Shrine of Shiloh or in the Jerusalem Temple.[3] If the
worship of Yahweh was older than the time of Moses and its
older form is reflected in the Decalogue of Exod. xxxiv, it would
appear that Yahwism was always an imageless faith.[4] Certainly
there is no reason to doubt that it was imageless in principle
from the time of Moses, however much declension there may
have been in practice in post-Mosaic days. For the breach of this
command in later times no more proves that the command could
not have been promulgated than the prevalence of adultery in
the modern world proves that the seventh commandment has
not yet been promulgated.

The most significant things that are taught about God's character are deeply stamped on the Bible as a whole, and they all spring
from Israel's experience of God in the period of the Exodus.
Underlying the whole thought of the Bible is the idea of a God
Who reveals Himself in history and experience. Such a thought
of God is not reached speculatively by a philosopher, but is born
of concrete history and experience through which men received
the revelation of the character of God. That God employs many
media of revelation is everywhere recognized in the Bible, but all
the others may be found in the thought of other religions. Other
faiths tell of the activity of God in Nature, and revelation through
dreams and omens is not confined to the Bible. Other religions,
indeed, offer examples of revelation through prophetic personality; nor is it peculiar to Israel to think of God as in control of

[1] There are, of course, some scholars who date the former of these later than the
document E, and the latter later than the document J. Cf. *B.J.R.L.*, *loc. cit.*, pp. 83 n.,
91 n. (*R.H.P.R.*, *loc. cit.*, pp. 9 n., 15 f. n.).   [2] Exod. xxxii.

[3] Cf. E. Sellin, *Introduction to the Old Testament*, E. Tr., 1923, p. 41: 'The absence of
any images which is so indubitably attested as regards the sanctuaries of Shiloh and
Jerusalem must, after all, have had some reason.'

[4] This is the view which is argued in the writer's paper on 'Moses and the Decalogue'.

history and intervening to help His people. What is peculiar to Israel is the idea of a revelation that is given in history and experience in a single complex. Here we do not have first the history and then its interpretation. We have first the announcement of the significant fact of the history through a prophetic person, speaking in the name of God, then the fulfilment of the announcement, and finally the interpretation of the event by one whose credentials were supplied by the fulfilment. The announcement, be it stressed, is not that of the soothsayer, who by his skilful technique wrests the secrets of the future to satisfy men's curiosity or their needs. It is the announcement of the prophet, who depends not on his own skill or technique, but on the complete assurance that it is God Who has put the word in his heart and in his mouth. History records many examples of leaders who have promised deliverance and have so infused their followers with confidence that they have wrought valiantly, and the deliverance has been achieved. Here, however, we find a different pattern. The deliverance from Egypt was not won by the superhuman valour to which Moses inspired his followers. Here the personal and the impersonal factors were inextricably woven together, and it was in the complex of the whole that the revelation was given.

It is quite inadequate, therefore, to represent this simply as revelation in history. Nowhere in the Bible is it taught that all history is the revelation of God, or that everything that happens reflects His will. If He is held to be active on the plane of history, He is not held to be the sole actor, or the only significant actor. To this we shall have to return, but for the present it is only necessary to draw attention to this important feature of the whole Exodus complex. The deliverance was not wrought by Moses, or entirely independent of him. His prophetic word and the fulfilment in history dovetailed into one another, and yet neither can be explained from the other; nor did either alone provide the vehicle of the revelation.

As for the revelation of God mediated through this complex of personal and impersonal factors, it may suffice to mention a few of its elements. The cry of the oppressed Israelites went up to God from Egypt and aroused Him to activity on their behalf. His hatred of the maltreatment of man by man did not have to wait to be announced by the eighth century prophets. It was already unfolded to men here. Moreover, God's compassion for the oppressed is as much revealed as His anger against the oppressor. It is in a passage assigned to the earliest document of the Pentateuch that we read: 'The Lord, the Lord, a God full of compassion and gracious, slow to anger and plenteous in mercy and truth';[1] and the same thought is echoed in one of the latest of the Old Testament prophets, in the book of Joel.[2] Nevertheless, there is development in the thought of the divine compassion. For while it is ever called forth by man's inhumanity to man, it was in time perceived to be called forth even by man's hostility to God. When Israel by her folly involved herself in ruin and failed to see that the way of her well-being lay in obedience to the will of God, she merited the stern rejection and the dire punishment of God. Yet His compassion for her was stirred and He sent His prophets to awaken her to the sense of her need,[3] and though He brought disaster on Israel it was less to punish her in wrath than to seek her in love. In such prophetic messages the compassion of God was lifted from something that concerned itself only with physical suffering and was seen to be called forth by the spiritual condition of men. With the widening of the prophetic horizon to include all mankind the way was prepared for the revelation in the New Testament of the divine compassion for men of every race who are in spiritual need.

Nor is the divine compassion that of the helpless spectator. Sometimes our heart is wrung with pity at the tragedy of the experience of some friend, and not the least poignant part of the pain for us is the recognition of our helplessness to do anything effective to meet the situation. But God is not alone a God of compassion. He is a saving God. His salvation manifests itself in

[1] Exod. xxxiv. 6.
[2] Joel ii. 13. Cf. also Psa. lxxxvi. 15, ciii. 8, cxlv. 8; Jonah iv. 2; Neh. ix. 17.
[3] Cf. Hos. xi. 8 f.; Jer. vii. 13, 25, xi. 7, xxv. 4, xxvi. 5, xxix. 19, xxxii. 33, xxxv. 14 f., xliv. 4.

a form appropriate to the need. Here again, therefore, while the thought of God as a saving God is constant throughout the Old Testament and lives on in the New, there is really a considerable development in the thought. At the Exodus He delivered Israel from the Egyptian bondage; at the other end of the development He is seen to deliver men from the corruption of sin. For with the perception that his compassion reached down beyond man's physical estate to his spiritual condition it was seen that His salvation reached as far as His compassion. Nowhere is He a helpless God. His resources are ever equal to His purposes.

It is a constant teaching of the Bible that He is a faithful God.[1] By this it is meant that He is to be relied upon, and that He is not arbitrary and changeable. There are some passages, indeed, where God is presented as unpredictable in His reactions, and where arbitrariness is attributed to Him. Such a passage is that already referred to, where He is represented as moving David to number the people in order then to blaze forth in wrath against him for the act. Such passages show traces of older and primitive ideas of God, which were only gradually eradicated in Israel. Far more characteristic of the thought of the Bible is the teaching that God is dependable. He is dependable in relation to His Covenant with Israel,[2] but He is also dependable in a wider context. The earliest source of the Pentateuch tells us that God made man free—free to make or to mar his own life, free to enjoy or to repudiate the divine fellowship, free to obey or to disobey the will of God. That freedom He always respects. He never reduces men to the status of puppets, and though He uses their acts to further His own purposes they are still their acts. He may make the Assyrian the rod of His anger,[3] but the Assyrian still stands under condemnation for the cruel purpose of his heart.[4] The Assyrian's intention is not to further the purpose of God; he may even cherish in his heart a boastful contempt for God.[5] On the other hand, God may claim for Himself men to share His counsel and to be the mouth-

---

[1] Cf. Deut. vii. 9; Isa. xlix. 7; Psa. lxxxix. 2 f., 9, 34; 1 Cor. i. 9; 2 Tim. ii. 13.
[2] Cf. Deut. vii. 9; Psa. lxxxix. 35.
[3] Isa. x. 5.
[4] Isa. x. 12.
[5] Isa. x. 7, 11.

piece of His message, and they may so strongly feel the constraint that is laid upon them that they declare themselves to be helpless in His hand.[1] Yet actually they are never helpless, or the false prophets and Judas would be beyond explanation. Their response in surrender is necessary, and it is the completeness of that response which makes it possible for them to be overwhelmed by the sense of the divine power. For all such service of God the initiative must ever be with God and not with man, and the call precedes the consecration. It is true that, in the case of Isaiah, the prophet-to-be heard the voice saying 'Whom shall I send? And who will go for us?'[2] and not a direct demand for his service. But before that he had experienced the divine initiative in the cleansing of every fibre of his being, laying upon him its claim.[3] His response in surrender and consecration was still response to the divine initiative.

This divine initiative in grace runs through the whole Bible, at whatever level that grace is seen to express itself, and the constraint it lays upon men is ever a moral constraint and not the compulsion of *force majeure*. When God brings Israel out of Egypt, the initiative is wholly His and the power is wholly His. Yet Israel is not brought out willy-nilly without respect to her freedom. Gladly she seizes the opportunity His grace provides and follows the prophet whom He had sent. And it is a firm constant of the prophetic teaching that while the initiative is ever with God in sending His prophets to recall Israel to the path of wisdom, that initiative is defeated until men freely respond in obedience and faith. God never overrides human freedom. His mercy and His love are bound in the unity of a single personality with His faithfulness and His dependability.

The same thing is seen in connection with His Covenant with Israel. This depends on the divine election of Israel, and the initiative is therefore with God. It calls for a response from Israel and the bringing of that response seals the Covenant.[4] From Israel's side the election seems arbitrary, since she recognized that there was nothing in her to justify it.[5] She was not better than

---

[1] Cf. Amos iii. 7 f.; Jer. xx. 7 ff.   [2] Isa. vi. 8.   [3] Isa. vi. 6 f.
[4] Exod. xix. 4 f.   [5] Deut. vii. 7 f.

other nations or more manifestly desirable as a heritage. But that does not mean that the election was arbitrary from God's point of view. The choice of the prophets always filled them with wonder and gave them the feeling that it was arbitrary, since they could not explain it. The issue in the case of the prophets who brought the response of true consecration showed that it was not arbitrary, and prompts the wonder what might have happened to the world if all those who were called to be prophets had brought the same response. Similarly the prophets lamented that every generation of Israel did not bring the same response in consecration to the Covenant that the generation of the Exodus had brought. God still respects the freedom of Israel, and though He Who showed the initiative in the making of the Covenant will show none in its breach, He recognized that Israel might show that initiative and break the Covenant. In so doing she would forfeit her claim on God, so that though He might still seek her in love and try to bring her back to the covenant relation, it would be because He was unchanging in His compassion for her in her need, and not because she had any claim on Him. Each succeeding generation of Israel inherited the blessings that the mercy of God had brought upon her; each succeeding generation inherited the revelation of the character and will of God that had been granted to her. Yet the freedom of each generation was respected and Israel was never forced into the covenant relation. Each generation had to make the Covenant its own by its response if it was to remain in that relation.[1]

It is sometimes supposed that early Israel was entirely collective in its thinking and later Israel became individualistic. It is true that there is a stronger emphasis on individualism and on individual responsibility in later times, but it is not true that there can be

[1] Cf. the present writer's *Biblical Doctrine of Election*, 1950, p. 48: 'The book of Deuteronomy represents Moses as saying to Israel: "Yahweh our God made a covenant with us in Horeb. It was not with our fathers that Yahweh made this covenant, but with us, even with us, all of us who are alive here today" (Deut. v. 2 f.). It is there implied that the Covenant with the patriarchs was not valid for the generation of the Exodus, but that only the Covenant into which they themselves entered could have validity and meaning for them. And by the same token their Covenant could not have automatic validity for the generations that followed.'

any sharp division of the kind just indicated.[1] Both early and late it was recognized that while there was a corporate soul of Israel, which might be obedient or disobedient to God, each individual shared the responsibility to maintain his own obedience and thus to contribute to the health of the soul of the people. Individual and corporate elements belonged together, for man was both an individual in the presence of God and a member of society with a responsibility for its life and well-being, as well as for his own. In days when men were regarding themselves as the helpless members of a society for which they felt no responsibility, the individual side of this double relationship had to be insisted on by prophets, but this was not to the neglect of the collective. Jeremiah, who insisted on the responsibility of the individual, did not forget that the individual was swept in the stream of the nation's life. He who urged men not to suppose that their misfortunes were the fruits of their fathers' sins[2] was assured that their follies would entail disaster for their children. In piteous terms he described how little children, who could not by any stretch of individualism be held responsible for the policies of their day, would be dashed to pieces by the ruthless foe in consequence of the false path the nation was treading.[3] That children could suffer for the deeds of their fathers Jeremiah fully realized, and he was far from offering any doctrinaire teaching that desert and fortune were nicely balanced for every individual. When his own kin plotted against him and sought his death, he did not suppose that he was meeting the just recompense of his deeds but cried out to God against them.[4] An arid and extreme individualism is nowhere part of the authentic teaching of the Bible, and Jeremiah was as far as any from offering teaching comparable with that of Job's friends, or of forgetting in his insistence on individual responsibility that man is also a member of a society, indissolubly bound in a single corporate whole with his fellow men. It is often noted that he expressed the New Covenant in individual terms. It must

[1] Cf. O. S. Rankin, *Israel's Wisdom Literature*, 1936, pp. 53 ff., J. Hempel, *Gott und Mensch im Alten Testament*, 2nd ed., 1936, p. 192; J. de Fraine, *Biblica*, xxxiii, 1952, pp. 324 ff., 445 ff.

[2] Jer. xxxi. 29 f.   [3] Jer. xvi. 4.   [4] Jer. xii. 3, 6.

nevertheless be remembered that though the laws of the covenant were to be written on the individual hearts of men, it was still the covenant with the house of Israel.[1] The individual and the corporate conception were held together in an indissoluble unity. Every man's obedience to the law of the covenant was both his personal responsibility to God as a member of the covenant people, and also his duty and his service to the people to which he belonged. By his obedience he was making his contribution to the collective soul of the nation. He who brought no obedience placed himself outside the covenant and was a peril to the whole community.

That this is a characteristic thought of the Old Testament, though understood at different levels, is clear when we remember the very ancient story of God's conversation with Abraham about the city of Sodom, where ten righteous men in the city might have caused it to be spared.[2] By their righteousness they would not alone have maintained their own relationship with God, but would have served the whole city. Here, too, we find the thought of the Remnant, which can be found throughout the Bible.[3] Though the city is destroyed a Remnant is saved. So in the story of the Flood. Sometimes there is the thought of a righteous Remnant, whose righteousness causes the whole community to be spared;[4] sometimes the thought of a righteous Remnant escaping itself from a destruction it is powerless to avert.[5] Sometimes there is even the thought of a Remnant spared not for its own righteousness, but spared in the divine mercy in order that it may transmit to another generation the heritage it does not value for itself.[6]

All of this far from exhausts the teaching about God which is constant and yet growing throughout the Old Testament, constant in its terms yet growing in the fullness of meaning that

---

[1] Jer. xxxi. 31 ff. [2] Gen. xviii. 16 ff.
[3] Cf. *The Biblical Doctrine of Election*, pp. 70 ff. E. W. Heaton, *J.T.S.*, N.S. iii, 1952, pp. 27 ff., raises a caveat against the use of the term 'doctrine of the Remnant', which may be misleading if it is forgotten that there is much variety in the conception of the Remnant in different passages.
[4] As in the passage cited from Genesis.
[5] Cf. Isa. iv. 3. [6] Cf. Amos iv. 11.

is given to them. Our present purpose is merely to illustrate that there is a fundamental unity, though a dynamic unity, in the thought of God that runs through the Bible. Over against the isolated passages that can be culled to illustrate divergences of view there is a far more significant body of passages which reveal a common view of the nature and character of God. Moreover, all of the qualities of God that have been noted, and others which have not been noted, are taken for granted in the New Testament. The divine compassion for men who are in need, and whose deepest need arises from their opposition to God's will, is expressed in the word, and in the life and death, of Jesus, in a revelation which is mediated in the context of history, where personal and impersonal factors are knit together in a single complex no less than in the Exodus complex. Moreover, here again the compassion is not a passive pity, but a power that expressed itself in saving grace, electing and delivering that by the election and the deliverance it might lay its constraint on men and claim their loyalty and devotion. To all this we shall have occasion to return.

In its teaching about man the Bible says many things which can be found also in other religions. He is the creature of God, and endowed with powers which God willed for him. If he is the crown and climax of all that lives in the world, it is not because he elevated himself to this position, but because God willed that he should be. All this, and much more that might be added, while it must have its place in a Biblical Theology, is of but passing interest to us here, where teaching more profoundly significant is what commands our interest. The purpose of man's creation is of more importance than the fact.

It is well known that we have two accounts of Creation lying side by side in the Bible, and it is commonly held that they come from widely separated ages. The second account stands in the oldest document in the Pentateuch,[1] and the first is in a document commonly dated nearly half a millennium later.[2] Many contrasts between the two accounts are frequently underlined. Some important elements which the two have in common are less

---

[1] Gen. ii. 4 ff.   [2] Gen. i. 1 ff.

frequently emphasized. The second account reveals unmistakably the conception of man as designed for God's obedience and fellowship. He was not designed to be the sport of the gods, or the nourisher of the gods, or the slave of the gods. The command of God was laid upon him,[1] but it was a command designed to further man's well-being, and not to bring some gain to God. Complete obedience was asked of him, but the reward of that obedience was the fellowship of God, and disobedience broke that fellowship and drove him forth from the presence of God and from the bliss designed for him.[2] In all the simplicity of this story there are profound teachings, which are accepted throughout Biblical thought as a whole. In the Garden Adam is represented as walking and talking with God in the simple intimacy of friendship. Many throughout the Old Testament are represented as living in that sort of intimacy with God, though it was an intimacy into which the element of reverence on the part of man must enter. Abraham is depicted as knowing such an intimacy,[3] and the prophets are set before us as men of God's council,[4] who were privileged to sit in on God's deliberations, and also as men who lived on terms of rich fellowship with God. Psalmists, again, express their relations with God in terms of fellowship, and though they worship Him in deep adoration, it is an adoration which is touched into intimacy by God's giving of Himself to them in fellowship. They worship Him not as men who lift their eyes to Him afar off, but as men who are privileged to draw nigh to Him and to rejoice in Him. When the New Testament emphasizes the thought of God as Father, it is not presenting some new thought which may be sought in vain in the Old. Even the term 'Father' is not limited to the New Testament, but is found already in the Old.[5] But beyond the terms used, when we penetrate to the thought we find this conception of the relation-

---

[1] Gen. ii. 16 f.   [2] Gen. iii. 23 f.   [3] Gen. xv. 1 ff.
[4] Jer. xxiii. 18, 22. Cf. H. Wheeler Robinson, *J.T.S.*, xlv, 1944, pp. 151 ff.
[5] Cf. Isa. lxiv. 8; Psa. ciii. 13. Cf. G. E. Wright, *J.N.E.S.*, i, 1942, pp. 404 ff., where, however, it is pointed out that the thought of God as Father is not common in the Old Testament. 'We must remember that the father-son conception is in continual danger of degenerating into sentimentality, as has so often happened in modern times. It needs to be united with the master-servant picture to give it backbone and support' (*ibid.*, p. 414).

ship between God and man designed by God and experienced by those who fulfil His purpose as one of intimacy and fellowship.

When now we return to the first account of Creation, we find none of the naïveté of expression that marks the second, but some notable agreements. Here man is said to be formed in the image of God.[1] By many writers this is understood to mean that man was formed in the physical likeness of God,[2] but this the present writer finds incredible. In the first place, the contrast between the naïve anthropomorphism of the second account and the absence of anthropomorphism in the first account—unless it is found here—is generally observed. If the emphasis in this reference to the image of God is physical, then there is a cruder anthropomorphism here than in the second account, where there is no emphasis on man's physical similarity to God. Moreover, in the very passage that states that man was made in the image of God it is added: 'male and female created he them'. Man is therefore made a creature of sex. It is alien to the teaching of the Old Testament in general that God is a Being of sex.[3] and certainly it is alien to the whole thought of the compilers of the Priestly document, and it would be nothing short of astonishing for the passage that stated man's likeness to God to specify his sex in that connection. For if the reference in the first part of the verse is

---

[1] Gen. i. 27.

[2] Cf. A. Jeremias, *Das Alte Testament im Lichte des Alten Orients*, 4th ed., 1930, p. 53; P. Humbert, *Études sur le Récit du Paradis et de la Chute*, 1940, pp. 153 ff.; L. Köhler, *Th.Z.*, iv, 1948, pp. 16 ff.; C. R. North, *The Thought of the Old Testament*, 1948, p. 27; C. Ryder Smith, *The Bible Doctrine of Man*, 1951, pp. 29 f. Ryder Smith says (*ibid.*, p. 37): 'The modern definition under which "the image of God" in man is described as "moral and spiritual likeness" does not root in the First Chapter of Genesis but in the teaching of the Prophets.'

[3] Cf. J. Hempel, 'Die Grenzen des Anthropomorphismus Jahwes im Alten Testament', *Z.A.W.*, lvii (N.F. xvi), 1939, pp. 75 ff. I. G. Matthews would not exclude the thought that God's sexuality is found here. He says (*The Religious Pilgrimage of Israel*, 1947, p. 75): 'That the gods should go in pairs, male and female, was normal in all early religions. Primitive man could not think of the creative powers in other terms, and even a late priestly writer has preserved the myth that must have been common among the Hebrews, viz., that God made man in his own image, "male and female created he them".' H. Gunkel, *Genesis* (H.K.), 5th ed., 1922, p. 111, says the meaning is not that man was created in the form of a single God, but in that of divine beings. It is, however, very improbable that the Priestly writer thought in other than monotheistic terms. Gunkel stresses the pronoun 'our', but however this is explained it is improbable that it implies any polytheism here.

physical, as that in the second half certainly is, the whole becomes a declaration of God's sexuality. This is in the highest degree improbable. The writer of the passage was doubtless sufficiently observant to know that neither in his physical frame in general, nor in his sexuality in particular, is man to be differentiated from the animals. Like them he has limbs and senses, like them he eats and breathes, is born and dies. To suppose that what the writer meant was no more than that man stands on two feet while most animals stand on four is to credit him with a triviality in his conception of the Being of God that is not impressive. What differentiates man from the lower creation most notably is not to be found here, as the Priestly writer must surely have known, and the image of God is something that significantly marks his uniqueness amongst created things.[1] That uniqueness is to be found in his spirit.[2] He has a quality of personality which distinguishes him from the lower creation and links him with God, and which makes him a creature designed for the fellowship and obedience of God. In accordance with this we find that immediately after his creation in the image of God, his Maker speaks to him and lays His command upon him,[3] thus lifting him into fellowship and laying upon him the law of obedience. To none of the lower creatures is God represented as speaking in the moment of their creation. It is only to man who is made in the image of God, and as the corollary of that creation in His image,

[1] Cf. P. Heinisch, *Theology of the Old Testament*, E. Tr. by W. Heidt, 1950, pp. 161 f.; also Th. C. Vriezen, *O.T.S.*, ii, 1943, pp. 87 ff., esp. p. 104

[2] Cf. S. R. Driver, *Genesis* (W.C.), 1904, p. 15: 'It relates, from the nature of the case, to man's immaterial nature'; H. Wheeler Robinson, *The Religious Ideas of the Old Testament*, 1913, p. 72: 'Made in His image, *i.e.* set in a similar relation of authority in regard to all other creatures'; H. Holzinger, *H.S.A.T.*, 4th ed., i, 1922, p. 11: 'The idea of the copying of the Physical form of God is quite excluded from P's conception of God'. G. E. Wright, *The Interpreter's Bible*, i, 1952, p. 368a: 'Man "in the image of God" means, therefore, that there is a correspondence between the total being of God and the total being of man. The thought cannot be confined to physical resemblance; indeed, it is improbable that the physical is in the centre of attention. Instead, the emphasis must lie on the self-conscious. . . . This, of course, does not exclude the corporeal. . . . Yet it does mean that the "image" in man must primarily be concerned with the deeper aspects of personal being' (cf. C. A. Simpson, *ibid.*, p. 485). F. Ceuppens, *Genèse I–III*, 1946, pp. 46 f., rejects the corporeal view of the reference, and holds that what is in mind is intelligence and will. Cf. also F. Horst, *Interpretation*, iv, 1950, pp. 259 ff.

[3] Gen. i. 28.

that He speaks. Once more the law that is laid on man is not a command to do anything which could be thought of as enriching God, but an ordinance which is for man's good and gain. It is permitted to him because God wills it for him. For God's will is the first law of his being.

When a prophet, at whose great word we looked in an earlier chapter, sought to express the deepest duty of man, he did so in the terms: 'What doth the Lord require of thee, but to do justly, to love mercy, and to walk humbly with thy God'.[1] While the terms of the obedience are different from those in Gen. i, where they would scarcely be relevant, it is of interest to note that here once more we find linked together obedience and fellowship, obedience as the demand of God and fellowship as its inevitable condition. Granting all the differences of level that are to be found within the Bible, it is characteristic of its thought as a whole that man is a creature capable of enjoying the fellowship of God and made to serve Him, and that these two belong together.

This may be expressed more generally in the principle that privilege carries responsibility, so that the repudiation of the responsibility involves the forfeiture of the privilege. This is a constant element of Biblical teaching everywhere. We have seen this in relation to Israel's election and the Covenant. Israel is chosen by God for a purpose, and when she repudiates the purpose she violates the Covenant and renounces her claim on God. In the hour of her election and the experience that demonstrated that election to her she received a revelation of God which she was charged to cherish and to pass on to her children, and at the same time the Covenant laid on her the obligation to conform her life to the will of God. Often men supposed that God was so tied to Israel that He must protect and preserve her even though she flouted His will, and that He must honour her though she dishonoured Him, but the prophets were tireless in denouncing such an idea. Great was Israel's privilege in being chosen to be the people of God; yet ultimately it was not for privilege but for service that she was chosen, and the greatness

[1] Mic. vi. 8. With this cf. Deut. x. 12.

77

of the privilege was matched by the greatness of the service to which she was called.

Nor is such an idea limited to the Old Testament. In the New Testament the Church is regarded as the elect of God, whose election fills with the sense of high privilege all who share it, but whose election lays on them an obligation to holy living which it is perilous to decline.[1] The elect are not the divine favourites who can do with impunity what others may not. They are subject to the sternest condemnation when they fall below the height of their calling. In the Old Testament Amos could say in the name of God: 'You only have I known of all the families of the earth; therefore will I visit all your iniquities upon you',[2] while in the New Testament to a Church that fails to fulfil the obligations laid upon it comes the word: 'I will spew thee out of my mouth'.[3] In the Old Testament the Servant of the Lord is elect from the womb,[4] but elect to shame and suffering,[5] and not to be the pampered of the Lord. In the New Testament Christ is elect,[6] but elect to a service that brings Him to the Cross.[7] The measure of the privilege and honour of the election is but the measure of the task it brings, and even of the suffering it entails. It is always election to do the will of God.

Stated in those terms the thought of the Bible is constant. Yet when we ask what is meant by the will of God we find development. Here once more we find a growing richness in the content of the constant terms, and must remember that historical sense whose importance has been earlier underlined. The duty of all men is to obey the will of God; the duty of God's elect is to obey His will. Reduced to these colourless terms, the teaching of the Bible is on a flat level, and elect and non-elect stand side by side. It is when we ask what is the will of God that the elect are distinguished, and the teaching of the Bible reveals diversity of level.

Every religion demands that men shall obey the will of its gods.

---

[1] Cf. Rom. xi. 13 ff.   [2] Amos iii. 2.   [3] Rev. iii. 16.
[4] Isa. xlix. 1.   [5] Isa. l. 6, liii. 5.
[6] Matt. xii. 18.   [7] Mark x. 45.

What is characteristic of Biblical religion is that God's demands spring out of His character, and that the measure in which man through fellowship is lifted into the very Being of God is the measure of His demand. God made man in His own image, and His essential law for man is that he shall reflect the image of God and become like Him in character. This was not perceived at first in all its clarity; neither was the character of God seen in all its fullness. In the wilderness loyalty to the Covenant was asked of Israel; but this was not simply because God laid the obligation of loyalty upon her. It was because He Who had initiated the Covenant in grace pledged His loyalty to it that hers was claimed. However loyal to it she might be, her loyalty would be but the reflection of His.

We have already seen that in that age it was perceived that God was compassionate and saving, not so much because these were abstract ideas about Him enunciated by Moses, as because they were deeply embedded in the experiences through which Israel had been brought. God's hatred of oppression and inhumanity had been declared in His acts, and not in His words alone. Through all the teaching of the eighth and seventh century prophets deeper insight into the character of God was given, and the corollaries of that character were underlined. Here Israel was taught that it is not enough for man to respond to God's goodness with gratitude; he must reflect in his dealings with his fellow man the same spirit that God had shown towards Israel. This already begins to appear in the Decalogue, where the demand is made that Israel's loyalty to the Covenant should be shown not only in devotion of spirit to God, but in fundamental loyalty to one another. Loyalty to parents, and loyalty to one's neighbour—expressing itself in counting sacred his life, his wife, his property and his reputation—and the cultivation of a loyalty of spirit as well as of act, provide the terms wherein loyalty to God can be expressed. When the prophets looked on the heart of God they saw His character more clearly, and in the light of that vision they perceived more fully what He asks of men. It is because God is inflexibly just that He hated all the injustice that was rampant in Israel, where every man was trying to get the better of his fellows and all means were counted good enough to achieve his end. When Amos looked around and saw men cheating in trade,[1] exploiting the misfortunes of others,[2] fouling the stream of justice with bribes,[3] even while they maintained with splendour the forms of religion,[4] he saw these things as one who had been lifted into the heart of God, and who saw all with the eyes of God. It was because of what God was that He must hate all this, and because this was the very antithesis of His justice that men who practised such things could not reflect His will. To reflect the heart of God and to reflect His will were one and the same, and since God is just all who worship Him acceptably must be just.

With each fresh insight into the heart of God, and each fresh emphasis in the conception of God, we find the same thing. It is the moral holiness of God which makes Isaiah conscious of the uncleanness of his own heart,[5] and makes him realize that these two cannot exist together. To live in that presence he must become pure; yet to purify himself is beyond his power. Only by the God-sent touch could he be cleansed, and the moral purity of God invade his very soul. What God is seen to be His people must become.

Here, as everywhere throughout the Bible, we see that revelation is given in the particular, yet transcends the particular. Through the historical experience of the Exodus and all associated with it there was given an enduringly valid revelation of the character of God. Through all the moral and social and political conditions of the eighth and seventh centuries there was given an insight into the character and will of God that was true for Israel, and that is just as true for men today. Some things must be translated into the terms of our modern life, and in another generation will call for retranslation into other terms; but fundamentally the message stands. It is a message about God; it is a message about man and his duty; it is also a message about the nature of religion.

---

[1] Amos viii. 5 f. [2] Amos ii. 8, iv. 1. [3] Amos v. 12.
[4] Amos v. 21 ff. [5] Isa. vi. 3, 5.

Religion is never conceived of as mere belief about God or mere ritual. This does not mean that ritual and belief were treated as negligible. So far as belief is concerned, if duty is defined in terms of the reflection of God's character, belief about Him is clearly of great importance. But a man's real belief is not that which his lips express; it is that whereby he lives. Similarly the ritual that has meaning is not that which is performed as a mere act, but that which is invested with his spirit and made the vehicle of his approach to God.[1] When his sacrifice has meaning he presents himself with it to God in humble surrender. Then, and then alone, is it charged with power to bless, enrich, and purify him. This means that his religion may come to a focus in the shrine, but it is not confined to the shrine. It belongs to all his life, and must express itself in every side of his experience. It sends him forth from the shrine filled with the spirit of God to reveal that spirit in all the relationships of his life. He will be merciful, gracious, and pure in all his life, and in so far as he fails will be filled with penitence and will repair to God that he may be renewed in spirit. Religion is not reduced to ethics. It is ethical religion because it expresses itself in ethical living, but it is religion because it springs from an experience of God and devotion to Him.

When in the New Testament we find the essence of the Old Testament law summarized in two of its provisions, it is made clear that they are set before the follower of Christ as valid for him no less than for the children of the old Covenant.[2] These two laws are: 'Thou shalt love the Lord thy God', and 'Thou shalt love thy neighbour as thyself'. The love of God, if it is to be the love of the God Who is revealed in the Bible, must issue in the love of man, because God loves man, and he who is lifted into the life of God must share that love. The love of man, if it is to be a true love expressing itself in loyalty and service, must arise from the love of God, Who is the only source of man's true life.

In the modern world we are much concerned with the problem

[1] Cf. what the writer has said on the essence of religion in the teaching of Jesus, in *An Outline of the Teaching of Jesus*, 1945, pp. 31 ff.   [2] Mark xii. 28 ff.

of the relation of the individual to the state, and various forms of totalitarianism have appeared. On these the Bible speaks with no uncertain voice. Man's first allegiance is to God and not to the state. When Micaiah is urged to say the word that will be welcome in the king's ear, he replies: 'What the Lord saith unto me, that will I speak'.[1] When Peter and John are charged not to teach in the name of Jesus, they reply: 'We must obey God rather than men'.[2] Neither in the Old Testament nor in the New is it taught that man is merely an individual, owing no more loyalty to the state than he cares to concede. It is recognized that the corporate body to which he belongs has a real claim on him, yet not an absolute claim. He has rights which none can legitimately infringe, and though they may be successfully infringed that success is the mark of disease in the life of the state. As to the basis of his rights, the Bible is equally clear. It is not because the state has granted them to him inalienably, or because he has fought and won them and in vigilance guards them, but because God has willed them for him. When Solomon's state pressed ruthlessly on men with its harsh demands it was prophets, acting in the name of God, who initiated the consequent Disruption.[3] When the powers of the state were used by Jezebel to eliminate Naboth and to give to Ahab the coveted vineyard, it was a prophet who declared that this was not merely an offence against Naboth's rights, but an offence against God.[4] The idea that might is right, and that the powerful state is entitled to bend to its will its weaker neighbours, is under divine condemnation in God's indignation against Egypt and deliverance of Israel, and in the vigorous condemnation by Amos and other prophets of those who oppressed and treated with inhumanity their weaker neighbours.[5] Everywhere we are brought back to the will of God as the only secure basis of life and liberty. Similarly, when the prophets denounce the social evils of their day, and all the harshness of the strong to the weak, it is not in the name of custom or constitution that they speak, but in the name of God. Every crime of man

---

[1] I Kings xxii. 14.   [2] Acts v. 29.   [3] I Kings xi. 29 ff., xii. 22 ff.
[4] I Kings xxi. 17 ff.   [5] Cf. Amos i. 3 ff.

against man is a sin against God. For whatever contravenes the will of God is sin.

To embark on a survey of the Biblical teaching on sin is impossible here. That we should find much variety of level is certain. We have already noted the large place that purely ritual offences and even involuntary acts have in the Law, and these should not be placed on the same level as moral offences. There are passages where old and primitive ideas which became transcended are expressed.[1] This is in no way surprising if we preserve that historical sense to which reference has been made. For while it is always seen that the will of God is man's law, there was development in the understanding of that will. But at every level it is seen that disobedience to God's will curses the disobedient. In the Garden of Eden Adam was disobedient, and his disobedience cut him off from the fellowship of God. It pained God; but it cursed man. Wherever men repudiated the will of God they could no longer walk with Him, and the true source of their life failed them. Their health was therefore forfeited and their life threatened. In the life of the state the same thing happened. When Israel did not walk in the way of God she went astray to her own hurt. Disaster threatened her life, and the prophets announced the disaster because they saw men treading the road that led to it. It is true that the social injustice rampant in Israel could not be related to the Assyrian onslaught as cause and effect in any mechanical way. But it is not true that the prophets saw the trouble that was coming merely because they were men of keener political insight, who could measure the strength of nations more objectively than their blinded contemporaries. They perceived that the social injustice meant that Israel's life was not directed by the spirit of God. It was a symptom of disease, and that disease must affect all its life. The nation that

---

[1] Cf. W. A. Irwin, *The Old Testament, Keystone of Human Culture*, 1952, p. 4: 'Israel's intellectual life bridges two worlds. Her primitivism is apparent, perhaps the most striking feature brought into relief by the critical studies of the last hundred years. . . . It is clear that the founders of the Hebrew nation and their heirs and successors for many generations brought with them and continued to live in the pervasive thought-life of the world of their times.'

walked by its own wisdom could not walk wisely in international affairs, when its internal life showed that it was not directed by the Spirit of God. Therefore it was not merely because a loving God must punish Israel for her defection in order to bring her to her senses and renew His claim upon her that disaster would come upon her. The prophets might so express it, in order to point the lesson of the trouble that was coming. But it was coming because Israel insisted on taking the way that led to it. The prophets were men who saw through the issues of their day to the ends towards which they must inevitably lead, because they saw all in the light of God's presence. They saw with clearness that the life of men and nations proceeds from the spirit, and that when the spirit is wrong the wrongness will manifest itself in every aspect of the life. They saw, moreover, that when men or nations sought to build their life on any foundation other than the will of God, springing out of true devotion to Him, they built on false foundations which must crumble beneath them.

In the New Testament we find some reflections of the same teaching, though in forms that are characteristic of itself. John the Baptist summoned all classes to a new righteousness and saw the ills of society as symptomatic of its sickness and portents of trouble. He saw the axe laid to the root of the trees,[1] the winnowing fan in the hand of God, and the consuming fire about to burn up the chaff.[2] On the individual side, Jesus could express the truth uttered by the prophets by saying that a tree and its fruits belong together,[3] and that out of the abundance of the heart a man's words proceed.[4] His life issues from his spirit, and is of a piece. If his spirit is not drawn from the Spirit of God, its evil effects will be seen in all his life.

The contrary of all this is insisted on everywhere. In doing the will of God is man's well-being. His obedience not alone delights the heart of God; it ministers to his own health. Similarly, when the life of the state is in fundamental harmony with the will of God, it treads the path of wisdom and finds blessing. In the book of Deuteronomy this is especially insisted on, and vividly do we

---

[1] Matt. iii. 10.　　　[2] Matt. iii. 12.　　　[3] Matt. vii. 16 ff.　　　[4] Luke vi. 45.

84

find depicted the blessings that obedience must bring to the state and the curses that disobedience must entail.[1] In this there is a measure of truth; yet it is not the whole truth. The individual who is well-pleasing to God does not always find prosperity and ease. Abel was well-pleasing to God, but was murdered.[2] Micaiah for his loyalty was cast into prison,[3] and Jeremiah for his was continually in bitter suffering.[4] Psalmists frequently lament that the righteous are afflicted, and the book of Job is a sustained protest against the idea that desert and fortune are so closely linked that desert can be deduced from fortune. Nowhere in the Bible is the easy doctrine taught that the good are always the fortunate, in the sense that their material well-being is always abundant. Nevertheless, it is always perceived that in a deeper sense their well-being is always secure. For on a truer view that well-being lies in the inner experience of God and not in material things. With all his suffering Jeremiah is more to be envied than all his contemporaries; for he was honoured of God beyond them all. Similarly Job, who cried out so often against his suffering, ended by resting in God even in his suffering, and in realizing that he had found a richer revelation of God in his misery than he had known before, so that it had actually ministered to his truest well-being.[5] In the New Testament we find the same thing with the Apostle Paul, who cried to God to deliver him from his thorn in the flesh, but who instead of being delivered was given such an experience of the grace of Christ that he could even thank God for the suffering.[6] In both Testaments it is perceived that the true well-being of man lies in a right relationship with God, and that without obedience to God he cannot know that relationship.

So far as the state is concerned, the Bible sets one important qualification on the thought that its righteousness will always bring prosperity. It recognizes that the final well-being of any is dependent on the well-being of all. That final well-being is expressed in terms of the Golden Age, when life shall be incomparably glorious and absolute righteousness shall everywhere

[1] Deut. xxviii.   [2] Gen. iv. 4, 8.   [3] I Kings xxii. 27.
[4] Cf. *e.g.*, Jer. xxxviii. 4 ff.   [5] Job xlii. 5 f.   [6] 2 Cor. xii. 8 ff.

prevail. That is why the Bible never speaks of the Golden Age, but in terms of the Kingdom of God. All its pictures of that age are drawn in terms of universalism. This is not the expression of Jewish nationalism, but of religious realism. Just as man's individuality and sociality are held together, so it is realized that the single nation is part of the larger society of nations. We sometimes suppose that this is a modern notion. Yet it is found in the Bible, which clearly recognizes that the final well-being of all peoples belongs together. Its basis is to be found not in human agreement, as we so often suppose, but in the will of God, and it is not supposed that the peoples will stumble by chance into the way of that will by trial and error, but only that they will find it when in their heart they seek Him and surrender themselves to His will.[1] When the Bible talks of nations beating their swords into ploughshares and their spears into pruning-hooks, it does not say that this will happen when they learn common sense, but when they go up to the house of the Lord and seek to know His will.[2] The Golden Age is none other than the Kingdom of God, and without God it cannot be.

It is widely held today that this thought of the Golden Age, and of its conditions and character, has its roots much farther back than was formerly believed.[3] There is no longer the same readiness to assume that all the passages which contain references to it must be late,[4] though it is certain that there are late passages in which

---

[1] Cf. The Rediscovery of the Old Testament, Chapter xi. [2] Isa. ii. 3 f.; Mic. iv. 2 f.

[3] Cf. S. Mowinckel, Psalmenstudien II. Das Thronbesteigungsfest Jahwäs und der Ursprung der Eschatologie, 1922 and Han som kommer, 1951; A. R. Johnson, 'The Rôle of the King in the Jerusalem Cultus', in The Labyrinth, ed. by S. H. Hooke, 1935, pp. 73 ff.; I. Engnell, 'Messias', S.B.U., ii, 1952, cols. 245 ff.; W. Eichrodt, Theologie des Alten Testaments, i, 3rd ed., 1948, pp. 252 ff. Cf. also W. C. Graham and H. G. May, Culture and Conscience, 1936, p. 102: 'In whatever particulars it may differ from this earlier messianism,' i.e. of the Palestinian city states—'that which is reflected so prominently in the Old Testament is a lineal descendant from it'; J. Morgenstern, Amos Studies, i, 1941, pp. 408 f. (= H.U.C.A., xv, 1940, pp. 284 f.): 'The roots of the concept of the Day of Yahweh were not new in any sense. They were embedded in the observance of the day of the fall equinox as the New Year's Day and in its ritual in Solomon's new Temple in Jerusalem.' Cf. also G. Pidoux, Le Dieu qui vient, 1947, pp. 49 ff., and J. Bright, Interpretation, v, 1951, pp. 9 ff. S. B. Frost, Old Testament Apocalyptic: its Origin and Growth, 1952, pp. 32 ff., gives a critical review of this line of modern study; so, more briefly, G. W. Anderson, The Old Testament and Modern Study, ed. by H. H. Rowley, 1952, pp. 304 ff.

[4] It may be noted, e.g. that whereas many scholars have rejected Isa. ii. 2 ff., ix. 2 ff. (Heb. 1 ff.), xi. 1 ff., as late and inauthentic (so, most recently, S. B. Frost, Old Testament

the thought was developed, and that the eschatological element in prophecy was the seed of apocalyptic. In the period between the Testaments apocalyptic flourished in some Jewish circles,[1] and in the New Testament we have eschatological and apocalyptic passages, and a whole apocalyptic book. The Kingdom of God is

---

Apocalyptic, 1952, p. 68, where the second and third of these passages are so rejected), a much larger number than is commonly recognized have allowed them to be from the period of Isaiah. So far as the first passage is concerned, since this is also ascribed to Micah we cannot be certain whether its author is Isaiah or Micah or a third writer, but the fact that both of the prophets to whom it is ascribed were contemporaries strengthens the probability that the tradition of its age has been rightly preserved. Cf. H. H. Rowley, *The Biblical Doctrine of Election*, p. 64, and J. Steinmann, *Le prophète Isaïe*, 1950, p. 129. Of writers who have ascribed this oracle either to Isaiah or to Micah or to an even earlier prophet, the following list of scholars of widely differing approach, while it could easily be largely added to, may suffice: B. Duhm (*Das Buch Jesaia* (H.K.), 2nd ed., 1902, p. 14), C. Cornill (*Introduction to the Canonical Books of the Old Testament*, E. Tr. by G. H. Box, 1907, pp. 269 f.), A. van Hoonacker (*Les douze Petits Prophètes* (E.B.), 1908, p. 381), G. H. Box (*The Book of Isaiah*, 1916, p. 31), E. Sellin (*Introduction to the Old Testament*, E. Tr. by W. Montgomery, 1923, p. 132), H. Schmidt (*Die grossen Propheten* (S.A.T.), 2nd ed., 1923, p. 112 n.), J. Fischer (*Das Buch Isaias* (H.S.A.Tes.), i, 1937, p. 36), J. Lippl and J. Theis (*Die zwölf kleinen Propheten* (H.S.A.Tes.), i, 1937, p. 200), E. J. Kissane (*The Book of Isaiah*, i, 1941, p. 22), A. H. Edelkoort (*De Christusverwachting in het Oude Testament*, 1941, pp. 194 ff.), L. Dennefeld (*Les grands Prophètes* (La Sainte Bible, ed. by A. Clamer, vii), 1946, p. 28a), J. Steinmann (*op. cit.*, pp. 128 f.). Similarly the other two above mentioned oracles have been accepted as genuine Isaianic utterances by the following: B. Duhm (*op. cit.*, pp. 62 f., 77), C. Cornill (*op. cit.*, p. 271), G. W. Wade (*The Book of the Prophet Isaiah* (W.C.), 1911, pp. 62 f., 81 f.), G. H. Box (*op. cit.*, pp. 54 f., 67 f.), E. Sellin (*op. cit.*, p. 132), H. Schmidt (*op. cit.*, pp. 114 ff.), O. Procksch (*Jesaia* (K.A.T.), i, 1930, pp. 150 f.), W. O. E. Oesterley and T. H. Robinson (*Introduction to the Books of the Old Testament*, 1934, p. 245—Isa. ix. 1–6 only; cf. pp. 245 f. on Isa. xi. 1–9), O. Eissfeldt (*Einleitung in das Alte Testament*, 1934, pp. 357 f.—where Isa. ix. 1–6 is held to be probably Isaianic; cf. pp. 358 f., where Isa. xi. 1–9 is held to be probably non-Isaianic), J. Fischer (*op. cit.*, pp. 83 f., 101), E. J. Kissane (*op. cit.*, pp. 105, 133), A. H. Edelkoort (*op. cit.*, pp. 228 ff., 242 ff.), L. Dennefeld (*op. cit.*, pp. 50b, 58b), J. Steinmann (*op. cit.*, pp. 125, 165 n.). J. Pedersen (*Israel III–IV*, 1940, p. 91) says: 'It is impossible to decide whether these utterances can really be ascribed to Isaiah, but it is highly probable that they date from the monarchical period'. Cf. S. Mowinckel, *Han som kommer*, 1951, pp. 22, 73 ff. A. C. Welch, *Kings and Prophets of Israel*, 1952, p. 250, says: 'There is nothing to prevent the oracles from being dated in the period of our prophet. What prompts men to relegate them to a post-exilic period is not, therefore, an unbiased criticism, but a criticism biased by an *a priori* opinion as to Isaiah's general position.' In writing of Isa. ix. 1–6, Oesterley and Robinson observe: 'It is impossible to resist the feeling that scholars have been too much influenced by the idea that Messianic prophecy is necessarily late' (*op. cit.*, p. 245). Cf. A. Bentzen: 'Often this'—*i.e.* the ascription of Messianic prophecies to post-exilic times—'was due to the dominant idea of the pre-exilic prophets being exclusively prophets of doom' (*Introduction to the Old Testament*, ii, 1949, p. 108). A. Alt, in *Festschrift Alfred Bertholet*, 1950, pp. 29 ff., has recently argued for Isaianic authorship, probably in 732 B.C., for Isa. viii. 23–ix. 6. H. L. Ginsberg, on the other hand, in *Alexander Marx Jubilee Volume*, 1950, pp. 357 ff., transfers ix. 1–6 to the time of Josiah.

[1] Cf. the present writer's *Relevance of Apocalyptic*, 2nd ed., 1947.

familiar New Testament phrase as well as an Old Testament concept. Its basis is always obedience to God, but an obedience that goes beyond the outward act to the inner source in the heart's relation to God. There is, however, here as so often a further development. Deutero-Isaiah realized that the Golden Age must be more than a hope; it must be an inspiration and a challenge to service. Israel must not wait until the nations rose of themselves to seek the Lord. She must carry through all the world in a mission of service the revelation which had been made to her. The book of Jonah finds its glory in the presentation of the same message. Nor was this wholly unheeded teaching. For though Judaism did not send out missionaries in the modern sense, many of the Jews of the Diaspora were effective missionaries, and large numbers of proselytes accepted the faith of Israel.[1] In the New Testament we find that the message of Deutero-Isaiah and Jonah is taken with even greater seriousness, and Paul and Barnabas are set apart for the specific task of spreading the faith of the New Israel.[2] To the Jews and their converts this message was first carried, but then to the Gentiles outside, and men were sought with a new energy and passion in the effort to claim all men for the Kingdom of God.

In not a few respects, then, we can find strands of unity running through the Old Testament, and occasionally we have traced them on into the New. The real bond of unity between the Testaments, however, is not to be found in the repetition of the message of the Old in the New, or even in the continuation of the tasks of Israel by the Christian Church. The message of the Old Testament is more often assumed and taken for granted than restated, and though much more could be added along the lines here adumbrated, the real foundation of the case for the unity of the two Testaments is other. Within the Old Testament, great though the span of time it covers may be, there are these manifest threads running through and uniting the whole, even though there is also much that is primitive and superseded before the end

---

[1] Cf. *The Biblical Doctrine of Election*, pp. 90 ff.
[2] Acts. xiii. 2 f.

of the journey is reached, much that comes from the distant past and that was shared with other peoples. The unity of the Old Testament is to be found in those things that were mediated to her through her own experience, and in such older and alien inheritance as she integrated into her faith and made its vehicle. The things she shed, or carried as fossils, are not fundamental to the faith of the Old Testament, though they must have their place in a history of the religion of Israel. For our present purpose the historical outlook can dispense with them, since they do not represent moments in the development of the message of the Bible. It is their supersession, or fading away, that is more significant here, since it was in their supersession that the inner dynamic of Israel's faith was seen.[1]

It would be wholly wrong to suggest, however, that the New Testament offers merely a development of Old Testament religion. Throughout the period covered by the Old Testament a thread of unity can be found, and much in the thought of the Old Testament is continued in the New. There is, on the other hand, a further sloughing of other elements of Old Testament teaching and practice, comparable with the sloughing that has just been noticed during the centuries covered by the Old Testament. The most significant bond of unity between the two Testaments, however, is not to be found in the continuity of development, but in the fundamental differences between the Testaments. To this paradox we must next turn.

[1] What is here in mind is such practices as blood revenge and levirate marriage. Both of these came out of a wider than Israelite background, and both came under limitation in Israel in the Old Testament period. Cf. the writer's *The Servant of the Lord*, 1952, pp. 169 ff. The genius of Israel's faith is seen in the limitation of this inheritance from the ancient past.

IV

THE FULFILMENT OF PROMISE

In the three preceding chapters we have looked at some aspects of the unity of the Old Testament in particular, though our thought has sometimes passed over to the New. It has throughout been insisted that unity does not mean uniformity, and that great diversity has also to be recognized within the compass of the Old Testament. All its parts are not on the same level of importance or of grandeur. Nevertheless, there are principles and ideas running through the whole, principles and ideas whose application would be differently pressed by different writers or spokesmen, yet still giving a real measure of unity to it all.

We come now to the bond that unites the two Testaments in the very act of distinguishing most clearly between them. This is not really so paradoxical as it may sound. In daily life we find a bond of unity between things which are antithetical to one another. Debtor and creditor are at opposite poles, yet they belong together, and the amount by which one is debtor is identical with the amount by which the other is creditor. There is promise which demands fulfilment, though it does not always find it. While the relation between the Testaments is quite other than this, of course, it is none the less the case here that the bond between them is consistent with wide differences between them. Again there is promise, which not alone calls for fulfilment, but finds it. Few things are more dangerous than the equation of the two Testaments, or the identification of the teaching of both. Jew and Christian alike recognize the differences, and though some teachings are continued from the Old into the New Testament, and there are fundamental ideas of God and man which belong to the teaching of both Testaments, there is also much in the Old which no longer belongs to the New. Nevertheless, the one belongs indivisibly to the other.[1] The New is neither a merely natural development from the Old, nor the substitution of something unrelated.

The Old Testament has always belonged to the Bible of the Church. Already by the beginning of the Christian era the Jews had a collection of sacred books, divided into three parts,[2] and the New Testament provides us with evidence that Chronicles was the final book of that collection,[3] as it is still in the Hebrew Canon. At the end of the first century A.D. there were still discussions amongst the Rabbis as to whether certain books of the Old Testament were rightly included in the collection, or should be rejected; but it is clear that they were not discussing the question *ab initio*. Already the disputed works had such a hold in the veneration of men that the scales were heavily weighted in favour of their reception as sacred. We may therefore say that though no rigid and binding decisions had been formally taken by the time of our Lord—or for that matter were even taken at the end of the century—for all practical purposes the Palestinian Jewish Canon was achieved by the beginning of our era.

There were certain other books, of Jewish origin, which were cherished in some circles.[4] There is no evidence that they were

---

[1] Cf. H. F. D. Sparks, *The Old Testament in the Christian Church*, 1944, p. 93: 'However much we may dislike it, and by whatever means we may seek to evade it, we are confronted always by a single incontrovertible, historic fact—the Old Testament and Christianity are inextricably woven together.'

[2] The Hebrew Canon of the Old Testament is divided into the Law, the Prophets, and the Writings. The first includes the Pentateuch, the second the historical books Joshua, Judges, Samuel and Kings, together with the four prophetical books, Isaiah, Jeremiah, Ezekiel, and the Book of the Twelve Minor Prophets, while the third includes the remaining books of the Old Testament, *i.e.* Psalms, Job, Proverbs, the five Rolls (Ruth, Song of Songs, Ecclesiastes, Lamentations and Esther), Daniel, Ezra, Nehemiah, Chronicles. Luke xxiv. 44 refers to a threefold division of the sacred books, called here Law, Prophets and Psalms.

[3] Luke xi. 51 says 'from the blood of Abel unto the blood of Zechariah, who perished between the altar and the sanctuary'. The latter reference must be to 2 Chron. xxiv. 20 f., which tells of the death of Zechariah the son of Jehoiada. Matt. xxiii. 35 wrongly says Zechariah was the son of Berechiah, by confusion with the prophet Zechariah (cf. Zech. i. 1). The Gospel reference is to be understood to be to every murder recorded in the Jewish Bible from Genesis to 2 Chronicles, *i.e.* from beginning to end.

[4] These are printed in the Apocrypha in our Bibles. The word Apocrypha has a different connotation in Roman Catholic and in Protestant works. Since the books referred to are part of the Roman Canon, the term Apocrypha is reserved in Roman

ever accepted by the Jews as a whole as on a comparable level with the books of the Hebrew Old Testament, though some of them were originally written in Hebrew or Aramaic. Nevertheless early in the Christian era these books were valued by many Jews, particularly in Greek speaking circles, for whose benefit they had been translated into Greek if they had not been composed in that language. From the Jews these books passed into the hands of Christians, who continued to value and use them after the Jews had ceased to be interested in them. Some of them are found in the great codices of the Bible which were copied for Christian use. Yet there was no uniform standard in this matter, and the codices are not in complete agreement in their choice of these works for inclusion, or in the order in which they placed them. It was only gradually that they secured their general acceptance in the Christian Bible, though powerful voices were raised against their recognition as fully canonical.[1] We may therefore leave these works out of our purview, since there is no evidence that they belonged to the Bible of the Jews in Palestine in the time of our Lord, or formed part of the sacred heritage which the Church took over from the Jews from its very inception. Of the importance and usefulness of these books for many purposes there is little doubt, but at no time do they appear to have been universally recognized as canonical throughout the Christian Church. Their canonicity was declared by the Council of Trent, and they are recognized as canonical by the Roman Catholic Church, though even there individuals have since expressed their

---

Catholic works for those books which Protestant writers include under the not very satisfactory term Pseudepigrapha. The Prayer of Manasseh, 1 Esdras, and 2 Esdras, are printed in the Appendix to the Roman Bible, where they stand after the New Testament and are called Apocrypha. It is only for these three books, therefore, that the word Apocrypha has a common meaning for Catholics and Protestants.

[1] Jerome, in the *Prologus Galeatus*, declares the books not found in the Hebrew Canon to be apocryphal (cf. H. Howorth, *J.T.S.*, x, 1908–09, pp. 481 ff., xi. 1909–10, pp. 321 ff., and L. Schade, *Die Inspirationslehre des heiligen Hieronymus*, 1910, pp. 158 ff.). Rufinus similarly observed that these books 'non canonici, sed Ecclesiastici a majoribus appellati sunt' (cf. Migne, *P.L.*, xxi, 1878, col. 374), but later abandoned this view (cf. Howorth, *J.T.S.*, xi, 1909–10, pp. 342 ff., xiii, 1912, pp. 1 ff.). Hilary of Poitiers also appears to recognize only the Hebrew Canon (cf. *P.L.*, ix, 1844, col. 241); but cf. Howorth, *J.T.S.*, xi, 1909–10, pp. 324 f.

doubts about them.[1] The Protestant Churches adopt varying attitudes towards them, some accepting them as profitable for edification though not canonical, and others adopting a more negative attitude to them by simply rejecting them.[2]

So far as the books of the Jewish Old Testament Canon are concerned, these were accepted as sacred by the Christians from the start. The New Testament makes constant appeal to them, and takes for granted their authority in such a way that it is not intelligible without reference to the Old. It is true that not every book finds specific reference, but it has been said above that there is a reference to the collection that ran from Genesis to Chronicles, and that doubtless then included all that is now in the Hebrew Canon. There is no evidence of Christian rejection of any of them, and, as has been said, the New Testament cannot be understood without the Old, to which it so frequently alludes.[3]

This does not of itself mean that the two Testaments belong together. Milton's *Paradise Lost* is so full of allusions to classical mythology that it is unintelligible without some knowledge of that mythology. We need, therefore, to consider in what respects the New Testament allusions to the Old differ from these in

[1] So Sixtus of Sienna (cf. *Bibliotheca Sancta*, 1586 ed., pp. 1 f.), Robert Bellarmine [cf. *De Verbo Dei* I, iv (*Disputationes de Controversiis Christianae Fidei*, i, 1613, cols. 9 f.)], B. Lamy [cf. *Apparatus Biblicus*, II, iv (E. Tr., 1723, pp. 292 ff.)], J. Jahn (cf. *Introductio in libros sacros Veteris Foederis*, 2nd ed., 1814, pp. 45 f.).

[2] Luther in 1534 declared that 'These are books not to be held in equal esteem with those of Holy Scripture, but yet good and useful for reading' (cf. F. Buhl, *Canon and Text of the Old Testament*, E. Tr. by J. MacPherson, 1892, p. 67). Similarly the Church of England in its Sixth Article states that these are books which 'the Church doth read for example of life and instruction of manners; but yet doth it not apply them to establish any doctrine'. On the other hand the Westminster Confession says 'The books commonly called Apocrypha not being of divine inspiration, are no part of the Canon of the Scripture, and therefore are of no authority in the Church of God, nor to be in any other wise approved or made use of, than other human writings' (cf. H. H. Howorth, *J.T.S.*, vii, 1906–07, pp. 35 f.). Apparently Tyndale accepted Ecclesiasticus and Wisdom for use in public worship (*ibid.* p. 4), though he separated Hebrews, James and Jude from the other books of the New Testament (*ibid.*), following Luther (*ibid.*, pp. 353 ff.). On the history of the Canon cf. S. M. Zarb, *De historia Canonis Utriusque Testamenti*, 2nd ed., 1934; also a series of articles by H. H. Howorth in *J.T.S.*, viii–xi, xiii, 1906–12, F. Buhl, *op. cit.*, pp. 1 ff., and L. Dennefeld, *Introduction à l'Ancien Testament*, 1935, pp. 195 ff.; in addition, on the attitude to the Apocrypha, cf. W. O. E. Oesterley, *An Introduction to the Books of the Apocrypha*, 1935, pp. 121 ff.

[3] Cf. A. J. B. Higgins, *The Christian Significance of the Old Testament*, 1949, p. 123, says of the Old Testament: 'It is still a part of the Word of God which is the Bible, for it, too, records the divine revelation and the divine message of salvation.'

fundamental character. Do they figure here just because the writers were familiar with the literature of the Old Testament, since it was the best-known literature of the world in which they moved? Was it just by the accident of the time and place of the birth of the Church that the Old Testament was taken over and these references made? The writer has heard such a view maintained, and some have suggested that it would be better for Chinese Christians to substitute the Chinese Classics for the Old Testament in their Bibles and for Indian Christians to substitute the sacred texts of Hinduism. This would still leave the New Testament allusions to the Old Testament unintelligible, apart from more serious objections. For the relation of the New Testament to the Old is not that of *Paradise Lost* to the literature of Greece and Rome. There is a fundamental unity, so that with all their diversity they belong so intimately together that the New Testament cannot be understood without the Old, and *neither can the Old Testament be fully understood without the New.* If this contention is sound, the difference between the case of Milton and Classical Mythology is at once clear; for no one would suppose that Classical Mythology could not be fully understood without the study of Milton.

It is by now obvious that it is here proposed to differentiate between the relation of the Old Testament to the New and its relation to Judaism and its literature. That Judaism is a development from the religion of the Old Testament is undeniable. Its literature abounds in references to the text of the Old Testament, and it always accepts it as authoritative and sacred. While post-Biblical Judaism is completely unintelligible without the Old Testament, however, it is not the case that the Old Testament is unintelligible without post-Biblical Judaism, whereas it is claimed that the Old Testament is not fully intelligible without the New Testament. For if the New Testament looks back to the Old which preceded it, the Old looks forward to something which should follow it, and *that something is not post-Biblical Judaism.*

We sometimes find a group of languages that have developed from a single language, known or assumed. Though the languages of the group are today distinct, each is a development along its own line from the parent language. Post-Biblical Judaism developed in that kind of way from the Judaism of the post-exilic period. But Christianity did not develop in that kind of way from early Judaism. The relation of Christianity to the religion of the Old Testament is quite different from that of post-Biblical Judaism to it.

The Old Testament continually looks forward to something beyond itself; the New Testament continually looks back to the Old. Neither is complete without something beyond itself. How far this interlocking of the Testaments can be pressed we shall have to examine. First, however, we may notice that there is nothing of this kind in the case of Judaism. The promise set forth in the Old Testament is not fulfilled in Judaism, which is a development out of the Old Testament and not the response to its hopes. In the Old Testament we find the hope of the Golden Age, in which people of every race should worship Israel's God and learn His law,[1] acknowledging as the head of the Kingdom of God amongst men the Davidic leader who would arise.[2] In no sense is this realized in Judaism. It is true that Judaism still cherishes the hope of the coming of the Messiah and the establishment of the Golden Age of peace and concord amongst men,[3] though some sections of it have shed the messianic hope.[4] Where this hope is retained, Judaism places the response to the expectations of the Old Testament still in the future, and does not even claim to be itself that response. Its claim is that it maintains the faith of the Old Testament, and is loyal to the heritage of Moses and the prophets. Yet in one great and important matter it does

[1] Cf. Isa. ii. 2–4; Mic. iv. 1–3.

[2] Cf. Isa. ix. 2 ff. (Heb. 1 ff.), xi. 1 ff.; Mic. v. 2 ff. (Heb. 1 ff.); Jer. xxiii. 5 f.

[3] Cf. J. H. Greenstone, *The Messiah Idea in Jewish History*, 1943, p. 276: 'The belief in a personal Messiah, whose advent is to be accompanied by many miracles and wonders, is still potent.'

[4] In the third century Rabbi Hillel—not the great Hillel—said that no Messiah was now to be expected, as he came in the days of Hezekiah. Cf. T.B. *Sanhedrin* 99a (ed. Goldschmidt, vii, 1903, p. 431). On this passage cf. Joseph Albo, *Sefer Ha-'Ikharim* (ed. I. Husile), i, 1929, pp. 44 ff. Cf. also L. Magnus, *The Jews in the Christian Era*, 1929, p. 397: 'There can be no more false Messiahs. . . . Pseudo-Messianism, as a force in Jewish life, is spent and done.'

not keep the law of Moses. That law prescribed animal sacrifices; yet for nearly nineteen centuries Judaism has not offered them. This is by sheer force of circumstances. It recognizes but one sacred place as the legitimate centre for sacrifice, and since the destruction of the Temple it has therefore had no legitimate altar and has offered no sacrifices. It claims no new revelation from God to dispense with the old law of sacrifice. The law which it holds to have been given to Israel by divine revelation is cancelled for nineteen centuries, not in response to the revealed will of God through a prophetic leader, but by the hand of circumstance. Judaism neither continues to obey the old law nor has it a new one, given to it with the same evident marks of the activity of God as accompanied the giving of the old Law.

Let it be quite clear that the writer speaks of Judaism with sympathy and respect. Of the loftiness of its teaching and of the life of many of its spiritual leaders he is not unmindful. He is not of those who depreciate the Judaism of the post-exilic period, or of subsequent ages. He recognizes with gratitude the rich heritage the Christian Church received from Judaism, and all that our Lord and the early Christians owed to the mother faith from whose womb the Church was born. Not in any spirit of hostility or of controversy, but as a simple statement of fact it must be observed that with all its cherishing of the high ethical values of the Old Testament post-Biblical Judaism is an interlude that neither continues to obey the law of Moses, nor yet offers in itself the fulfilment of the hopes which the Old Testament holds before men. It is an interlude that is worthy of high respect, and marked by a noble spirit which calls for deep admiration. Nevertheless, it is an interlude, in which the sacrificial element that is of such importance in the thought and teaching of the Old Testament is suspended, and Israel's task to win the world to the worship of her God is also suspended.[1]

It is when we turn from this to the New Testament and the

---

[1] Cf. C. G. Montefiore, *The Old Testament and After*, 1923, p. 455: 'Any sign of a desire or of a duty to *go out* and *seek* proselytes soon became wanting'. On this cf. *The Biblical Doctrine of Election*, pp. 89 ff.

Christian Church that we see how different is the relation to the Old. Here we find a new revelation from the same God Who revealed Himself in the Old. In so far as there is modification of the old law, therefore, it claims to rest on the revealed will of God, and not merely on the relentless compulsion of circumstance. And the first thing we observe is that the basis of revelation in the New Testament is the same as that in the Old. By this is meant that the revelation is given in a combination of personal and impersonal factors. It is given through a Person, yet it is guaranteed by historical events which could not be controlled by any impostor. If we rightly found this to be the evidence of the hand of God in the Mosaic revelation, it is equally that evidence here. Moreover, it is wholly consistent with the claim that the same God is to be found in both that this same unique medium of revelation should be again adopted.

It will be remembered that it has not been argued above that the uniqueness of the Biblical revelation is to be found in its mediation through history, or in its mediation through prophetic personality. It is in the structure of the combination of both that the uniqueness lies. Moses claimed that by Divine initiative he was sent to deliver Israel. Though he promised deliverance he could not effect it by human power, and it was not to the achievement of freedom by Israel's own efforts that he summoned them. It was to faith in his promise that he called them, and then deliverance was achieved by forces beyond his and their control. His promise was fulfilled by circumstances, and his claim to have spoken in the name of God was vindicated in history. No intelligent anticipation could offer the explanation, and the vindicating circumstances can no more explain his prior faith and promise than his prior faith and promise can explain the vindicating circumstances.

In the New Testament we find that our Lord appears before men with claims and promises. To examine them all is unnecessary. Suffice it to say that He believed that His work was of wide and enduring importance to men, and that His death would be of unique significance and power. If He was no more than a

97

village carpenter and His word arose from no deeper source than His own heart, and if His claim that he delivered the word of God Who had spoken through Moses was false, then there could be no power in that word to effect its own fulfilment. Yet it has undeniably been fulfilled, and whether we like it or not the fact remains that His word has been of uniquely enduring importance to men, and His death has proved the uniqueness of its power in the experience of men. His confidence could not of itself give power if it were falsely based, and it is quite impossible to explain His confidence from its subsequent vindication. The vindication was given in verifiable history, and there is precisely the same evidence for the hand of God in this complex of personality and event as there was in that of the period of the Exodus.

In finding the same pattern of revelation here and in the Old Testament we are not resorting to typology, and arguing that the old revelation was a foreshadowing of the new. That is far from our thought here. The old revelation had a reality and a validity in its own right. The new, too, had a validity and a reality in its own right. If both were revelations of the same God, as they claimed to be, then in the common pattern of the revelation in personal and impersonal factors, where neither could explain or control the other, we have the signature of God.

In many other ways we have similar patterns in the New Testament and the Old. Yet the new pattern is never a mere repetition of the old. It is on a new level, or in terms of new conditions, and it brings a new message and a new power. It brings the evidence of the personality of the same God, Whose initiative is never limited by His past revelation. The community of pattern does not mean that all could have been predicted beforehand, but that when the new pattern appears its community with the old can be perceived. It is as the revelation unfolds itself that the pattern becomes evident. For the divine signature is not given merely through some human voice that claims to be prophetic; it is given in the texture of the revelation.[1]

[1] G. E. Wright, *Interpretation*, v, 1951, p. 305, refers with approval to Filson's rejection of 'the oversimplified attempts of those who find the basic unity in the Bible in terms

In the Old Testament we found that God chose Israel for Himself in her weakness and need, and then delivered her. The initiative in grace and compassion was wholly His, and through it all His character as a gracious, compassionate, electing and saving God was manifested. When Israel thereafter committed herself to Him in the Covenant, her consecration to God was but her response to the deliverance which He had already achieved, and it was a consecration as absolute in its promise as the deliverance she had experienced had been absolute. The bond between Israel and God would never be broken from God's side; it might be broken from Israel's. Here, again, we find the same pattern in the New Testament. The divine initiative is taken in the Person and Work of Christ. His grace and compassion for men in a deeper need than the Egyptian bondage is manifested. The pattern is lifted to a new level, indeed; nevertheless it is a pattern of grace and compassion, and a pattern of election. For election is as deeply written on the New Testament as on the Old. Moreover, we have here not merely a message of grace and compassion; we have an act of deliverance. Its instrument is the Cross of Christ, which responds to Old Testament patterns in ways at which we shall look later. But the power of the Cross is the power of God, which by its means brings deliverance to men. The New Covenant into which men then enter is the response of gratitude to the deliverance which God has wrought in Christ. It pledges them to an absolute and enduring loyalty. The deliverance has been achieved and the response it demands is an absolute consecration. The New Covenant which is sealed in this consecration is one which is never to be broken by God, but which men may violate by disloyalty. The new deliverance and the New Covenant are in different terms from the old; yet the pattern is still the same. No one could deduce it from the old, and there cannot be the slightest suggestion that by the careful study

of certain patterns (for example, Phythian-Adams and Hebert)', and adds: 'The primary unity is to be found in the activity of the independent, sovereign God.' With this the present writer is in agreement. While he recognizes recurring patterns, and looks beyond them to God, he does not find the hand of God only in these patterns. These form but a part of his argument, and are not to be seen out of relation to the whole.

of the Old Testament anyone could have written the New before its context of history took place. Nevertheless, the lines of correspondence are impressive.

It is not unreasonable, therefore, to find the hand of God as manifestly active here as in the events in which Moses figures, and through both to find revelation which is authoritative because its source is God. In the content of the revelation there is both continuity and newness, as could only be expected. If the Old Testament revelation was from God, then it could not be so completely repudiated by the same God in a new revelation that every element of the old was done away, and something wholly new was put in its place. Accordingly we find that while in the New Testament the old law is superseded, there is yet great respect for the Law, and many of its principles and teachings are carried forward. The fundamental character of God is still seen to be the same. For if the New Testament thinks of God's relation to men characteristically in terms of fatherhood, that is not alien to the thought of the Old Testament, as has been said. Nor is this merely a matter of the occasional use of the word Father in relation to God in the Old Testament. There men were exhorted to walk humbly with God, and it was perceived that power to fulfil His demands could only arise from intimate fellowship with Him.

The unity and onliness of God are never questioned in the New Testament, and any supposition that the Christian doctrine of the Trinity is inconsistent with the strictest monotheism rests on misunderstanding of the doctrine of the Trinity. In the Old Testament no less than in the New the Spirit of God is perceived to be active in the human spirit. It can enter a man's personality and give power and direction to his life and make him the instrument of the divine will amongst men. And if the New Testament can use the language of sonship of God in relation to Jesus and others, such language is found also in the Old Testament. That the Sonship of our Lord is held to be unique is, of course, true; but if it is possible for others to become the sons of God without challenge to monotheism, it is possible for One

to be 'the first-born of many brethren',[1] and in a special sense the
Son of God, without such challenge. In the wholeness of His
Person He is other than the Father; yet in so far as He is Divine
He is one with the Father, and not a second God. The Spirit of
God was uniquely in Him, so that His humanity was lifted into
perfect accord with the Father's will and became the vehicle
of divine activity amongst men in a way that transcends that of
all others who became the garment of God's spirit. There is here
no break with monotheism, and the seeds of all this thought are
to be found within the Old Testament.

It is sometimes suggested that the monotheism of Islam is too
rigid to allow of a doctrine of the Trinity. It is thus gently implied
that in the Christian doctrine monotheism is somewhat loosely
held. The fact is that Christian monotheism is as completely
monotheistic as it is possible to be. Islamic monotheism has no
place for a doctrine of the Trinity, not because it is too rigid, but
because its God is too remote. It is not the *fact* of its monotheism
which provides an obstacle, but the *nature* of its conception of
God as a Being afar off, and wholly other than man. In the
Biblical doctrine throughout God is both other than man and
akin to man, making man in His own image and for His own
fellowship, and giving of His intimacy to him. Job can speak of
God as his next-of-kin,[2] and Deutero-Isaiah can speak of Him as
the kinsman of Israel,[3] Who will not shrink from all the obligations that kinship lays upon Him.

In the whole conception of religion as man's response to God's
initiative in grace, the thought and teaching of the Old Testament

[1] Rom. viii. 29.
[2] Job xix. 25. The word rendered 'redeemer' means 'kinsman', and is used especially
of the next-of-kin on whom the responsibilities of kinship particularly fell. One of his
duties was to avenge a violent death, and Job boldly looks to God to take up his case when
death overtakes him.
[3] Cf. Isa. xliii. 1, xliv. 22 f., xlviii. 20, lii. 9. In all these passages verbal forms from a
root meaning fundamentally 'to play the part of kinsman' are found. In addition there
are a number of passages where the participial form found in Job xix. 25 is found: Isa
xli. 14, xliii. 14, xliv. 6, 24, xlvii. 4, xlix. 7, 26, liv. 5, 8. In Trito-Isaiah the verb is found
in Isa. lxiii. 9, and the participle in Isa. lix. 20, lx. 16, lxiii. 16. A passive participle, rendered
'redeemed', and meaning fundamentally 'those who are given a kinsman's protection,
help, or vindication' is found in Deutero-Isaiah in Isa. li. 10, and elsewhere in Isa. xxxv.
9, lxii. 12, lxiii. 4.

is continued in the New. That was the new conception of religion which was mediated to Israel through Moses, and which succeeding generations were slow to understand. Its bond was not an inevitable one, but one willingly accepted. It began in constraint laid upon man by the grace of God, but it was in the free response to that constraint and in the freely pledged loyalty of the heart that it was sealed. Such a conception of the nature of religion is basic to the New Testament. It rests on a covenant relation, and the basis of the Covenant is what God has done, while from man's side it is the absolute committal of the self to Him in response.

All of this and much more might be regarded as a development out of Old Testament teaching, similar in character though different in form as compared with the development in post-Biblical Judaism. Within the period covered by the Old Testament there had been not a little development of the principles which were incipient in Israel's religion from the start, and such development as has been so far indicated could be regarded as a particular stream of development without involving the conclusion that the Old and New Testaments belong peculiarly together. It is when we turn to some other matters that we find the most significant evidence for the bond between the Testaments. For our Lord not merely continued to validate for His followers much that is in the Old Testament. He claimed that much was superseded in the New Covenant. 'Ye have heard that it was said . . . But I say unto you' are words that we hear on His lips.[1] Old commands are modified or lifted to a new level, and an authority equal to that of the old lawgiver is quietly assumed by Him. It is in the supersession of the old that the bond with the old is particularly to be found. This may seem to be patently absurd; but it is in paradox that the deepest truth is commonly to be found.

For many of the supersessions of the old law which we find in the Gospels there is no conflict with the principles of the Mosaic law. When our Lord supersedes the law of 'an eye for an eye, and a tooth for a tooth' by the law of love, the roots of the new law are already found in the Old Testament. The Law had long

[1] Matt. v. 21 f., 27 f., 33 f., 38 f., 43 f.

taught that man's first duty was to love God,[1] and that his next duty was to love his neighbour.[2] The principle of the Golden Rule was not first enunciated by our Lord, and it is not legitimate to press the negative form in which it was stated by others as against the positive form He used, in order to establish superiority.[3] With Him it was no mere abstract principle, but something that He set before men in Himself, as well as in His word; and He brought to men a spring of power that would enable them to make it realizable in their experience. But as a principle its roots lie already in the Old Testament.[4]

So, too, when He taught that the avoidance of adultery was insufficient, and that the deeper law of the avoidance of lust was the divine law for man, He was merely giving a particular application to what was already implicit in the tenth commandment. This penetrated beneath action to its root in desire. Much as we cherish the teachings of Jesus, we should not see things of this kind out of focus, and falsely represent the originality of His teaching, or look in the Old Testament only for those things which we can set as a foil to Christ's words.

Much more significant was His supersession of the old Law in less direct ways. Here we may select a single example, but in a matter of particular importance. Our Lord seems to have been in the succession of the great pre-exilic prophets in his attitude to the ritual forms of religion. Like them He was often found in the Temple, and there is no reason to think that He opposed the

---

[1] Deut. vi. 5.

[2] Lev. xix. 18. It is true that Jesus gives a wider connotation to the word 'neighbour' in the Parable of the Good Samaritan (Luke x. 30 ff.), but He is nevertheless building on the Old Testament passage which He is interpreting. In Matt. v. 43, Jesus says: 'Ye have heard that it was said, Thou shalt . . . hate thine enemy'. No specific command in these terms stands in the Old Testament, though Deut. xxiii. 6 comes very close to it. In extending the meaning of neighbour to include even a Samaritan, and in positively commanding men to love their enemies and to pray for their persecutors, Jesus is carrying the principle of Lev. xix. 18 further rather than contradicting or rescinding the old Law.

[3] Cf. the writer's essay on 'The Chinese Sages and the Golden Rule', in *Submission in Suffering and other Essays*, 1951, pp. 74 ff.

[4] It had already been stated in the negative form 'What thou thyself hatest, do to no man' in Tob. iv. 15 (Vulg. 16), and by Hillel in the words 'What is hateful to thee, do not to thy neighbour; this is the whole Law, all else being but commentary' (T.B. *Shabbath* 31a, ed. Goldschmidt, i, 1897, p. 388).

whole Temple cultus root and branch, and regarded it as a thing evil in itself, and always alien to the will of God. He sent cleansed lepers to offer the prescribed sacrifices,[1] and clearly regarded the sacrificial cultus as still binding on the Jews. Yet His followers, even before the destruction of the Temple, had ceased to be concerned with sacrifices, and for them all the forms of sacrifice were superseded. Yet their indifference to the Temple ritual of sacrifice rested on their regard for sacrifice.

In a previous chapter it has been observed that the deepest word on sacrifice to be found in the Old Testament speaks of no sacrifice that was offered in the Temple, but of the death of the Servant of the Lord. The passage telling of this is not found in the Law, but in the Prophets.[2] There the death of the Servant is presented as a sacrifice transcending in its character and in its effect any animal sacrifice on the altar of the shrine. This was the willing sacrifice of one who gave his back to the smiters, and his cheeks to them that plucked out the hair.[3] It was the sacrifice of one who was without moral blemish, instead of the sacrifice of an animal without physical blemish. 'He had done no violence; neither was deceit found in his mouth.'[4] Its effect was greater than that of any ordinary sacrifice, or even of the sacrifice of the great annual Day of Atonement. In the presence of the Servant men are depicted as confessing that he was bruised for their iniquities,[5] and finding healing and cleansing through his death.[6] Moreover, the range of the effectiveness of this sacrifice was greater than that of any sacrifice prescribed in the Law. It went beyond the borders of Israel, and as the mission of the Servant was a universal one,[7] so the power of his death was depicted as universal.[8]

It is quite clear that our Lord was much influenced by this

---

[1] Luke v. 14; cf. xvii. 14. S. M. Gilmour, in *The Interpreter's Bible*, viii, 1952, p. 104, observes that the former passage 'assumes that Jesus contemplated no break with Jewish sacerdotalism.'

[2] Isa. lii. 13–liii. 12.   [3] Cf. the preceding Servant Song, Isa. l. 4–9.   [4] Isa. liii. 9.
[5] Isa. liii. 5.   [6] Isa. liii. 5, 8, 10, 11, 12.   [7] Isa. xlii. 2, 4, xlix. 6.
[8] Isa. lii. 15 reads in R.V. 'So shall he sprinkle many nations', where commentators have understood the meaning to be the sprinkling of ritual purification. Most modern writers reject this view since the Hebrew would not mean that he would sprinkle something upon the nations, but that he would pour out the nations. Hence some have found the sense given in the R.V. marg. 'He shall startle', justifying this by recourse to an Arabic

passage, and thought of His death before it took place in terms of the death of the Servant.[1] It was not until after His death that His followers realized that with that death all other sacrifice was superseded. Yet it was implicit in His teaching. If His death was a sacrifice that far transcended in significance and effect all other sacrifice, and was valid for all men,[2] then no other sacrifice was needed. The Church was not long in perceiving

meaning of the verb, which is not found elsewhere in Hebrew (so E. König, *Hebräisches und aramäisches Wörterbuch zum A.T.*, 6th ed., 1936, p. 270b, and most recently, I. W. Slotki, *Isaiah*, 1949, p. 261, and R. J. Tournay, *R.B.*, lix, 1952, p. 492). This sense is not very suitable, and convincing arguments against it were advanced by G. F. Moore, in *J.B.L.*, ix, 1890, pp. 216 ff. The Septuagint version has 'Many nations shall wonder at him', and R. Levy (*Deutero-Isaiah*, 1925, p. 259) changes the Hebrew to secure this meaning. Other conjectural changes which have been proposed would yield the sense 'shall be aroused' (so G. F. Moore, *loc. cit.*), 'shall bow down' (so T. K. Cheyne, *The Book of the Prophet Isaiah* (S.B.O.T.), 1899, p. 149, and K. Marti, *Das Buch Jesaja*, 1900, p. 346; earlier Cheyne changed the text to agree with Hab. iii. 6, yielding the sense 'he made the nations to start', cf. *The Prophecies of Isaiah*, ii, 1889, pp. 42, 166 f.), 'shall be struck dumb' (so E. J. Kissane, *The Book of Isaiah*, ii, 1943, p. 184, reading the word which stands in Exod. xv. 16), 'shall gaze (with amazement)' (so first Vogel, according to P. Volz, *Jesaia II*, 1932, p. 170; also P. Humbert, in *La Bible du Centenaire*, ii, 1947, p. 416; L. Koehler, *Lexicon in V.T. libros*, x, 1951, p. 604b, reads another form of the same verb and finds the same meaning), 'shall utter an inarticulate cry' (so A. Cohen, *A.J.S.L.*, xl, 1923–24, p. 176, retaining the present Hebrew consonants, but assuming an else unknown Hebrew verb, which is found in Aramaic). Th. C. Vriezen retains the Massoretic text, but holds that the verb had an elsewhere unexampled meaning 'scatter in fear' (*O.T.S.*, vii, 1950, pp. 203 f.). Some writers accept the sense of the Septuagint, but without specifying by what change of the reading they secure this (so J. van der Ploeg, *Les Chants du Serviteur de Jahvé*, 1936, p. 13; A. H. Edelkoort, *De Christusverwachting in het Oude Testament*, 1941, p. 394; C. R. North, *The Suffering Servant in Deutero-Isaiah*, 1948, p. 123). H. S. Nyberg, *S.E.Å.*, vii, 1942, p. 47, takes 'many nations' as the subject of the verb, which then has the meaning 'shall make ritual purification'. This is rejected as improbable by J. Lindblom, *The Servant Songs in Deutero-Isaiah*, 1951, p. 40, who suggests that the verb does not come from the root *nāzāh*, but from a root *yāzāh*, which survives in Hebrew only in some Proper Names, and which means 'be-sprinkle', *i.e.* purify from sins. He thus returns to the meaning of R.V. Some editors arbitrarily delete the word 'nations' from this verse, but there is no evidence for this, and the reference to 'kings' in the following line favours its retention. In the view of the majority of scholars the speakers in Chapter liii are the Gentiles, who confess that the sufferings and death of the Servant are for them.

[1] Cf. H. W. Wolff, *Jesaja 53 im Urchristentum*, 1942, pp. 49 ff. (2nd ed., 1950, pp. 55 ff.); V. Taylor, *Jesus and His Sacrifice*, 1943 ed., pp. 39 ff.; W. Manson, *Jesus the Messiah*, 1943, pp. 30 ff. Cf. also now C. Maurer, *Z.Th.K.* l, 1953, pp. 1 ff.

[2] The contrast between 'for many' of Mk. x. 45 and 'for all' of 1 Tim. ii. 6 (cf. also 'for the whole world' of 1 John ii. 2) has frequently been pressed. If it could rightly be pressed it would tell in favour of the earliness of the form of Mk. x. 45. It is very doubtful if it should be so pressed, and probable that it is a reminiscence of the 'many' which recurs several times in the fourth Servant Song. Jerome held that the text has 'for many' and not 'for all' to indicate that the death of Christ was only for those who believe (cf. Migne, *P.L.*, xxvi. 1884, col. 150), but H. B. Swete rightly says that this is unwarranted (cf. *The Gospel according to St. Mark*, 1898, p. 226b).

this, and it does not seem to have asked that those who joined its ranks from paganism should go to Jerusalem to offer a sacrifice. Judaism always asked this, so long as the Temple stood. It welcomed interested foreigners to its synagogues and places of prayer,[1] but it did not recognize them as proselytes unless they had offered sacrifice.[2] The Church accepted into the company of the elect, and recognized as full brothers and sisters in Christ those who found in the death of Christ their sufficient sacrifice and the final sacrifice.

Two things are here to be noted. The first is that we have here the fulfilment of something that was promised in the Old Testament, and something that by promise and fulfilment binds the two Testaments firmly together. Of no other than Christ can the terms of the fourth Servant Song be predicated with even remote relevance; it would be hard for even the most sceptical to declare them absurd in relation to Him. For whether we like it or not, and whether we can explain it or not, countless numbers of men and women, of many races and countries, and of every age from His day to ours, have experienced a major change of heart and life when they have stood before the Cross of Christ, and have felt that no words but those of Isa. liii. 5 were adequate to express their thought. 'He was wounded for our transgressions, he was bruised for iniquities; the chastisement of our peace was upon him, and with his stripes we are healed.'

[1] Cf. E. J. Bickerman, in *The Jews*, ed. by L. Finkelstein, i, 1949, p. 76: 'The Jews were first of all peoples we know to open wide the gates to proselytes'; p. 104: 'It seems that in early Hellenism the people who completely accepted Judaism by circumcision and baptism, and refused to take part any longer in pagan ceremonies, were rather rare. But there were numerous Hellenes who revered the Most High without observing all the prescriptions of the Torah.'

[2] This, of course, was no longer the case after the destruction of the Temple. The tradition that this was the rule while the Temple stood is well preserved. Cf. T.B. *Kerithoth* 9a (ed. Goldschmidt, ix, 1935, p. 497); *Sifre* on Numbers § 108—on Num. xv. 14 (ed. H. S. Horovitz, *Corpus Tannaiticum, Siphre ad Numeros*, 1917, p. 112, or E. Tr. by P. P. Levertoff, *Midrash Sifre on Numbers*, 1926, p. 92); *Mekilta de R. Simeon ben Yoḥai* on Exod. xii. 48 (ed. D. Hoffmann, *Mechilta de Rabbi Simon b. Jochai*, 1905, pp. 29 f.); *Gerim* ii. 4 (ed. M. Higger, *Seven Minor Treatises*, 1930, Hebrew part, p. 72, English part, p. 50); Maimonides, *Issure Biah* xiii. 1 (ed. H. Prideaux, *De jure pauperis et peregrini apud Judaeos*, 1679, p. 113). This tradition is generally accepted as trustworthy. Cf. E. Schürer, *G.J.V.*, 4th ed., iii, 1909, pp. 181 f.; G. F. Moore, *Judaism*, i, 1927, pp. 331 f., 334; J. Bonsirven, *Le Judaïsme palestinien*, i, 1934, pp. 29 f.

Whether we like it or not, the Cross of Christ stands as the greatest source of spiritual power the world has seen. When we look at Isa. liii in the light of the Cross we can only say that the two correspond impressively, and that nothing else can be brought into relation with the fourth Servant Song and show any similar correspondence. If the hand of God is found in the promise, then fulfilment it ought to have, and here fulfilment is to be seen. If the hand of God is denied in the promise, then it is passing strange that it should find so remarkable a fulfilment.

The second thing to be noted is that here the suspension of sacrifice is quite different in character from that of post-Biblical Judaism. Within the course of the period covered by the Old Testament many primitive practices, which went back to the remote past, and which in many cases Israel shared with her neighbours and drew from her common heritage with them, had fallen away.[1] They were not born of the particular faith of Israel, and though they were continued in her Law, they were not the expressions of its essential character and spirit, and could gradually be outgrown and dropped. Sacrifice was not of the number of these things. It is true that sacrifice came from a wider than Israelite background, and was not in itself peculiar to the faith of Israel; but it was not dropped because men had come to realize that it was superfluous to the real essence of Judaism. It was dropped because it had to be, and for no other reason. The one legitimate sanctuary had been destroyed and there could be no other. In the Mishnah we find evidence of the treasuring of the memories and traditions of the ritual of the Temple, and it is abundantly clear that Judaism had not terminated sacrifices because they were no longer thought to have meaning or value. For the Church, on the other hand, sacrifice was suspended

---

[1] The custom of the wholesale massacre of a defeated enemy and the destruction of all his animal and material possessions figures in the earlier history of Israel, but becomes obsolete in the later period. This custom was not peculiar to Israel, but was shared with her neighbours. On the Moabite Stone Mesha records that he put the Israelites to the ban in this way (line 17; cf. G. A. Cooke, *A Text-Book of North Semitic Inscriptions*, 1903, pp. 1 ff.). Similarly the customs of blood revenge and levirate marriage were shared with other peoples, but were limited and controlled in Israel. Cf. H. H. Rowley, *Servant of the Lord*, pp. 167 ff.

because it had been superseded by a sacrifice which corresponded to one promised in the Old Testament and achieved in history in a setting which bore the signature of God no less clearly than the earlier revelation in the Mosaic period. The one suspension had no relation to the Old Testament and none to the revealed will of God; the other is closely knit to the promise of the Old Testament and rests on a new revelation of God, whose guarantee is similar in kind to that of the guarantee of the old revelation.

Nor does the case for the unity of the two Testaments rest there. Many were the forms of the hopes set before men in the Old Testament. The promise of the Kingdom of God is sometimes linked with the great descendant of David,[1] and sometimes he is not especially mentioned.[2] It is always in terms of a world-wide kingdom, in which righteousness is to prevail, and which consequently will know peace and perfect well-being, since the will of God will be perfectly done. In one passage, as has just been said, the death of the Servant of the Lord is associated with the universal extension of submission to God. All of these hopes come together in our Lord in a remarkable way. In the confluence of the streams there is necessarily mutual modification,[3] as there was bound to be if all were to be in any sense fulfilled. His kingdom is truly world-wide, though not universal, but it is a spiritual kingdom and not one resting on material force, and it asks for the willing acceptance of the rule of God in the heart. All of this and more has been so often said that there is no need to enlarge on it here.[4] There is a broad correspondence, though not

---

[1] So, e.g., Mic. v. 2 ff. (Heb. 1 ff.); Isa. ix. 2 ff. (Heb. 1 ff.), xi. 1 ff.; Jer. xxiii. 5 ff

[2] So, e.g., Isa. ii. 2 ff.; Isa. li. 4 ff.; Isa. lxv. 17 ff.; Dan. ii. 44, vii. 14, 22, 27; Psa. xxii. 27 f (Heb. 28 f.).

[3] Cf. G. A. Smith, *The Book of Isaiah*, i, 10th ed., 1897, p. 143: 'The Messianic prophecies of the Old Testament are tidal rivers. They not only run . . . to their sea, which is Christ; they feel His reflex influence.' In *Israel's Mission to the World*, 1939, p. 97, the present writer cited this from memory, but was unable to recall where he had read it.

[4] F. C. Grant holds that the identification of Jesus in the Gospels with the Son of Man, the Son of David, and the Suffering Servant offers evidence of the reflection of more than one type of Christology in the Early Church, and cannot derive from the 'messianic consciousness' of Jesus, since they are incompatible concepts (*An Introduction to New Testament Thought*, 1950, pp. 22 ff.). He is conscious of the difficulty that later Christian thought, even in the New Testament, succeeded in fusing these concepts, but thinks it improbable that Jesus could have so fused them. The present writer has elsewhere argued

a detailed correspondence, with the promise of the Old Testament, a correspondence that is significant and impressive, and one that is quite unique in history. If the hopes were in any sense given to men by revelation from God, then they ought to be realized, and here is a significant realization; if the hopes were not given by revelation from God, but were merely the expression of the delusive hopes of men, then it is surely remarkable that such delusive hopes proved not to be delusive, but had so impressive a measure of fulfilment.

It cannot for one moment be claimed that the hopes have been completely fulfilled, however, and it is unwise to concentrate on the things that are convenient and to ignore the rest. That is far from being our intention here. The Kingdom of our Lord is by no means universal, and universal peace is not even on the horizon. Instead of beating swords into ploughshares men make ever larger and sharper swords, and ever more deadly and destructive weapons. The full consummation of the hopes of the Old

---

that the Davidic Messiah and the Suffering Servant are different concepts, though both related to the Golden Age, as also is the concept of the Son of Man (*The Servant of the Lord*, pp. 61 ff.). Nevertheless he holds that it is not without reason that they came together in Christ, since both are probably derived ultimately from the royal cultic rites. The Davidic Messiah concept derived from the victorious and regnant elements in those rites, while the Suffering Servant concept derived from the elements of humiliation in them. Separated they yield different concepts, which were not brought together until the time of our Lord. There is, however, no reason why they could not have come together in His mind. W. F. Howard observes: 'The more we study the primitive Christian tradition and the earliest Christian preaching the more we must acknowledge that the creative mind in the Church was that of Jesus Himself. . . . The outstanding assertion made by Jesus in the whole tenor of His teaching and example is that the Messiah must be interpreted in the light of the Servant of Jehovah' (*E.T.*, l, 1938–39, p. 108b). The incompatibility between the regnant and the humiliated aspects is removed by the thought of Christ as both having come and yet to come, and as achieving His triumph through His suffering. Such an idea was already found in the fourth Servant Song, and it does not seem improbable that in the Gospels we have an accurate picture. John the Baptist heralded the Kingdom of God and Jesus took up his message, but as the Leader of the Kingdom and no longer its Herald. The perception that suffering lay before Him, and that it would be the organ of His mission and not merely incidental to it, inevitably meant that His triumph lay beyond the Cross. To the disciples this implied that His Messiahship was imperilled, but since there is no suggestion that Jesus wavered in His messianic consciousness, which had preceded His intimations of His sufferings, the reconciliation must have been effected in His mind before it was effected in the minds of any others. Any other view must involve far too serious and arbitrary a rewriting of the Gospels. If, as the Gospels narrate, Jesus declared that His death would be followed by resurrection and return in power, even though the disciples quite naturally were puzzled at the time, the fusing of the concepts would seem to be complete.

Testament lies still in the distant future, so far as human prescience can guess. Nor does the New Testament fail to perceive this. The Early Church did not suppose that the Kingdom of God in all its universality and final glory was established on earth in the ministry and death of Christ. It still placed the final glory in the future. It believed that Christ was living and that He would one day reappear to rule His kingdom in the day of its universality. This is quite different from the Jewish hope that the Messiah will one day appear. The Church found in the significant measure of fulfilment of the old hopes the evidence that the Messiah *had* appeared and had begun His work. The Kingdom of God had been established, but the task of its extension was one that could be achieved but slowly, and the final glory could only come with the universality of the Kingdom. This was really in accordance with what the Old Testament had itself taught. It had declared that before the Golden Age could be attained by any it must be attained by all, and that its attainment would rest on a spiritual change in men. All men must go up to the house of the Lord and freely seek to learn His way ere the Golden Age could dawn.[1] Such a spiritual change could not be effected in the twinkling of an eye, but must take time. Moreover, it had been taught in the Old Testament that Israel was called to be the light of the Gentiles,[2] and had a mission to the world. The winning of all men to seek the Lord waited for the response of Israel to her mission.

It is frequently observed that the prophet who looked into the future could not perceive the temporal relation of the things of which he spoke. Just as one who gazes at the stars sees them as on a domed surface and is unable to distinguish their depth in space, so the prophet in his visions of the Golden Age could not distinguish depth in time. Hence to the prophets the beginning and the consummation of the Messianic Age could be linked together, though at other times they perceived the spiritual processes of conversion that stood between the two. To the Church that stood between the beginning and the consummation a period divided the two. It is true that the Early Church did not rightly

[1] Isa. ii. 3; Mic. iv. 2.   [2] Isa. xlii. 6.

estimate the period, and men who have since sought to estimate it have continually erred.[1] But the recognition of a period between the beginning and the consummation is not inconsistent with the teaching of the Old Testament as a whole, though it is often not manifest from the individual word. With the recognition of such a period the Church looked forward to the Second Coming of Christ in the consummation to bring to completion that which He had begun in His first coming.

Such extravagances of view on the Second Coming have been expressed by some that in modern times others have reacted strongly against the whole idea, and cease to cherish the thought of it as a living hope This seems to be unwise, and to make sense neither of the Old Testament nor of the New, and to suggest a half-hearted faith that Christ is living.[2] If in any real sense He is believed to be living and to be present in His Church today, it would seem to be not unreasonable to expect that in the consummation of the Kingdom He will be more gloriously manifest. The fundamental hope seems to belong to the thought of the Bible, and to be essential to the finding in the New Testament of the fulfilment of the Old. It is quite distinguishable from the extravagances that seek to define the time and place and manner of the consummation—matters on which the New Testament expressly warns that speculation is vain.[3]

We have far from exhausted the case for the binding together of the two Testaments. It is not merely that we have the blending

[1] P.-H. Menoud, *La Vie de l'Église naissante*, 1952, p. 43, observes that the Early Church expected the Second Coming in the immediate future, and Paul believed that he was of the number of those who would be still alive at the time of the Parousia (cf. 1 Thess. iv. 15). Nevertheless the delay of the Second Coming did not precipitate a crisis in the Church because the hope was not tied to any specific chronology, and the believers were not apocalyptists busy with calculations.

[2] Cf. O. Cullmann, *Le Retour du Christ, espérance de l'Église, selon le Nouveau Testament*, 1943, where it is argued that to reject the hope of the Second Coming is to mutilate the New Testament message of salvation (pp. 12 f.). Cf. what the present writer has written in *The Relevance of Apocalyptic*, 2nd ed., 1947, p. 148: 'I do not regard the belief in the Second Advent as a delusion of primitive Christianity, but as something which is inherent in the fundamental Christian beliefs. I would deprecate all attempts to determine when it is to take place, or to define its manner, but it seems to me eminently reasonable to believe that if the Kingdom of God is ever to be realized on earth, Christ will have the manifestly supreme place in it.' Cf. also *ibid.*, p. 122.

[3] Cf. Mk. xiii. 21, 32 f.; Matt. xxiv. 23 f., 36; Lk. xxi. 8.

of the expectation of the Messiah and the Suffering Servant and other forms of the thought of the Golden Age in relation to Christ and His work. Many other Old Testament streams of thought run to Him and to His Church; or, if they do not run to Him, run nowhere. That is why it can be claimed that the Old Testament requires the New no less than the New requires the Old. Streams which do not in any sense run to Judaism run to Christianity, and unless they have meaning in relation to the Church they can have no meaning at all.

First, however, we may note a remarkable fact which can claim significance. It has been said that Jesus, Who believed Himself to be the Messiah, also believed that His death would achieve what the death of the Servant was expected to achieve, and that in the experience of men His death has indeed achieved this. It is to be noted that the Crucifixion took place at the time of the Passover, and that it was determined and carried through by His enemies. We are not concerned with the controversy as to whether the Last Supper was a Passover meal, or whether our Lord died in the hour when the Passover lambs were being slain. Whether His death is associated with the death of the Passover lambs, whose blood sprinkled on the doorposts was a reminder of the ancient deliverance, or whether His death, like that of the firstborn of Egypt, followed the eating of the Passover, matters little for our present purpose. In either case the death of Jesus is related to that ancient deliverance by the time at which it took place.[1] At the time of the Exodus, in the deliverance from Egypt and in all that preceded and followed it, there was given a revelation of God, and there lay the foundation of Old Testament religion as it was established by Moses. Whatever significance the Passover may have had before, from the time of the Exodus on its significance for Israel was a new one. Now once more it is in connection with the same festival that a new and profounder deliverance is wrought and a new revelation

---

[1] Cf. F.-J. Leenhardt, *Le Sacrement de la Sainte Cène*, 1948, p. 14: 'The paschal interpretation of the Last Supper of Jesus does not seem to us to depend directly on the solution of the chronological problem.'

of God given. Here, too, the New Covenant is established, so that here again for the followers of Jesus a new significance attaches henceforth to this festival. What may once have had apotropaic significance as a spring festival for a pastoral people, warding off evil influences and perhaps associated in some way with moon worship, had for centuries had for all Israel, whether pastoral, agricultural or urban, a memorial significance and a sacramental significance. Whatever association with moon worship it may once have had, it lost it for Israel from the time of the Exodus, and became instead a time when men remembered what God had done for their fathers and the heritage of freedom and of faith that had become theirs in consequence, and a time when gratitude called for the solemn renewal of the Covenant in recommitment to God in loyalty. Now for the followers of Jesus every observance of this festival is charged with a new commemorative significance. It preserves the memory of the deliverance wrought by Christ, and calls for new gratitude and new consecration. If someone had sat down to create a story that should be dramatically appropriate, one could understand his lighting on the time of the Passover for this climax of his story. If the hand of God was at work, carrying the old revelation forward into a new one, lifting the old deliverance to a new plane of deliverance, filling the ancient festival a second time with fresh significance, one could understand it. But if it were merely the accident of the choice of Christ's foes that caused this remarkable coincidence, it would be both surprising and beyond all explanation. For to declare a thing an accidental coincidence and to leave it at that is to offer no explanation, but to declare that it is incapable of explanation.

To add to the remarkable nature of this fact we have the prior declaration of our Lord that His foes were about to strike, and His linking of His death with the New Covenant.[1] The New

---

[1] Lk. xxii. 20. This verse is omitted from the Western text, and its originality has therefore been contested. Cf. J. Jeremias, *Die Abendmahlsworte Jesu*, 2nd ed., 1949, pp. 67 ff., where the evidence is presented and examined, and where it is held that the longer text is original. In its reference to the New Covenant it agrees with the Pauline account, 1 Cor. xi. 25, from which it is sometimes held to have been borrowed. A. J. B. Higgins,

Covenant had been spoken of by Jeremiah.[1] By its very name it pointed back to the old Covenant of Sinai, which sprang out of the deliverance from Egypt, and pointed forward to the future. Here, at the Last Supper, on an occasion that itself points back to the old Covenant, and on the eve of His death which his enemies were at that moment planning, Jesus picks up the thought of the New Covenant. Jeremiah had said that this was to be written on men's hearts, and not on external tables of stone, and that it was to spring from deep intimacy with God, in which the children of the New Covenant would know Him in living fellowship. When Jesus spoke to His followers of the New Covenant He called them to eat and to drink of Him, and to experience a union of themselves with His spirit. In Him God was revealing Himself anew to them, so that in His spirit they saw God's Spirit, and in union with Him they were experiencing union with God. So many Old Testament streams run together here that only a blinding prejudice can hide their significance. And even prejudice could not produce any other confluence of these streams that could show a comparable impressiveness.

Nor have we yet finished. Throughout the Old Testament we have the idea of the Remnant.[2] Though all Israel would not rise to the full glory of its high calling and fulfil the purpose of Israel's vocation, it was perceived that the stream of the election might be narrowed to the Remnant, who alone should inherit the promises and who alone should bring true loyalty to the

---

The Lord's Supper in the New Testament, 1952, pp. 37 ff., argues that both Luke and Paul used a common tradition. F. C. Grant, An Introduction to New Testament Thought, 1950, p. 204, observes that the identification of the covenant with the 'new' covenant is peculiar to Paul's interpretation of the rite. To the present writer it seems that very heavy weather is made of the word 'new'. In Mk. xiv. 24 the saying reads 'This is my blood of the covenant'. This form is held to be older than the Pauline form, though it stands in a later work (cf. Grant, ibid.; so also Jeremias, op. cit., p. 85). It can scarcely be supposed that in the Marcan form the covenant could be the ancient covenant of Sinai. It must therefore necessarily be a new covenant, and the Lucan and Pauline form, whether original or not, is legitimate interpretation of the meaning. Cf. J. Héring, La première Épitre de St. Paul aux Corinthiens, 1949, pp. 101 ff., where it is argued that the thought must be of Ex. xxiv. 8, and of another covenant conceived in those terms.

[1] Jer. xxxi. 31 ff.
[2] On the Remnant cf. H. Dittmann, T.S.K., lxxxvii, 1914, pp. 603 ff.; R. de Vaux, R.B., xlii, 1933, pp. 526 ff.; E. W. Heaton, J.T.S., N.S. iii, 1952, pp. 27 ff.; also the present writer's Biblical Doctrine of Election, pp. 71 ff.

tasks of the election. While sometimes the Remnant is thought of as spared not for its own loyalty,[1] but for the sake of a future generation, that it might transmit the heritage it did not itself value to a generation that should value it, its end and purpose was still a loyal and consecrated people.[2] At other times the Remnant is thought of as itself loyal, spared because it is the true heir of the Covenant.[3] In either case it is perceived that the heritage of election and the privileges of the Covenant belong only to the faithful in Israel who bring to the Covenant their loyalty and fulfil the purposes of the election. It is not the automatic inheritance of all who are born into the Israel after the flesh. The line of election is limited to the faithful. Yet alongside this we have the widening of the stream to include those who were not of the Israel according to the flesh, but who came to share the worship of Israel's God, and the perception that it belonged to the mission of the elect to carry the faith of Israel and the Law of God to all men.[4]

Here again we have factors in the Old Testament pointing to the future, and factors which have not pointed to post-Biblical Judaism. By New Testament times Judaism had won large numbers of converts from paganism, and we should never forget how much the Early Church owed to this fact. Though the Apostle Paul was often persecuted by the Jewish communities to which he went in many cities it was the synagogues to which he first went, and they provided him with his first forum and often brought him face to face with his first converts. While Judaism was never a missionary faith in the sense in which the Church became missionary almost from its inception, it had a solid missionary achievement to its credit.[5] But soon it ceased

[1] Cf. Amos iv. 11.   [2] Cf. Isa. x. 20 f.
[3] Cf. 1 Kings xix. 18.
[4] Cf. *The Biblical Doctrine of Election*, pp. 81 ff.
[5] Cf. C. G. Montefiore, in *The Beginnings of Christianity*, edited by F. J. Foakes Jackson and K. Lake, i, 1942 ed., pp. 42 ff., and the editors, *ibid.*, pp. 164 ff. A. Causse, *Israël et la vision de l'humanité*, 1924, pp. 129 ff.; Bousset-Gressmann, *Die Religion des Judentums im späthellenistischer Zeitalter*, 1926, pp. 76 ff.; G. F. Moore, *Judaism*, i, 1927, pp. 323 ff.; J. Bonsirven, *Je Judaïsme palestinien*, i, 1934, pp. 22 ff.; M. Simon, *Verus Israel*, 1948, pp. 315 ff.; J. Jeremias, *S.N.T.S. Bulletin*, 1952, pp. 1 ff.

to be missionary in any effective sense, and many of its leaders deprecated the winning of converts.[1] The message of Deutero-Isaiah and of Jonah cannot be said to point to post-Biblical Judaism for its serious adoption as a programme. Nor can Judaism in the centuries that have followed be said to have spread the Law of God as given to it in the Old Testament specially widely amongst men.[2] No Jewish society comparable with the British and Foreign Bible Society has ever been formed. The oldest surviving translation of the Old Testament into another language is the Greek version known as the Septuagint. This was prepared by Jews, as also were some other ancient versions. But these were prepared for the use of Jews in the first instance, and not as a means of making the Jewish Scriptures known amongst the heathen. No Jew has ever set to work, as William Carey did, to translate the Bible into language after language and to send it forth to be its own ambassador to peoples too numerous to be reached by his voice, and to whom he had no means of sending forth living ambassadors.

The Church, on the other hand, has been thus missionary from the time of the Apostles until today. It has sent forth men and women set apart for the specific task of winning others to share its faith, and it has been instrumental in winning vast numbers from innumerable nations to worship the God of Israel. It has translated the Jewish Bible into countless tongues and has spread it throughout the earth, so that no book is so widely known and loved amongst men as the Scriptures of the Old Testament, and the New Testament that belongs so intimately to it. The mission committed to Israel, according to the teaching of the Old Testament, has been accepted and carried out by the Church on

[1] Cf. C. G. Montefiore, *The Synoptic Gospels*, ii, 1909, p. 728: 'The Palestinian Rabbis were on the whole not particularly favourable to proselytes'; C. J. Cadoux, *The Historic Mission of Jesus*, 1941, p. 150: 'Certain it is that this main line of Jewish life represented by Rabbinism paid very little regard to the universalistic ideals represented in the Old Testament, and became eventually so self-centred that even the zeal for proselytism faded away.'

[2] L. I. Newman holds that though Jewish opinion as a whole did not favour the making of proselytes, and the Rabbis sometimes denounced would-be converts to the authorities, nevertheless the Jews did not wholly cease to make converts in the Middle Ages. Cf. *Jewish Influence on Christian Reform Movements*, 1925, pp. 394 ff.

a scale incomparably greater than anything that can be found outside the Church.[1]

Moreover, the Church consisted of a Remnant of Israel, together with Gentiles who were won to the faith by them. The first Christians were all Jews, undeniably a Remnant of Israel, whether they be thought to be the Remnant of Promise or not. Soon they had communicated the faith to non-Jews who entered whole-heartedly into it and took its obligations seriously. Either this was the fulfilment of the hope and promise of the Old Testament or it was not. If it was not, then where shall we look for the fulfilment ? And if it was not, how comes it to pass that here we find so remarkable a correspondence with the promise that had been set forth? If this was not the Remnant of Promise, then how comes it to pass that the obligations of the Covenant, including the obligation to make the Only God of all men known throughout the world, and to carry His Law to the nations, were so enthusiastically taken up by this Remnant, while the Remnant of Promise is still to seek? The faith of the Church that it was the Remnant of Promise is surely supported by the testimony of history, in which its inner hope has found such signal vindication in demonstrable fact.

Here, then, are a few of the ways in which the New Testament may be said not alone to spring out of the Old, but to respond to the faith and promise of the Old. We have not merely a development that did in fact follow from the Old. Expectations and promises are set before men in the Old Testament, and in the New Testament and in the Church we have the only response to them so far seen, which can be taken seriously. It is not that we have in the New Testament and in the Church a response which the Church believes to be superior to the response that can be found in Judaism. With all its nobility and grandeur, which may be recognized with the utmost sincerity, Judaism does not

---

[1] Cf. L. Finkelstein, *The Pharisees*, ii, 1938, pp. 498 f.: 'The Pharisees traveled over land and sea to win converts to their views, and proselytes to Judaism were to be found in Rome, in Egypt, and in the midst of Arabia. And finally, when Judah, weary with its struggle against Rome, was beginning to withdraw into itself, the task was taken over by the apostles of Christianity.'

even claim to be the response to these hopes. It has no Messiah to offer, no Suffering Servant that can gather to Himself the things predicated of the Servant in the fifty-third chapter of Isaiah, no new revelation of God to authorize the dispensing with sacrifice, no vital sense of a mission to win the world for its God, no overmastering passion to communicate the Law of God to all men. All of these things, and more that could be added to them, are offered in the New Testament and in the Church, where the response to the promises is impressive indeed.

To ignore all these elements in the Old Testament and yet to regard it as the vehicle of divine revelation seems impossible. To ignore them and to dismiss the Old Testament as a human document in which no hand of God is to be seen seems equally impossible. For neither of these attitudes can account for the remarkable correspondences which have been noted, correspondences which in part belong to the texture of events and not to the design of any human mind, which of itself could be supposed to be linked with a will capable of achieving it. On the other hand, to regard the New Testament with veneration and to find in Christ the supreme revelation of God, and at the same time to ignore the Old Testament and the correspondences at which we have looked, seems also impossible. The Old Testament is wanted not alone to provide the background of the New. It offers its contribution to the guarantee of the authority of the New Testament no less really than the New Testament brings its guarantee of the authority of the Old Testament. The promise of the Old could not by itself ensure its fulfilment in the New; yet since it was written before the fulfilment it was necessarily independent of that fulfilment. Neither Testament can be explained from the other alone; yet both find their sufficient explanation if the hand of God is in both. Just as Moses promised a deliverance he could not achieve, and a power beyond human control answered with the deliverance; and as our Lord promised that His death would release unique power, but could not by His promise give that power to His death if He were no more than a village carpenter, yet did in fact achieve by His death all that

He promised; so here we find a prior word and a subsequent fulfilment, where the word, if it had no higher source than a human thought, could not effect the fulfilment.

The argument from prophecy has hardly seemed respectable to many modern writers, and an apology is almost required if one uses such an argument. It has a legitimate use, though we should be careful not to pass beyond its legitimate use. Sometimes men have torn isolated words out of their context and wrested their meaning, or resorted to a convenient version for a meaning that could be pressed into service. The use of the Septuagint translation in Isa. vii. 14 is a familiar case of the latter,[1] while the New Testament offers several instances of the former. That kind

[1] The Hebrew word which is translated by 'virgin' in R.V. neither requires nor excludes virginity, and the American R.S.V. accordingly renders by 'young woman'. The Greek renders by a word which limits the meaning to 'virgin', and the New Testament accordingly cites the verse in Greek in this form in Matt. i. 23. Since the primary reference in Isa. vii. 14 must be to a child about to be born, if this birth was to be a sign to King Ahaz, it is improbable that a virgin birth was in the prophet's mind. Father C. Lattey (*C.B.Q.*, viii, 1946, pp. 375 f.) holds that the primary reference was to Isaiah's own son, Maher-shalal-hash-baz, though he holds that by the principle of compenetration there was also a reference to our Lord's birth. This recognizes that in the primary reference the child of a human father is intended, and so justifies the rendering of the R.S.V. Since Father Lattey firmly believes in the Virgin Birth of our Lord, it is clear that there is no necessary danger to that doctrine in this translation, though Father Lattey still translates by 'virgin' since he applies the principle of compenetration to the mother as well as to the child. On this passage cf. *The Biblical Doctrine of Election*, p. 150 n., and the literature there referred to. F. C. Grant, *An Introduction to New Testament Thought*, 1950, p. 231, holds that the belief in the Virgin Birth as reflected in the New Testament is secondary and inferential, and that it is derived from Isa. vii. 14, and supported by it. It is more probable that men who believed in the Virgin Birth seized on the Greek rendering of Isa. vii. 14 to support the view by a prophecy, in accordance with rabbinical methods of exegesis, which allowed what was useful to be torn from its context and used without regard to the context, than that this verse gave the starting point, and the story of the Annunciation was then created to justify the doctrine. Such a view implies that the doctrine first arose in Greek-speaking circles, since it rests on the Septuagint rendering, whereas the Hebraic character of Luke i.–iii. and of the First Gospel, where alone the Virgin Birth is recorded, is generally recognized. Cf. J. Moffatt, *Introduction to the Literature of the New Testament*, 3rd ed., 1918, pp. 266 f., where the view is expressed that Luke i. 5–ii. 52, iii. 23–38, represents an early Palestinian source which Luke translated and worked over, perhaps inserting i. 34 f., and p. 255 f., where it is held that the author of the First Gospel is a Jewish Christian, acquainted with rabbinic learning, and employing Palestinian traditions. It is improbable that Luke was himself the free creator of Luke i. 34 f., since the passage shows the parallelism of Hebrew poetry, and it is probable that it was taken over from a Hebrew or Aramaic source. For the view that these verses are a later addition, cf. A. Harnack, *Z.N.W.*, ii, 1901, pp. 53 ff., and on the other side M.-J. Lagrange, *Évangile selon Saint Luc*, 7th ed., 1948, pp. 31 ff. For a discussion of the rendering of R.S.V. cf. J. J. Owens, *Review and Expositor*, l, 1953, pp. 56 ff., and Dale Moody, *ibid.*, pp. 61 ff., and for a defence of the rendering 'virgin' cf. J. Coppens, *E. Th.L.*, xxviii, 1952, pp. 648 ff.

of argument may have a homiletic or psychological value; it has no logical value. Much Rabbinic exegesis was of this kind, and it is not surprising that we have some traces of it in the New Testament.[1] So far as the Virgin Birth of Christ is concerned it is neither proved nor disproved by reference to Isa. vii. 14, which promised King Ahaz a sign, and which therefore gave assurance of a fulfilment that he should live to see. We have not resorted to such examples here, in order to force the argument from prophecy beyond its legitimate limits.[2] We have rather been content with the broad outlines of the hope and with the fulfilment, where we are moving in a common context.[3] Moreover, when reference has been made to a common texture in the revelation of the Old and New Testaments, there has been no resort to typology or the argument that the purpose of the one revelation was to prepare the way for the other.[4] Where a

[1] Cf. J. Guillet, *Thèmes Bibliques*, 1950, p. 22: 'There are certainly some disconcerting arguments in Pauline exegesis.' Cf. also J. Bonsirven, *Exégèse rabbinique et exégèse paulinienne*, 1939, pp. 327 ff. T. W. Manson, *B.J.R.L.*, xxxiv, 1951-52, p. 312; says: 'In some cases the connection between the supposed prediction and its fulfilment is of the flimsiest character, and when we get into the field of allegorical interpretation and typology, it often seems as if the only limits to what can be done are set by the resource and fertility of invention of the expositor.' Cf. also Manson's article 'The Argument from Prophecy', *J.T.S.*, xlvi, 1945, pp. 129 ff.

[2] Cf. W. Zimmerli, *Evangelische Theologie*, xii, 1952-53, pp. 34 ff., esp. p. 58.

[3] The writer has been criticized on the ground that he is undermining faith by seeking to offer rational 'proof' in the argument from prophecy. The reader who has followed his argument will be aware that this is not so. Cf. what he has written elsewhere: 'I am not attempting to replace faith by a logical demonstration that will make it superfluous. I have already said that man is more than mind, and I do not forget that religion touches every side of his being. I am only seeking to show that though man is more than mind he is also mind, and that he need not suspend that side of his being when he speaks of the authority of the Bible. . . . What I am concerned to say is that the authority of the Bible rests on objective evidence that God was active in event and personality, and that both belonged together, and that the whole process culminated in the death and resurrection of Christ, which were charged with demonstrably unique power. Faith is not rendered superfluous. But faith is the subjective response to the authority of the Bible and of the God Who is recognized to speak through it, just as loyalty is the response of the good citizen to the authority of the state. And faith opens the heart to the entrance of the Spirit, by Whose operation the riches of the Word of God are increasingly seen and appropriated' (*The Authority of the Bible*, 1949, p. 20). To show that faith is reasonable is not to destroy faith; nor is the establishment of its reasonableness to be confused with 'proof'.

[4] Cf. W. Eichrodt, *Israel in der Weissagung des Alten Testaments*, 1951, where allegory is rejected but substance found in the broad hope of Old Testament prophecy. Cf. also H. W. Hertzberg, *Werdende Kirche im Alten Testament*, 1950, where other aspects of the relations between the Testaments are studied. For a fuller treatment of this theme cf. N. A. Dahl, *Das Volk Gottes*, 1941.

common signature is to be found in the texture of the revelation, the purpose of the first was not merely to ensure the identification of the second. Each message that bore the signature was a significant message of God. With the broad hope and its fulfilment, however, there is a more direct interlocking and mutual guarantee of authority.[1] From both the community of pattern and the interlocking we may reasonably conclude that there is a profound and important unity running through both Testaments, and that it is the unity of the thread of the revelation of the One God.

[1] Cf. J. W. Bowman, *J.R.*, xxv, 1945, p. 58b: 'To say that Jesus consciously fulfilled the prophetic concepts (not "predictions") with which we have been dealing is simply to say that we live in a theistic world and that there is such a thing as a divine purpose in history.'

V

THE CROSS

HITHERTO we have considered some aspects of the unity of the Old Testament and some of the things which bind the Old Testament and the New securely together. Little has been said of the inner unity of the New Testament, and on this little will be here said.[1] The New Testament consists of books which were written within a relatively short space of time, and it presents quite a different problem from that which the Old Testament raises. The compilation of the various books of the Old Testament occupied many centuries, whereas the books of the New Testament were all composed within a period of about half a century.

That there are differences of emphasis even within the New Testament is neither to be denied nor surprising.[2] For if divine inspiration came through the medium of human personality, the inspired writings bore the marks of that personality, and the differing outlook, thought and interest of the various writers may be seen, as well as the truth which is unfolded through them. It is well known that each of the Gospels has its special interests and character, and by their study we can learn something of the personality of the evangelists. Even within the Synoptic Gospels, despite all that they have in common, there are differences, and between the Synoptic Gospels and the Fourth Gospel there are much greater differences. While all tell the story of the life and death of Jesus, each has its own particular purpose. Nevertheless the space they all give to the record of the last few days of the life of our Lord, and particularly to His trial and death, reveals a significant common interest that outweighs all their differences.

[1] Cf. A. M. Hunter, *The Unity of the New Testament*, 2nd ed., 1944; also V. Taylor, *E.T.*, lviii, 1946–47, pp. 256 ff. E. F. Scott, *The Varieties of New Testament Religion*, 1947, emphasizes the differences which must never be lost sight of in the recognition of unity.

[2] Cf. V. Taylor, *loc. cit.*, p. 256: 'This unity does not mean that the same teaching is to be found in every part of the New Testament, but rather that the distinctive ideas which are characteristic of individual writers rest upon a common basis, bringing out points which are wanting or latent elsewhere and so establishing an organic whole.'

Between the Gospels and the rest of the New Testament there are yet more obvious differences. For if the Gospels tell the story of the life and death and teaching of Jesus, the rest of the New Testament may be said to record the teaching ot the Early Church about Him. Here we might have found as great a difference as there is between the teaching of Buddha and the teaching of Buddhism about him. We find nothing of the kind. It is true that the Gospels represent Jesus as saying very little about the mystery of His Person, whereas the Epistles contain much on this subject. Yet within the Gospels we find that Jesus quietly assumes a uniqueness of His Person and His authority that is far more impressive than a theological disquisition about His Person would have been. In the Fourth Gospel we find on our Lord's lips such words as 'I and my Father are one';[1] 'He that hath seen me hath seen the Father';[2] 'I am the light of the world';[3] 'I am the way, the truth, and the life'.[4] But in the Synoptic Gospels we find that Jesus spoke with authority, and not as the scribes,[5] and that He claimed quite simply and not self-assertively to be charged with power to forgive sins,[6] and assumed the authority to supersede the law of Moses.[7] He could say 'Come unto me all ye that labour and are heavy laden, and I will give you rest'.[8] And if in the Fourth Gospel He says 'I am the bread of life',[9] in the Synoptic Gospels He gives bread to His disciples and says 'Take, eat; this is my body'.[10] While there are many contrasts between the Synoptic Gospels and the Fourth Gospel, which need be in no way minimized or forgotten, there is a yet greater measure of unity in the impression which they make of the uniqueness of Christ's Person. There is an implicit theology in

---

[1] John x. 30.   [2] John xiv. 9.   [3] John viii. 12.   [4] John xiv. 6.
[5] Mk. i. 22; Matt. vii. 29.
[6] Mk. ii. 5, 9 f.; Matt. ix. 2, 5 f.; Luke v. 20, 23 f.   [7] Matt. v. 21 ff.
[8] Matt. xi. 28. On the suggestion that we have here a quotation from a Jewish wisdom book, and that it has been put into the mouth of Jesus, cf. T. W. Manson, *The Sayings of Jesus*, 1949, pp. 185 f. Manson concludes: 'It does not seem necessary to assume that the words are a quotation. If the author of Ecclesiasticus could think of such words, so might Jesus. Further, it is not necessary to suppose that there is any reference to Wisdom in the text. . . . It is surely more natural to suppose that Jesus is here speaking as the representative, not of the divine Wisdom, but of the Kingdom of God.'
[9] John vi. 35.   [10] Matt. xxvi. 26; cf. Mk. xiv. 22, Luke xxii. 19.

the Gospels and an explicit theology in the Epistles; but they are not unrelated to one another. Nor should we forget that for the record of the Virgin Birth we rely on two of the Synoptic Gospels, while all the four Gospels record the Resurrection, to which frequent reference is made in the other books of the New Testament. All make it plain that Jesus is presented as unique in His Person as well as in His Work. In all the Gospels Jesus assumes a relation to God that is different from that of others, even though He addresses Him as Father and teaches others to address Him by the same term. The theology of the Gospels is not something wholly other than the theology of the Epistles.

To this it may be replied that while all may be in a measure true, we have yet to recognize that we cannot get back from the Gospels to Jesus. He is effectively screened from us, and we can only confess that we have reports about Him, whose accuracy we cannot check. Where we have a threefold witness in the Synoptic Gospels, it can be discounted on the ground that all of these go back to a single witness, and the mere fact that it was copied by more than one writer gives it no added authority. Where we have our Lord's words differently recorded in the different Gospels, they may be again discounted on the ground that we cannot be sure which, if any, of the versions gives us His *ipsissima verba*. We therefore have a Morton's Fork that can with equal skill dismiss the common testimony and the differing testimony.

Such dialectic skill will fail to satisfy those who reflect that the purpose of the Gospels is not to present us with the *ipsissima verba* of our Lord, but to bring us face to face with Him, that we may see Him as men saw Him and feel the impression which He made on those with whom He lived. The revelation of God came in the totality of His personality, and not in particular words alone. Of His words and deeds we have but a very small selection. Yet by the study of the Gospels we can know Him, and the Jesus Whom we come to know in the Gospels is the same in all of them. Moreover, if the Synoptic Gospels can sometimes be reduced to a single witness, we should not forget that in their totality they present more than a threefold witness. Beyond these three books, or rather behind them, we have the common source of Matthew and Luke and the special sources on which Matthew and Luke severally drew. Moreover, these sources carry us back beyond the date of our present Gospels to somewhere much nearer to the time of our Lord.

While much might be said on all these subjects, it is not our purpose in this chapter to dwell on the Person of Christ, or to emphasize at length the measure of unity on this question that is to be found in the teaching of the New Testament as a whole, or to show what preparation it had in the teaching of the Old Testament. In the previous chapter brief reference was made to this. In the Synoptic Gospels Jesus is represented as thinking of Himself in terms of the Messiah, and thus claiming to be the answer to the hope of the Old Testament. He also gathers to Himself all that is associated with the term Son of Man. He uses this term of Himself and specifically refers to Dan. vii. 13,[1] where the Son of Man is brought into connection with the establishment of the Kingdom of God. Similarly, His thought of Himself was in terms of the Suffering Servant of the Lord,[2] and the prophet's conception of the Servant became actualized in Him. All of these streams go back to the Old Testament, and if the thought of the rest of the New Testament is linked to that of the Synoptic Gospels, that of the Synoptic Gospels is linked in innumerable ways to the thought of the Old Testament.

[1] Matt. xxvi. 64. On this cf. C. J. Cadoux, *The Historic Mission of Jesus*, 1941, p. 293. T. W. Manson, *The Teaching of Jesus*, 2nd ed., 1935, pp. 227 ff., argued that the individualizing of the figure of the Son of Man and equation with Jesus was the outcome of the ministry of Jesus, and that on His lips the term had precisely the same meaning as in Daniel, where it indicates 'the manifestation of the Kingdom of God on earth in a people wholly devoted to their heavenly King'. More recently Manson has modified this view by the recognition that more weight should have been allowed to the oscillation between the individual and the collective (*B.J.R.L.*, xxxii, 1949–50, pp. 190 ff.). Cf. *The Biblical Doctrine of Election*, p. 157, and *The Servant of the Lord*, pp. 81 f. n. J. M. C. Crum, *St. Mark's Gospel*, 1936, pp. 102 ff., holds that the use of the term 'Son of Man' goes back almost, but not quite, to the time of our Lord. He thinks it was first used by the Early Church as a formula with reference to the Second Advent, and then applied to Jesus and ascribed to Him. Since the term is found outside the Gospels only in Acts vii. 56, there is scanty evidence for this theory. Already the term had become obsolete on the lips of the Church by the time of Paul's earliest writings, and it is highly improbable that it had been created and died in the Church in so short a time, to survive only in the unhistoric ascription to Jesus, which this theory postulates.

[2] Cf. A. M. Hunter, *op. cit.*, pp. 99 f.

Here, however, our thought will be limited more particularly to the Cross. Clearly this was of supreme importance in the eyes of all the Evangelists, since they give it so large a place. In the preaching of the Early Church, as recorded in the Acts, it had prominence. Similarly, in the teaching of the Epistles and of the Apocalypse we again find emphasis on the death of Christ and the significance it had. Here is one of the outstanding marks of the unity of the New Testament, and the thought of the New Testament is set in a wider context in the teaching of the Old Testament as well.

Much modern thought on the Cross is set in an Abelardian mould. It repudiates the forensic and the commercial approaches which have been characteristic of some interpreters, whereby the death of Christ was thought of in penal terms or in terms of the satisfaction of a debt. It cannot suppose that the justice of God was satisfied by the most flagrant injustice. For vicarious suffering is by its very nature not to be expressed in terms of justice. Nor can it think of God as a creditor only concerned with securing His pound of flesh, but indifferent whether it comes from the bankrupt debtors or from another who volunteers to settle the debt on their behalf. Nor can it press the metaphor of the ransom in the way that so many interpreters have pressed it. Much of the early thought of the Church seized on the text 'The Son of Man came . . . to give his life a ransom for many',[1] and interpreted the ransom as a price paid to the Devil, so that by His death Christ bought us out of the power of the Evil One. Respectable theologians went so far as to suppose that the Cross was the bait by which God hooked the Devil,[2] and that though

[1] Mk. x. 45; Matt. xx. 28.

[2] So Gregory of Nyssa. Cf. Migne, *P.G.*, xlv, 1863, col. 65; J. H. Srawley, *The Catechetical Oration of Gregory of Nyssa*, 1903, p. 93. W. Moore translates this passage as follows: 'In order to secure that the ransom in our behalf might be easily accepted by him who required it, the Deity was hidden under the veil of our nature, that so, as with ravenous fish, the hook of the Deity might be gulped down along with the bait of flesh.' Cf. *Nicene and Post-Nicene Fathers*, ed. by H. Wace and P. Schaff, Second series, v, 1893, p. 494. Similarly Ambrose can speak of a fraud practised by God on the Devil (cf. Migne, *P.L.*, xv, 1887, col. 1699; *Corpus Scriptorum Ecclesiasticorum Latinorum*, xxxii, Part 4, 1902, p. 145). Ambrose regards the death of Jesus as the satisfaction of a bond which the Devil held against us (cf. Migne, *P.L.*, xvi, 1880, cols. 313 f.; cf. col. 1299, translated in *The Letters of S. Ambrose* (Library of Fathers), 1881, p. 426).

the ransom was paid to him he found he could not hold it and so lost both ransom and prisoners. One of the latest writers to present this type of view said: 'What did the Redeemer do to our captor? He extended to him His Cross as a mouse-trap (*muscipulam*); He set there as a bait (*quasi escam*) His blood'.[1] Small wonder that such views cannot commend themselves to men today!

With such views the sacrificial view of the Cross has also gone largely out of fashion in modern times. This has probably been due in part to the prevalence of the view that sacrifice was abolished in the teaching of the pre-exilic prophets. If God had already revealed through His prophets that He did not desire sacrifice and never had desired it, then it could not be supposed that He could find satisfaction in the sacrifice of Christ. Implicit in such a view is the conception of sacrifice in terms of a single element of its complex character. If sacrifice were no more than a gift to appease an angry God, the sacrificial view of the Cross might with advantage be abandoned. Such a view also implies a false emphasis in the conception of God. Too often in the sacrificial interpretation of the Cross God and Christ have been set over against one another in complete antithesis. God has been depicted as the stern embodiment of justice, and Christ as the gentle embodiment of love; and the drama of redemption has been set forth in terms of love's triumph over justice, and the appeasing of the wrath of God by the noble self-surrender of Christ.[2]

As against this the texts in the New Testament which have been most stressed by many of those with an Abelardian approach are such words as 'God was in Christ, reconciling the world unto Himself';[3] 'God commendeth his own love toward us in that while we were yet sinners Christ died for us';[4] 'God so loved the world that He gave his only begotten Son that whosoever

---

[1] So Peter Lombard (cf. Migne, *P.L.*, cxcii, 1880, col. 796).
[2] Cf. E. Masure, *The Christian Sacrifice*, 1944, p. 169: 'This doctrine some have mis-interpreted by making an opposition between the God of Mercy who desires to pardon and the God of Justice who refuses pardon. But Scripture does not speak of such a tension.'
[3] 2 Cor. v. 19.   [4] Rom. v. 8.

believeth in him should not perish but have everlasting life'.[1] All of these texts stress the thought of the Cross as the manifestation of the love of God. It was not merely Christ's love that was there revealed, but the love of God, so that Christ in His love is not to be set over against God in His justice.

With all this the present writer has the fullest sympathy. It cannot be that He Who in His life was the revelation of God was in His death the antithesis of God. It cannot be true that there was an inner tension between the love and the justice of God, leading to their distribution between two Persons of the Trinity. The very foundations of monotheism are threatened by such a view. We must therefore stand quite firmly with those who find in the love which is revealed in the Cross the expression of the love of God no less than of Christ, and give the fullest weight to those elements in the teaching of the New Testament on which they rely.

We do little justice to the teaching of the New Testament, however, if we pick out certain elements and ignore the rest.[2] Moreover, we forget the teaching of the Old Testament if we think of justice and love warring against one another. When Amos said in the name of God 'You only have I known of all the families of the earth; therefore will I visit your iniquities upon you',[3] he linked the justice of God with His love. Similarly Hosea was a prophet of judgement, but also a prophet of love, and the love and the judgement were not in conflict. God's justice is the expression of His love, and His discipline of Israel was designed to awaken her to the folly of her way and to restoration to Himself. We must therefore beware of thinking that all interpretations of the Cross in terms of judgement are

---

[1] John iii. 16.

[2] Cf. V. Taylor, *E.T.*, lviii, 1946–47, p. 259b: 'It is significant that almost all the great theories have been based on (New Testament) teaching, and that, in so far as they have failed, their failure has been due to an excessive dependence upon certain elements in it and the consequent neglect of others.'

[3] Amos iii. 2. Cf. *The Biblical Doctrine of Election*, p. 53 n.: 'The sense is clearly not merely "recognized", but "recognized as mine", or "chosen".' A. Neher, *Amos*, 1950, pp. 34 ff., discusses this at length, and notes that the mediaeval Jewish commentators Rashi and Ḳimḥi rendered 'known' by 'loved' and 'chosen' respectively.

inconsistent with interpretation in terms of love. The two belong together, and if we tear them apart we have a one-sided view of the significance of the Cross and a one-sided view of God, that fits the teaching of the New Testament no more than that of the Old.

To review all the teaching of the New Testament is here impossible, and it lies beyond our purpose to offer a complete theological interpretation of the meaning of the Cross. All that can here be done is to emphasize certain elements in the teaching of the New Testament, and particularly the sacrificial elements, and to show how they take up Old Testament ideas which, rightly understood, fill them with rich meaning. So long as we think of sacrifice in terms of that which the pre-exilic prophets condemned, it is rightly objectionable. They condemned a sacrifice which was offered as an external and merely ritual act, without relation to the heart and will of the offerer, and without either arising from his life or exercising any influence upon his life. But if we have rightly said that in the teaching of the Old Testament sacrifice must bear a two-way traffic or none, and that it could not be charged with power to bless the offerer unless it was also charged with his surrender of himself in humble submission and obedience to God, the position is greatly changed.

It is easy to think of all that differentiates the death of Christ from a sacrifice. He was not slain in the Temple and consumed on the altar. The men who crucified Him and drove the nails through His hands were not priests, and those who delivered Him to death could not be thought of as offering unto God a sacrifice well pleasing unto Him and fraught with blessing to themselves. Yet before we dismiss the thought of the death of Christ in terms of sacrifice, let us remember that in the fifty-third chapter of Isaiah the death of the Servant is presented as a sacrifice. As has been already said, this is not merely in the word 'āshām, or sin-offering, but in the whole thought of the chapter. The Servant is led as a lamb to the slaughter and bears the sins of many. Yet his death was not effected in the Temple with priestly ritual. The sacrifice of the Servant was the most potent sacrifice referred to in the Old Testament, wider in its efficacy than any sacrifice offered in the Temple, and extending its benefits to the nations. Moreover, this sacrifice surpassed any that was offered on the altar of the Temple in that here one who was without moral blemish yielded himself freely to death as the organ of his mission to others. It is with that climax and crown of Old Testament sacrifice that the death of Christ is to be linked, and is linked in the thought of the New Testament.

In an earlier chapter it has been said that Israelite sacrifice came out of a background of primitive sacrifice and of Canaanite sacrifice. It took many forms and served many purposes.[1] Here in the concept of the Servant we have the richest development of the thought on sacrifice found within the compass of the Old Testament. It was linked with all the background of sacrifice in Israel and beyond in the far past, but it marked an Israelite development, associated with the characteristic ideas of the Old Testament but moving forward under that dynamic power which is so marked a feature of the Old Testament revelation. It is with this most advanced point that the New Testament thought of the Cross is to be connected. It is, besides, to be remembered that it is not only in relation to sacrifice in general that the two-way traffic of sacrifice is emphasized in the Old Testament, but in relation to this sacrifice in particular. Men must stand in awe and confession before the Servant ere his death is potent to bless them. They must say 'Surely he hath borne our griefs and carried our sorrows. . . . He was wounded for our transgressions, he was bruised for our iniquities; the chastisement of our peace was upon him, and with his stripes we are healed'[2] and charge the martyred Servant with their penitence and surrender, before they could be of the transgressors for whom he made intercession,[3] and of those whose iniquities he bore and who were refashioned in righteousness by his sacrifice.[4]

We may now turn to underline some elements in the teaching

---

[1] Cf. *B.J.R.L.*, xxxiii, 1950–51, pp. 83 ff.; also G. B. Gray, *Sacrifice in the Old Testament*, 1925; W. O. E. Oesterley, *Sacrifices in Ancient Israel*, 1937, pp. 75 ff. On the variety of Old Testament sacrifices and the purposes they served cf. further E. Dhorme, *La Religion des Hébreux Nomades*, 1937, pp. 201 ff., and A. C. Welch, *Kings and Prophets of Israel*, 1952, p. 182.　　　　[2] Isa. liii. 4 f.　　　　[3] Isa. liii. 12.　　　　[4] Isa. liii. 11.

of the New Testament which point to this kind of sacrificial thought. Jesus Himself, especially in the latter part of His ministry, spoke to His disciples about His approaching death. 'He began to teach them that the Son of Man must suffer many things, and be rejected by the elders, and the chief priests and the scribes, and be killed and after three days rise again.' [1] Here the fact of His coming death is emphasized, and it is not presented in terms of the love of God but in terms of the hostility of men. There is no suggestion here of sacrifice, but in the reference to the Resurrection there is the implication that the death of Christ will not be the death of defeat, but will be charged with power. Later we read: 'Verily the Son of Man came not to be ministered unto but to minister, and to give his life a ransom for many'.[2] Here we have the ransom metaphor which has so much obsessed some theologians, and has been so much abused. However the metaphor is to be understood, it is clear that the thought is of service which should be rendered to others through the organ of Christ's death. The same thought is brought out again at the Last Supper, where Jesus says: 'This is my blood of the covenant, which is shed for many'.[3] When Matthew adds 'unto the remission

[1] Mk. viii. 31; Matt. xvi. 21; Luke ix. 22. F. C. Grant, *The Earliest Gospel*, 1943, p. 179 n., and *The Interpreter's Bible*, vii, 1951, pp. 767 f., denies that this is a genuine utterance of our Lord's, and holds that it has been created from the Passion narrative, on which it depends. C. J. Cadoux, *The Historic Mission of Jesus*, 1941, pp. 286 ff., is doubtful of the originality of the references to the Resurrection, but apparently accepts the genuineness of the prediction of the Passion. He observes: 'We are not, however, bound to go so far as to suppose that *all* Jesus' references to his Resurrection were created by the early Church in the light of the Easter experience' (p. 297). M. Goguel, *The Life of Jesus*, E. Tr. by O. Wyon, 1933, p. 390, while doubtful of the triple announcement of the suffering, death and resurrection of the Son of Man, owing to its theological bias, finds that Lk. xvii. 25 'falls into an entirely different category. This saying cannot have been invented by tradition, for it does not mention death or resurrection.' For a fuller acceptance of the historical reliability of these passages cf. J. Denney, *The Death of Christ*, ed. by R. V. G. Tasker, 1950, pp. 25 f.

[2] Mk. x. 45; Matt. xx. 28. On the suggestion that the saying in Mark is of Pauline origin, cf. V. Taylor, *The Gospel according to St. Mark*, 1952, pp. 445 f. F. C. Grant, *The Earliest Gospel*, 1943, p. 151, observes that it is more un-Pauline than Pauline. Cf. also M.-J. Lagrange, *Évangile selon St. Marc*, 1947 ed., pp. 281 ff.

[3] Mk. xiv. 24. F. J. Leenhardt, *Le Sacrement de la Sainte Cène*, 1948, pp. 51 ff., holds that the Pauline form in 1 Cor. xi. 25, is older than the Marcan, but J. Jeremias, *Die Abendmahlsworte Jesu*, 2nd ed., 1949, p. 85, favours the Marcan form as the earliest. Cf. also A. J. B. Higgins, *The Lord's Supper in the New Testament*, 1952, pp. 29 ff. For our present purpose either form would be equally relevant. On the grammatical difficulties of the Marcan form as a translation from Aramaic, cf. Jeremias, *op. cit.*, p. 99.

of sins'[1] he makes explicit what is implicit in the words of Mark.

Of these two passages Vincent Taylor says: 'Here it is sufficient to say that certainly the second, and probably also the first saying, indicates that, when Jesus spoke of His death, His thought was influenced by Old Testament teaching regarding sacrifice. In the case of the first passage, this conclusion cannot be established on linguistic grounds, but depends on whether the phrase "a ransom for many" reflects the influence of Isa. liii.'[2]

There are some scholars who deny that our Lord was influenced by the conception of the Suffering Servant, and who attribute to later thought all in the Gospels which points to such an influence.[3] This the writer finds it hard to believe,[4] and it can only be established by first dismissing the evidence we have. That Jesus taught His closest disciples that He would suffer seems to belong too closely to the texture of the Gospel story to be torn out in this way, and from no passage in the Old Testament can any basis for such teaching more relevant than Isa. liii be found. Hence it is probable that Moffatt is right when he says:

[1] Matt. xxvi. 28. Cf. V. Taylor, *The Gospel according to St. Mark*, 1952, p. 546: 'The addition is interpretation, but valid interpretation, for the connexion of forgiveness with the idea of the new covenant is distinctive of Jer. xxxviii. (xxxi.) 31-4.'

[2] Cf. *Jesus and His Sacrifice*, 1943 ed., p. 74.

[3] Cf. J. Weiss, *Die Schriften des Neuen Testaments*, 3rd ed., edited by W. Bousset and W. Heitmüller, i, 1917, pp. 174 f.; H. Rashdall, *The Idea of Atonement in Christian Theology*, 1919, pp. 49 ff.; B. W. Bacon, *J.B.L.*, xlviii, 1929, pp. 59 ff.; C. T. Craig, *J.R.*, xxiv, 1944, pp. 240 ff.; B. H. Branscomb, *The Gospel of Mark*, 5th imp., 1948, pp. 190 f. F. J. Foakes Jackson and K. Lake, *The Beginnings of Christianity*, i, 1942 ed., pp. 383 f., say: 'The most probable theory is that Jesus spoke of his future sufferings in general terms, and that his disciples developed his sayings in accordance with the event. . . . The fact that Jesus did suffer preceded the discovery of suitable prophecies.' Cf. A. Loisy, *L'Évangile selon Marc*, 1912, p. 403, where it is maintained that two essentially different ideas are combined in Mk. x. 45.

[4] Cf. A. E. J. Rawlinson, *St. Mark*, 1925, pp. 146 ff.; H. Wheeler Robinson, *The Cross of the Servant*, 1926, pp. 64 ff.; G. Kittel, *Deutsche Theologie*, 1936, pp. 166 ff.; A. M. Ramsey, *The Gospel and the Catholic Church*, 1936, p. 17; W. F. Howard, *E.T.*, l, 1938-39, pp. 107 ff.; R. Otto, *The Kingdom of God and the Son of Man*, E. Tr., by F. V. Filson and B. Lee-Woolf, 1943 ed., pp. 244 ff.; V. Taylor, *Jesus and His Sacrifice*, pp. 39 ff., and *The Gospel according to St. Mark*, 1952, pp. 445 f.; C. J. Cadoux, *The Historic Mission of Jesus*, 1941, pp. 253 f.; H. W. Wolff, *Jesaja 53 im Urchristentum*, 1942, pp. 49 ff. (2nd ed., 1950, pp. 55 ff.); W. Manson, *Jesus the Messiah*, 1943, pp. 30 ff.; J. W. Bowman, *J.R.*, xxv, 1945, pp. 56 ff.; C. R. North, *The Suffering Servant in Deutero-Isaiah*, 1948, pp. 24 f.; J. Schniewind, *Das Evangelium nach Markus* (Das N.T. Deutsch), 5th ed., 1949, p. 144.

'The suffering Servant conception was organic to the consciousness of Jesus.'[1] Similarly Vincent Taylor finds unmistakable echoes
of Isa. liii in a number of passages in the Gospels, and expresses his
belief in their genuineness, and consequently concludes that
'Jesus was profoundly influenced by the Servant-conception'.[2] He
finds it particularly significant that we have allusions rather than
quotations, and says 'It is probable that the Servant-conception
would be much more obvious in the Gospel tradition if it were
not an authentic element which goes back to Jesus Himself.'[3]

It is curious to observe that some recent scholars have gone to
the other extreme. Instead of finding the hand of the Church in
the allusions to the Suffering Servant, and so making the bringing
of this concept into association with the Messiah concept later
than the ministry of Christ, they have held that the union of
the Suffering Servant with Messianic thought antedated the time
of Jesus.[4] This seems to be as great an error, and it is far more
likely that the first linking of these concepts should be ascribed
to our Lord.[5] This is, indeed, the common view,[6] and it is borne

[1] Cf. *The Theology of the Gospels*, 1912, p. 149.
[2] Cf. *Jesus and His Sacrifice*, p. 47.
[3] *Ibid.*, p. 48. Cf. Th. Preiss, *E.Th.R.*, xxvi, 1951, p. 52: 'If the Early Church had
invented the application of Isa. liii. to Jesus, it would have made more extensive use of
the prophecies; and would have attributed quotations to Him.'
[4] Cf. J. Jeremias, *Deutsche Theologie*, ii, 1929, pp. 106 ff., and *Aux Sources de la Tradition
Chrétienne* (Goguel Festschrift), 1950, pp. 112 ff.; W. Staerk, *Soter*, 1933, pp. 77 f.;
N. Johanneson, *Parakletoi*, 1940, pp. 113 ff.; H. Riesenfeld, *Jésus transfiguré*, 1947, pp.
81 ff., 314 ff.; W. D. Davies, *Paul and Rabbinic Judaism*, 1948, pp. 274 ff. I. Engnell
maintains that the Suffering Servant in Deutero-Isaiah was already in the prophet's mind
identified with 'the Messiah himself, the Saviour king of the dynasty of David' (*B.J.R.L.*,
xxxi, 1948, p. 58). A. Dupont-Sommer holds that the Teacher of Righteousness of the
Dead Sea Scrolls and of the Zadokite Work in the first century B.C. already combined
in himself the roles of Suffering Servant and Messiah, and that his martyrdom gave rise
to a whole theology of the Suffering Messiah (*Aperçu préliminaires sur les manuscrits de
la Mer Morte*, 1950, pp. 116, 121 f., E. Tr. by E. M. Rowley, 1952, pp. 96, 99 f.). C. C.
Torrey holds that the conceptions of the Davidic Messiah, the Suffering Servant and the
Son of Man 'had been combined, speculated upon, and fashioned into a many-sided
doctrine, held and cherished by the Jewish people long before the beginning of the
Common Era' (*J.B.L.*, xlviii, 1929, p. 25).
[5] Cf. the writer's essay on 'The Suffering Servant and the Davidic Messiah', in *The
Servant of the Lord and Other Essays*, 1952, pp. 61 ff. (also in *O.T.S.*, viii, 1950, p. 100 ff.).
[6] Cf. G. F. Moore, *Judaism*, i, 1927, pp. 551 f., iii, 1930, p. 166; M.-J. Lagrange,
Le Judaïsme avant Jésus-Christ, 1931, p. 385; P. ⸀olz, *Die Eschatologie der jüdischen Gemeinde
im neutestamentlichen Zeitalter*, 1934, p. 228; Strack-Billerbeck, *Kommentar zum N.T
aus Talmud und Midrasch*, ii, 1924, p. 274.

out by the fact that the disciples, even when they thought of Jesus in terms of the Messiah, were completely nonplussed by the thought of His possible suffering. Wheeler Robinson says: 'Accepting the form' (sc. of the messianic hope) 'He transformed the content of Messianic belief, by interpreting His Messiahship in the light of the Suffering Servant of Isaiah 53'.[1] Whatever our conclusion on this issue, Vincent Taylor observes that the sacrificial interpretation of the other passage which is quoted above, Mark xiv. 24, is inescapable, and that therefore 'whatever explanation of the death of Jesus we may give today, there can be no doubt at all that Jesus Himself understood its meaning in terms of sacrifice.'[2]

The Fourth Gospel thinks of the death of Jesus rather in terms of the Passover lambs than in terms of the Suffering Servant. This is easily understandable since it was at the time of Passover that the Crucifixion took place. This Gospel represents our Lord as slain at the very time when the Passover lambs were being slain,[3] and therefore as not having eaten of the Passover at the Last Supper, and it antedates to the beginning of His ministry and ascribes to John the Baptist the perception that He was 'the lamb of God which taketh away the sin of the world.'[4] Here there is a clear interpretation of the death of Christ in terms of sacrifice, though it is found in the Gospel which emphasizes the thought of the death of our Lord in terms of the expression of the love of God. It is here that we find the most familiar text in the whole of the New Testament, John iii. 16, where the context clearly indicates the thought of the Cross and where this is declared to be the evidence of the surpassing love of God. We

[1] Cf. *Revelation and Redemption*, 1942, p. 198. Cf. also pp. 199, 251 f., and J. W. Bowman, *The Intention of Jesus*, 1945, p. 10: 'Jesus and he alone was responsible for the fusion of the two prophetic concepts noted'—*i.e.* the Suffering Servant and the Messiah.

[2] Cf. *Jesus and His Sacrifice*, p. 74.   [3] Cf. Jn. xviii. 28.

[4] Jn. i. 29. H. W. Wolff, following C. J. Ball (*E.T.*, xxi, 1909–10, p. 93a), C. F. Burney (*The Aramaic Origin of the Fourth Gospel*, 1922, pp. 107 f.), and J. Jeremias (*Z.N.W.*, xxxiv, 1935, pp. 115 ff.; cf. *Th.W.B.*, i, 1949 ed., p. 343) finds here a reminiscence of the Servant Songs, since the saying probably goes back to an Aramaic utterance, and in Aramaic *ṭalyā'* may mean *servant* or *lamb*. Cf. *Jesaja 53 im Urchristentum*, 1942, p. 72, 2nd ed., 1950, p. 81. Against this cf. R. Bultmann, *Das Evangelium des Johannes*, 11th ed., 1950, p. 67.

should be very careful before we set the ideas of love and sacrifice as the keynotes for the interpretation of the Cross over against one another as antithetical.

Elsewhere in the New Testament the Cross is frequently referred to in sacrificial terms. There are several passages where the necessity for Christ's sufferings is insisted on, sometimes with a probable allusion to Isa. liii, though without an explicit indication that the sufferings are the organ of His mission.[1] There are others where it is made clear that Christ's death is the organ of His redemption. 'Without shedding of blood there is no remission of sins' we read in the Epistle to the Hebrews,[2] in a context where the whole thought of the Cross is sacrificial. Here, however, it is not directly in terms of the Suffering Servant, or of the Passover Lamb, but in terms of the ritual of the Temple. 'If the blood of goats and bulls, and the ashes of a heifer sprinkling them that have been defiled, sanctify unto the cleanness of the flesh: how much more shall the blood of Christ, who through the eternal Spirit offered himself without blemish unto God, cleanse your conscience from dead works to serve the living God?'[3] Nevertheless it is to be observed that there are some reminiscences of Isa. liii in the chapter in which these words occur, and there may be some allusion to the Servant here.[4] Vincent Taylor notes that even in the Epistle to the Hebrews it is not claimed that Christ's death is to be explained in terms of any one of the sacrifices of the Old Testament,[5] and thinks it probable that here and in the New Testament generally 'the sacrificial element . . . is to be found, not so much in the specific rites of the cultus, as in the underlying ideas of sacrifice.'[6] When we considered the Servant Songs in Deutero-Isaiah we noted that the Servant was presented as one freely yielding himself to suffering and without

---

[1] Cf. Acts xvii. 2, xxvi. 23; Luke xxiv. 26 f.   [2] Heb. ix. 22.   [3] Heb. ix. 13 f.

[4] C. H. Dodd, *The Old Testament in the New*, 1952, p. 9, observes that of the twelve verses in Isa. liii. 'there is only one which does not reappear, as a whole or in part, somewhere in the New Testament. . . . This surely means that the writers of the New Testament . . . all considered this chapter, taken as a whole, to have outstanding significance for the understanding of the Gospel.' Cf. also *id., According to the Scriptures*, 1952, pp. 92 ff.

[5] Cf. *The Atonement in New Testament Teaching*, 1940, p. 273.   [6] *Ibid.*, p. 274.

moral blemish. It is possible that in the words 'who . . . offered himself without blemish unto God'[1] we have an allusion to this here. Elsewhere in the same Epistle it is emphasized that Christ was One Who needed not to offer sacrifice on behalf of Himself, since He was holy, guileless and undefiled.[2]

In the Pauline Epistles we have not merely the already noted thought of the Cross as the expression of the love of God. Christ is said to have been delivered up for our trespasses, and raised for our justification,[3] and we are declared to be justified by His blood and reconciled unto God by the death of His Son.[4] Here, as in the Old Testament, the idea of justification is sometimes given a forensic interpretation.[5] It is probable, however, that in this passage it has a profounder meaning, and speaks of the miracle of the making righteous of the unrighteous. God is not content with a false declaration, and when He declares men righteous it is because they have become righteous.[6] This is quite certainly the thought of the New Testament as a whole whatever may be the etymological meaning of the term used here.[7] For elsewhere

[1] Heb. ix. 14. Similarly Heb. ix. 28 embodies reminiscence of Isa. liii. 12.

[2] Heb. vii. 26 f.

[3] Rom. iv. 25. C. H. Dodd, *The Epistle of Paul to the Romans*, 1942 ed., p. 70, observes: No antithesis is intended between "delivered for our trespasses", and "raised that we might be justified". Somewhat after the manner of Hebrew parallelism, the meaning is "He died and rose again in order that we might be delivered from the guilt of our sins".'

[4] Rom. v. 9 f.

[5] Cf. Grimm-Thayer, *Greek-English Lexicon of the New Testament*, 4th ed., 1901, p. 150b; A. C. Headlam, in Hastings's *D.B.*, ii, 1899, pp. 826 ff. Headlam says (p. 826b): 'In Biblical literature the word δικαιοῦν is always used, or almost always, in the forensic sense, and its proper meaning is to pronounce righteous. . . . It may be taken as certain that it cannot mean to *make* righteous.' Cf. also C. H. Dodd's careful discussion in *The Bible and the Greeks*, 1935, pp. 46 ff.

[6] Cf. L. Cerfaux, in *S.D.B.*, iv, 1949, col. 1485: 'The divine intervention involves more than a simple declaration. . . . Righteousness is not simply "imputed", but constitutes an actual condition of the man who is justified.'

[7] Headlam (*ibid.*) cites Godet, who 'goes so far as to say that there is not a single example in the whole of classical literature where the word=to make righteous'. To make this consideration conclusive it would be necessary to adduce evidences of the concept 'to make righteous' from classical literature to show how such an idea was expressed. The miracle of recreation which is characteristic of Biblical thought was not one which would occur readily to a Greek, and he is not likely to have felt the need for such a term. On the other hand when the Biblical writers wished to express such a thought, they had to do the best they could with the terms they could find. Missionaries could give many examples of the way in which they have had to use inadequate terms in vernacular languages.

we read of the necessity for the death of the old self and the birth of a new self. 'If any man is in Christ', says Paul, 'He is become a new creature';[1] while in the Fourth Gospel we read 'Except a man be born anew, he cannot see the kingdom of God.'[2] How this miracle is thought to be effected we shall consider later. Here it will suffice to note that this justification is effected by the death of Christ, which is thus thought of in sacrificial terms.[3]

Even more directly sacrificial terminology is used in the Epistle to the Ephesians, where it is not merely said that our redemption is through the blood of Christ,[4] but where the death of our Lord is explicitly referred to as an offering and a sacrifice unto God.[5] In the Epistle to the Colossians the bond standing against us by reason of our sins is said to have been nailed to the Cross[6] and therefore removed from us. It lies beyond our province to consider the question of the authorship of these Epistles, and since we are considering the teaching of the New Testament as

[1] 2 Cor. v. 17.

[2] Jn. iii. 3. The Greek could here be rendered 'from above', instead of 'anew', but as R. Bultmann (*Das Evangelium des Johannes*, 11th ed., 1950, p. 95 n.) says, it can only mean 'anew' here, and it is so rendered in most translations. Cf. F. Büchsel, *Th.W.B.*, i, 1949 ed., p. 378.

[3] On the place of sacrifice in Paul's thought on the Cross, cf. W. D. Davies, *Paul and Rabbinic Judaism*, 1948, pp. 230 ff.

[4] Eph. i. 7. Cf. S. D. F. Salmond, *The Expositor's Greek Testament*, ed. by W. R. Nicoll, iii, 1912, p. 254b: 'It is a *sacrificial* term, based on the use of the blood of victims, offered under the Old Testament Law.'

[5] Eph. v. 2. Cf. also Rom. iii. 25, on which M. Goguel, *The Life of Jesus*, E. Tr., 1933, p. 110, observes that Paul 'appears to conceive the redemptive death in terms of the Levitical sacrifice'. C. H. Dodd, *op. cit.*, p. 55, observes that 'propitiation' is a misleading rendering, and that the meaning is 'a means whereby guilt is annulled' (cf. also his *The Bible and the Greeks*, 1935, pp. 84 ff. and *J.T.S.*, xxxii, 1930–31, pp. 325 ff.). Cf. also M.-J. Lagrange, *Épitre aux Romains*, 1950, pp. 75 f., L. Morris, *E.T.*, lxii, 1950–51, pp. 227 ff., L. Cerfaux, *Le Christ dans la Théologie de St. Paul*, 1952, pp. 114 ff., and the long note in Strack-Billerbeck, *Kommentar zum Neuen Testament aus Talmud und Midrasch*, iii, 1926, p. 165 ff. W. D. Davies, *op. cit.*, pp. 232 ff., discusses this passage, and says (p. 236): 'We are justified in finding in the Pauline application of the term "blood" to Christ the use of a sacrificial concept.' T. W. Manson, *J.T.S.*, xlvi, 1945, pp. 1 ff., argues that the reference is to the 'place of propitiation', and that the background of the thought is the ritual of the Day of Atonement. Cf. further W. G. Kümmel, *Z.Th.K.*, xlix, 1952, pp. 154 ff.

[6] Col. ii. 14. A. Deissmann, *Paul*, E. Tr. by W. E. Wilson, 2nd ed., 1926, p. 172, says: 'Anyone who has seen one of the numerous records of debt on the papyri that have been discovered, will realize that the metaphor, which Paul carries out so strikingly, of the bond nailed to the cross, after being first blotted out and so cancelled, was especially popular in its appeal.'

a whole it matters not whether they are from the hand of Paul or not. Indeed, if they are not Pauline the evidence is even stronger. For in addition to the Synoptic Gospels and the Fourth Gospel, the Epistle to the Hebrews and the genuine Pauline Epistles, we should then have these evidences of yet another author or authors to show that the Cross was thought of in sacrificial terms. Nor have we yet finished. For in 1 Peter we similarly read that Christ bore our sins in His own body on the tree,[1] and in 1 John that He is the propitiation for our sins and for those of the whole world.[2]

While few of these interpretations of the Cross are directly linked with any Old Testament passage, and while some think in terms of the Passover or of the Temple ritual, there can be no doubt from the number of allusions to Isa. liii in the New Testament that that chapter had a large place in the thought of the Early Church, and that Christ was believed to have fulfilled the mission of the Servant. Leaving aside allusions which stand on the lips of our Lord in the Gospels, we may note that the First Gospel declares that in Him was fulfilled the saying 'Himself took our infirmities and bare our diseases',[3] and also finds the first Servant Song fulfilled in Him.[4] The Fourth Gospel applies to Him the opening words of Isa. liii,[5] and in the early preaching of the Apostles, as recorded in the Acts, Jesus is sometimes referred to as 'the Servant'.[6] Moreover, in the passage recording the baptism of the Ethiopian eunuch everything depends on the identification of Jesus with the Servant.[7] The reference to Jesus taking upon Him the form of a servant, in Phil. ii. 7, may also

---

[1] 1 Pet. ii. 24. On this passage, V. Taylor, *The Atonement in New Testament Teaching*, 1940, p. 42, says: 'In order to express the meaning of Christ's death, it draws upon the underlying ideas of the sacrificial system, rather than the special associations of any one rite.'

[2] 1 Jn. ii. 2. C. H. Dodd, *The Johannine Epistles*, 1946, pp. 26 f., says: 'The reference in i. 7 to the blood of Christ suggests that the author is thinking . . . of the death of Christ as analogous to animal sacrifices. . . . The term used, however, does not in itself connote a blood sacrifice.' Cf. J. Chaine, *Les Épitres Catholiques*, 2nd ed., 1939, pp. 153 f.

[3] Matt. viii. 17. Cf. Isa. liii. 4.

[4] Matt. xii. 18 ff.   [5] Jn. xii. 38.

[6] Acts iii. 13, 26, iv. 27, 30. Cf. F. F. Bruce, *The Acts of the Apostles*, 1951, pp. 107 f.

[7] Acts viii. 32 ff.

be an allusion to the Deutero-Isaianic Servant, as may Paul's reference elsewhere to the death of Christ as being 'according to the scriptures'.[1] Further, the context of the verse already quoted from 1 Peter abounds in allusions to Isa. liii. 'Christ suffered for you, leaving you an example, that ye should follow his steps: who did no sin, neither was guile found in his mouth . . . who his own self bare our sins in his body on the tree . . . by whose stripes ye were healed. For we were going astray like sheep.'[2]

Despite the particular place which this chapter had, however, it is clear from the references to other sacrifices[3] that to the Early Church Christ had superseded the need for all sacrifices. In giving reality to the highest thought on sacrifice found in the Old Testament He had gathered into Himself all the enduring significance of all sacrifice. 'We have been sanctified through the offering of the body of Jesus Christ once for all.'[4]

In considering the Old Testament sacrifices we have observed that they were believed to be charged with power when rightly offered. In the New Testament the sacrifice of Christ on the Cross was similarly believed to be charged with power unto them that are called.[5] Yet like the power of the old sacrifices it became effective only when the sacrifice was the organ of man's approach to God. It was not something automatic and unrelated to the spirit of those whose sacrifice it was. Whether the sin offerings of the Law, or the offering of the Day of Atonement, or the sacrifice of the Servant, all had to be charged with confession and surrender and to become the organ of submission to the will of God before they could become the organ of divine blessing. In the New Testament we find that this aspect of the meaning of sacrifice is not forgotten, but on the contrary continually stressed. The Cross is potentially effective for all the world; yet for some it is the organ of condemnation. Just as sacrifices in Israel that were not the organ of the soul's approach

---

[1] 1 Cor. xv. 3. The allusion to Isa. liii. here is not, however, certain. Cf. V. Taylor, op. cit., pp. 31 f., J. Héring, La première Épitre de St. Paul aux Corinthiens, 1949, pp. 134 f.
[2] 1 Pet. ii. 21 ff. Cf. E. G. Selwyn, The First Epistle of St. Peter, 1946, pp. 92 ff.
[3] E.g. Passover (1 Cor. v. 7), and the Day of Atonement (Heb. ix. 6 ff.).
[4] Heb. x. 10.   [5] 1 Cor. i. 24.

to God brought condemnation on men, so those for whom the sacrifice of Christ is not the organ of their approach to God stand under condemnation. 'God sent not the Son into the world to condemn the world; but that the world through him might be saved. He that believeth on him is not condemned: but he that believeth not is condemned already.'[1] Many who did not live in the days of Christ's flesh may find blessing and salvation through His Cross; but by the same token others who never saw Him may be guilty of the body and blood of Christ,[2] or may crucify afresh the Son of God.[3] While salvation is an external act, wrought by the power of God through the death of Christ, it is not wholly an external act, without relation to the spirit of men. Those who reject Christ, or who repudiate His way, share the iniquity of the crucifixion and stand before God in the company of Christ's crucifiers.

That is why the New Testament insists so much on faith. For faith is no mere intellectual belief, though it inevitably includes an intellectual element. But fundamentally it is not an integrated system of theology but the surrender of the person.[4] When Jesus said to men 'Thy faith hath saved thee', He was not thinking in terms of a creed. He meant such a belief in Him that it involved the abandonment of the whole personality to Him, to be re-created by His touch and transformed into His own likeness. The woman who was a sinner and who bathed His feet with her tears heard Him say 'Thy faith hath saved thee; go in peace'.[5] She did not return to her sin, for she went forth a changed woman. The self that loved the sin had died, and one now marked with the purity of Christ went forth to live in newness of life. This is what is meant by faith elsewhere in the New Testament. It is faith into Christ, faith that so identifies a man with Him Who was crucified that instead of being numbered with His crucifiers he becomes one with Christ, and the Cross becomes the organ of his submission of himself to God. Paul said 'If we have become united with Him by the likeness of his death,

---

[1] Jn. iii. 18.　　　　[2] 1 Cor. xi. 27.　　　　[3] Heb. vi. 6.
[4] Cf. the writer's *Outline of the Teaching of Jesus*, 1945, pp. 30 f.　　　[5] Lk. vii. 50.

we shall be also by the likeness of his resurrection; knowing this, that our old man was crucified with him, that the body of sin might be done away.'[1]

The Fourth Gospel, which also emphasizes the importance of faith and in a passage whose context clearly links it with the Cross of Christ says 'God so loved the world that He gave his only begotten Son that whosoever believeth in him should not perish but have everlasting life',[2] stresses elsewhere the importance of the complete identification of the whole person with Christ. The union with Him must be as intimate as the union of the branch and the vine,[3] so that in a profound sense a man abides in Christ, and Christ in him.[4] Such a thought is also characteristic of Paul, and it is always brought into relationship with the Cross.[5] 'That I may gain Christ, and be found in Him, not having a righteousness of mine own, even that which is of the law, but that which is through the faith of Christ, the righteousness which is of God by faith: that I may know him and the power of his resurrection and the fellowship of his sufferings, being conformed unto his death'.[6] In a vital sense the believer must die with Christ,[7] so that the death of Christ on the Cross becomes the organ of his death to the past and to all that separated him from God. 'I have been crucified with Christ, nevertheless I live; and yet not I, but Christ liveth in me: and the life which I now live in the flesh, I live by the faith of the Son of God, who loved me and gave himself for me.'[8] The Cross is not alone the power of God effective on behalf of a man. It is something into which he must in a profound sense enter. At its foot the old self dies and Christ bears his humble surrender of himself to God; and in the same moment He bears to him from God the renewed self, marked with the presence and the purity of Christ. The miracle of rebirth is achieved, and he who one moment stands numbered

---

[1] Rom. vi. 5 f.   [2] Jn. iii. 16.   [3] Jn. xv. 5.
[4] On the Johannine thought of union with God in Christ cf. C. H. Dodd, *The Interpretation of the Fourth Gospel*, 1953, pp. 187 ff.
[5] Cf. J. Schneider, *Die Passionsmystik des Paulus*, 1929, pp. 21 ff.   [6] Phil. iii. 8 ff.
[7] On the Pauline thought on dying and rising with Christ cf. A. Schweitzer, *The Mysticism of Paul the Apostle*, E. Tr. by W. Montgomery, 1931, pp. 101 ff.
[8] Gal. ii. 20.

with the crucifiers of Christ is the next moment identified with Him, dying with Him[1] and passing through death to newness of life in Him.[2] There is no suggestion that he is saved by his own surrender, or his own resolve, or even by his own faith. He is saved by the power of God, and his surrender is but the condition which he must fulfil. It is precisely as we found it in the Old Testament, where forgiveness and cleansing are ever represented as the act of God and not of man. When the sacrifice was charged with power, it was not a power that the offerer communicated to it by his touch. It was the power of God. This is integral to the thought of both Testaments, and is one of the strongest marks of the unity of the Bible. It is this which more than anything else links the sacrificial thought of the Cross with the thought of the Old Testament. For while in the Old Testament sacrifice for purely ritual offences might be thought of as having a mechanical or magical power, in all other cases the teaching of the Old Testament is uniformly that it has no efficacy as a mere *opus operatum*; and in the teaching of the New Testament the Cross is never thought of in terms of magic, or as effective through the mere *opus operatum*. Hence the sacrificial interpretation of the Cross does not commit us to the idea of a loving Christ wresting from a just and reluctant God the boon of salvation. It permits, nay requires, us to find the power of its love to awaken our hearts to repentance to be but the power of God, and the cleansing and renewing power which lifts our lives into the life of Christ to be equally the power of God. 'And you did he quicken when ye were dead through your trespasses and sins, wherein aforetime ye walked according to the course of this world. . . . But God, being rich in mercy, for his great love wherewith he loved us, even when we were dead through our trespasses, quickened us together with Christ . . . and raised us up with him.'[3] Salvation is born of the love of God, but it requires the yielding up of the self to die with Christ and to rise with Him to newness of life. It is therefore clear that the Cross must bear a two-way traffic or it can bear none. From God's side there is ever the readiness to operate

[1] Rom. vi. 8. [2] Rom. vi. 4. [3] Eph. ii. i ff.

that two-way traffic, but it cannot operate until there is readiness on man's side and the inevitable condition is fulfilled. It cannot be a two-way traffic until there is faith, and faith is not compelled.

Not seldom faith is thought of as the organ of salvation, and a man is thought to save himself by his repentance and faith. The difference between condition and organ is a profound one. If I want electric light in my room I must press the switch, but I deceive myself if I suppose that my pressing the switch produces the light. If there has been a power cut I shall soon be disillusioned. Nevertheless the pressing of the switch is necessary as the condition of the becoming available of the power, which I do nothing to create. In a comparable way, in the teaching of the Bible the power of salvation is the power of God, and man's right approach to God is but the condition of its release.

The fundamental truth of the two-way traffic of the Cross is expressed differently in the New Testament when it uses the metaphor of the Mediator for Christ. We read: 'There is one God and one mediator between God and men, the man Christ Jesus, who gave himself a ransom for all.'[1] A mediator is essentially one who represents each side to the other, and here Christ is thought of as representing us to God and God to us. There is thus a measure of truth in the idea that Christ is set over against God in the drama of redemption. In so far as He represents us He stands in our stead over against God; in so far as He represents God He stands over against us. It is not in His love that He represents us, however, for such love is not the reflection of our hearts. In His love and in His power to cleanse and renew He represents God to us. 'God so loved the world', and that love of God is manifested to us in the love of Christ. It is in His sin that He represents us to God. For 'Him who knew no sin he made to be sin on our behalf, that we might become the righteousness of God in him.'[2] Here again we probably have a reminiscence of Isa. liii, for this is very much what we read of the Servant there. 'The Lord hath laid on him the iniquity of us all . . . though he had done no violence, neither was any deceit found in his

[1] 1 Tim. ii. 5.   [2] 2 Cor. v. 21.

mouth'.[1] Christ, our Mediator, bears our sins to God and so represents us to God, and with it bears our surrender in penitence, and bears to us the cleansing touch of God that delivers us from sin to newness of life.

It is hard to overemphasize how much of the Old Testament thought runs together here. There is not merely the conception of the meaning of sacrifice, caught up at its highest point, and particularly in the thought of the Servant, and the insistence on the double character of sacrifice. Nor is there merely the response to the hope of the Old Testament in a sacrifice which has become indeed the organ of salvation to countless myriads of men of every race, and in relation to which men have said simply and humbly and with demonstrable appropriateness 'He was wounded for our transgressions, he was bruised for our iniquities: the chastisement of our peace was upon him, and with his stripes we are healed'.[2] There is the renewal of so much of the pattern of Old Testament thought. The fundamental nature of religion is here, as throughout the Old Testament, recognized to lie in a life of obedience to the will of God, whose spring lies in fellowship with God. In the Old Testament doing justly and loving mercy rested on the humble walk with God; and here the newness of life to which men are called is the newness to which they are lifted when the Spirit of God, mediated to them through Christ, so fills their hearts that they can say: 'I have been crucified with Christ; nevertheless I live, and yet not I, but Christ liveth in me.'[3] Religion does not consist merely in the observance of religious forms, but penetrates to the very spring of life, and issues in a quality of life which marks its every aspect. To Jesus all life was aglow with God, and He would have His followers similarly conscious of God's presence with them in every experience. He taught them to pray to the Father 'Thy will be done on earth as it is in heaven'.[4] None can pray that prayer sincerely if he is indifferent whether the will of God is done in his own life or not. And none can live in intimate union with Christ who is

---

[1] Isa. liii. 6, 9.   [2] Isa. liii. 5.
[3] Gal. ii. 20.   [4] Matt. v. 10.

thus indifferent. 'If Christ is in you, the body is dead because of sin; but the spirit is life because of righteousness.'[1]

Moreover, when men are lifted into Christ and share His Spirit, they share His sufferings and His task. In a profound sense they are called to know 'the fellowship of his sufferings',[2] to 'suffer with him that they may be glorified together',[3] or to make up that which was lacking in the sufferings of Christ,[4] entering into His agony for the world and taking the burden of the world's need upon them, and becoming the instruments whereby His work for all men becomes known to all.[5]

Here again we have something that links closely with Old Testament thought. The Servant was both Israel and a representative of Israel in whom its mission should be supremely expressed. Yet that mission was still the mission of Israel, to which all were summoned. And He in Whom the individual hope became realized and Who was the supreme Servant of the Lord, lifted His followers to share His mission, so that the Church was missionary from the start, and was in a real sense the extension of the personality of its Lord, the body of Christ. The Servant narrowed down from Israel to Christ, to open out then to the New Israel that is identified with Him in love for God and for men, and that shares something of the very agony of the Cross in its yearning for the salvation of the world.

Again, as in the Old Testament the act of God in history, whereby Israel was delivered from Egypt, preceded Israel's committal of herself to Him in the Covenant, so here the historical act which is the basis of salvation, the death of Christ, precedes our committal of ourselves to Him in faith. We have an event of history, yet more than an event of history. We have a revelation

---

[1] Rom. viii. 10.   [2] Phil. iii. 10.   [3] Rom. viii. 17.
[4] Col. i. 24. Cf. 2 Cor. i. 5. On Col. i. 24 cf. J. B. Lightfoot, *Epistles to the Colossians and Philemon*, 1900, pp. 103 ff., where the view that the meaning is 'the sufferings imposed by Christ', or 'sufferings endured for Christ's sake' is rejected, and where it is maintained that the meaning is 'the sufferings which Christ endured'. C. Masson, *L'Épitre de S. Paul aux Colossiens*, 1950, p. 115, says the thought of this verse is quite alien to Paul, and maintains that we have here an interpolated passage from the hand of the author of the epistle to the Ephesians.
[5] Cf. A. Schweitzer, *op. cit.*, pp. 141 ff., on this aspect of Paul's thought.

of the heart of God and of the need of man, and an enduring symbol which rests securely on history. We may respond to the revelation of the divine love with faith, but the revelation is the basis of our response. 'We love him because he first loved us.'[1] The initiative was God's, and it was an initiative expressed on the plane of history. When we respond in faith, the New Covenant becomes real for us in our experience. When Jeremiah spoke of the New Covenant he said it was to be written on the tables of men's hearts.[2] It was to be a covenant with the house of Israel, yet its law was to be inscribed on the individual hearts of men and not on external tables of stone. It would belong to the very texture of their personality, yet they would not cease to belong to a community, and Jeremiah was far from preaching an arid individualism. Here in the New Testament the New Covenant is expressed in terms of union with Christ, whereby He lives in the heart. Its law is graven in the substance of personality, for He is its law. The covenant of faith in Him is the response to the achieved act of God in Christ, and on man's side it consists in the yielding of the entire being unto God. It is a covenant which is unbreakable from God's side, as was the old Covenant of Sinai. It is formed to be an eternal covenant,[3] laying upon man the eternal bond of obedience and bringing to him the eternal gift of God's blessing. Nevertheless, like the old Covenant, it may be broken from man's side. And when he breaks it, it is broken. The covenant is trampled underfoot and God Himself is spurned.[4] For no man can continue to live in the Covenant, with Christ as the spring of his life and the treasure of his heart, who will have none of Christ and His way.[5] All the message of the Old Testament about the obligations of the Covenant is here relevant. When it found no response in obedience it was broken, and though God in His grace might still seek to renew it, rising up early and sending His servants the prophets to men, they who broke it had no claim upon Him, but stood outside the Covenant until they brought their response. The New Covenant, like the

---

[1] I Jn. iv. 19. [2] Jer. xxxi. 31 ff. [3] Heb. xiii. 20.
[4] Heb. x. 29. [5] Heb. vi. 6.

old, is inviolable from God's side, but is violable from man's. The grace of God is never indifferent to man's response.

It is further vital to remember that all this is not just a weaving together of Old Testament strands of thought into a pattern of fancy. It is the expression of the experience of men in relation to a historical person and the event of history that His death marked. In the Old Testament the Suffering Servant was a concept; in the New a figure of history, Who gathered these strands together to Himself and gave them meaning in the context of human experience.

It is not supposed that a complete interpretation of the Cross of Christ is contained in the foregoing pages. To offer such is far from our present purpose. All that has been attempted here is to illustrate the unity of the Bible with reference to the Cross, and to emphasize that to apprehend all its significance we must not limit ourselves to this or that aspect of New Testament thought, but must find a place for it all. There are many sides of that thought which have not been here touched upon, and which could only be dealt with if a whole volume were devoted to the theme. It must not be supposed that they are implicitly rejected because unmentioned here, where our aim is not to expound the significance of the Cross, but to underline the ties which bind the two Testaments together, and to say that any interpretation which ignores those ties does less than justice to the New Testament, and fails to perceive that the New Testament is but a part of the Biblical revelation that includes both Testaments. In particular, the sacrificial interpretation of the Cross, which is deeply inscribed in the New Testament but which has been widely ignored or rejected in modern thought, ceases to involve unworthy ideas of God and becomes of rich significance, once it is studied in the light of Old Testament teaching. It avoids a merely declarative view of the Cross, which leaves a man's salvation still to be achieved by himself, and equally so objective a view that the spirit of him who is saved is of no consequence. Subjective and objective factors belong together here as in so much else, and grace and faith are both involved. With God is the initiative in grace, yet the divine grace is impotent until it finds its response in faith. In that moment its power is released, and he who is saved does not preen himself on the potency of his faith, but glories in the power of God which he experiences within himself.

It has been observed above that in modern times it has sometimes been argued that the Old Testament should be abolished, at least on the Mission Field, and the Churches of India and China should be encouraged to find in the Scriptures of their ancient faiths the preparation for Christianity. While all sympathetic study of other religions is to be welcomed, and a merely negative attitude to them is to be deprecated, it is certain that only the Old Testament could provide the background for the understanding of the Cross as it is set forth in the New Testament. It would be unfair to seek to deprive any Church of this. To teach it to understand the Old Testament may be hard, but it is richly rewarding, and understanding of the New is at the same time deepened and enriched. At home not a few have given up the effort to understand the Old Testament, to the impoverishment of their grasp of the New, and this in turn leads to a selective use of the New Testament. The Old Testament provides the necessary background of the New Testament, and makes imperative the preservation of grace and faith in our interpretation of the New. There is a wholeness in the teaching of the Bible, which should guard us against the one-sided emphasis to which we so often incline, and nowhere more disastrously than in relation to the Cross. Nowhere in the New Testament is it taught that the Cross operates independently of belief; and if it were the Old Testament would rise up to condemn it. The Cross is the power of God, but the power of God unto every one that believeth.[1]

[1] Rom. i. 16.

VI

THE CHRISTIAN SACRAMENTS

O UR final study is of the Christian sacraments of Baptism and the Lord's Supper in the light of the aspects of Biblical thought which have engaged our attention. Here we come to what ought most to unite Christians, but what in fact most divides them, and what in earlier days could only be discussed with violence and sometimes abuse. At first sight it might appear to some readers that we are merely following the pattern of the Baptist preacher in the story, whose last division of every sermon, no matter what the text might be, was always: 'Finally, my brethren, a few words about baptism'. The Christian sacraments belong so wholly to the New Testament that they would seem to have no place in a study of the unity of the Bible. Moreover, it can hardly be claimed here, as it has been claimed in relation to the Work of Christ, that we have the response to hopes that are set forth in the Old Testament. For apart from such typological arguments as the claim that the crossing of the Red Sea was a prophecy of baptism,[1] there can be no claim to find prophecies of the sacraments in the Old Testament. It has been said in a former chapter that while that kind of argument may sometimes have a certain homiletical value, it has no logical value and is not appealed to in our study. It is wholly different from those recurring patterns in which the signature of God may be found, to which attention has been drawn. Some Roman Catholic writers find in the book of Malachi a prophecy of the Mass,[2] but

---

[1] So J. Calvin, *Institutes of the Christian Religion*, E. Tr. by H. Beveridge, ii, 1869, p. 517; and, most recently, O. Cullmann, *Die Tauflehre des Neuen Testaments*, 1948, pp. 40 f., E. Tr. by J. K. S. Reid, 1950, pp. 45, 47. Cf. 1 Cor. x. 1 f., where in a rabbinical manner Paul uses the word baptism of the passing through the Red Sea, but is really concerned to stress the contrast between that crossing and baptism, and to urge that the example of the Israelites who came out of Egypt is not to be followed by the Church, since it was an example of disobedience.

[2] Mal. i. 11. Cf. C. Lattey, *The Book of Malachy*, 1934, pp. xix ff., esp. p. xxiii: 'If all the points of the prophecy be taken into careful account, it will be seen that it is fulfilled

again it is not on that ground that the sacraments are brought in here. They are included because they must be, because they are only to be understood in the light of Biblical thought as a whole, and because those aspects of the unity of the Bible to which we have given attention are vital for their understanding. Though they are Christian sacraments, fundamental Biblical principles which run all through both Testaments cannot be forgotten in their interpretation.

Actually the writer would expose himself to reproach from members of other Churches far more than from his own if he were to leave the sacraments without consideration. For it is common to connect baptism with circumcision, and to define its significance with reference to the significance of circumcision. It is therefore important to ask whether this is a mark of the unity of the Bible, and whether the old meaning is expressed with a new form. Moreover, where the sacrament of the Lord's Supper is interpreted as a sacrifice it is linked with the sacrifices of the Old Testament, and so brought into connection with Biblical thought as a whole. The sacrificial interpretation of this sacrament is not characteristic of the Baptist Church, and therefore attention to this subject is demanded by claims made elsewhere, and not by the writer's own Church. It is, indeed, probable that most

---

in the holy sacrifice of the Mass. . . . Nothing else can be said to fulfil this prophecy.' Cf. the present writer's *Israel's Mission to the World*, 1939, p. 31: 'The prophet is here claiming for Yahweh worship that is not offered in His name, worship that is offered to other gods. He is claiming that men who did not call themselves worshippers of Yahweh were really worshipping Him, that worship offered to idols could be accepted by Yahweh as offered to His name.' Similarly S. R. Driver, *The Minor Prophets* (Cent.B.), ii, 1906, p. 304: 'The passage is a tribute to the truer and better side of heathen religion, a recognition of the fact that "in every nation he that feareth God, and worketh righteousness, is acceptable to Him" (Acts x. 35).' With this interpretation cf. Tosephta *Sanhedrin* xiii. 2: 'There must be righteous men among the heathen who have a share in the world to come' (E. Tr. by H. Danby, *Tractate Sanhedrin, Mishnah and Tosefta*, 1919, p. 122). For a different interpretation of the passage in Malachi, cf. J. M. Powis Smith, *The Book of Malachi* (I.C.C.), 1912, pp. 30 f. It should be added that the interpretation of the passage in relation to the Christian sacrament is very ancient, and appears already in *Didache* xiv. 3 (cf. J. B. Lightfoot, *The Apostolic Fathers*, ed. by J. R. Harmer, 1891, pp. 224, 234), Justin Martyr, *Dialogue with Trypho* xli, cxvii (cf. *P.G.*, vi, 1884, cols. 564, 745 ff., E. Tr. by A. Lukyn Williams, 1930, pp. 81 f., 241 f.), and Irenaeus, *Against Heresies* IV, xvii. 5 f. (cf. *P.G.*, vii, 1882, cols. 1023 f., E. Tr. by A. Roberts and W. H. Rambaut, *The Writings of Irenaeus*, Ante-Nicene Christian Library, i, 1874, pp. 430 f.; ed. W. W. Harvey, IV, xxix. 5, xxx, cf. *S. Irenaei Libros quinque adversus Haereses*, ii, 1857, pp. 199 f.).

Baptists would say that the sacraments have no direct links with the Old Testament, since they would repudiate both of the claims just mentioned, and would put no similar claims drawn from the Old Testament in their place. It is, therefore, necessary first to examine these claims, and then to show in what sense the context of Biblical thought as a whole may be found illuminating for the understanding of these sacraments.

For the discussion of the origin of Christian baptism various rites have to be considered.[1] In the first place there were Jewish lustrations. These are referred to in the Old Testament, and were designed to cleanse the body of ritual pollution. They had to be performed on a variety of ordinary occasions. They cannot be compared with the Christian rite of baptism, since they were private rites which had to be repeated on many occasions, whereas baptism is an unrepeatable ceremony which is administered and witnessed. Nevertheless it is probable that Jewish lustrations have some historical connection with Christian baptism to the extent that the form of the ceremony developed out of the form of the lustrations.

Next there was Jewish proselyte baptism. It is disputed how far we can accept this as older than Christian baptism,[2] but the evidence, though less full than might have been desired, points

---

[1] Cf. the writer's paper 'Jewish Proselyte Baptism and the Baptism of John', *H.U.C.A.*, xv, 1940, pp. 313 ff., and 'The Origin and Meaning of Baptism', *B.Q.*, xi, 1942–45, pp. 309 ff.

[2] S. Zeitlin maintains that Jewish proselyte baptism was not practised before A.D. 65, though he holds that it is older than Christian baptism (cf. *H.U.C.A.*, i, 1924, pp. 357 ff., *J.B.L.*, lii, 1933, pp. 78 f.; cf. *J.Q.R.*, N.S. xiv, 1923–24, pp. 131 f.). This view involves so great a scepticism towards the New Testament evidence that it is unlikely to be accepted, and L. Finkelstein has exposed its difficulties (*J.B.L.*, lii, 1933, pp. 203 ff.; cf. also A. Büchler, *J.Q.R.*, N.S. xvii, 1926–27, p. 15 n., against whom cf. Zeitlin, *Historical Study of the Canonization of the Hebrew Scriptures*, 1933, pp. 33 f. n.). H. A. W. Meyer declared that 'the baptism of proselytes . . . did not arise until after the destruction of Jerusalem' (*Critical and Exegetical Handbook to the Gospel of Matthew*, E. Tr. by P. Christie and F. Crombie, 1877, p. 109). Many writers have held that Jewish proselyte baptism was copied from the Christian rite. So M. Schneckenburger, *Über das Alter der jüdischen Proselytentaufe und deren Zusammenhang mit dem johanneischen und christlichen Ritus*, 1828. This view is generally abandoned, despite the absence of positive evidence, since it is improbable that Judaism would have adopted a practice from the Christian Church. So, already, A. Calmet, *Commentaire littéral sur tous les livres de l'Ancien et du Nouveau Testament*, vii, 1726, p. 288. J. Thomas, however, still thinks it is improbable that any rite of proselyte baptism was generally recognized amongst the Jews before the end of the first century A.D. Cf. *Le Mouvement Baptiste en Palestine et Syrie*, 1935, p. 364.

to the probability that it is older.[1] It doubtless sprang from the background of the ordinary lustrations, but it was different in significance. It was concerned with a spiritual experience, and not with physical impurity. It was therefore symbolic rather than cleansing in itself, and it marked the experience of conversion from paganism to Judaism. Moreover, it was a sacrament and not merely a lustration.[2] It was an administered and a witnessed rite, which was performed once for all, and it involved a clear recognition by the person baptized of the significance of the act.[3]

[1] This is the view of W. Brandt (*Die jüdischen Baptismen*, 1910, pp. 58 f.), W. Heitmüller (*R.G.G.*, 1st ed. v, 1913, col. 1088; so also E. Stauffer, *ibid.*, 2nd ed., v, 1931, col. 1003), J. Coppens (*S.D.B.*, i, 1928, col. 893), and the view for which the writer argued in *H.U.C.A.*, xv, 1940, pp. 314 ff., though without claiming more than probability for it. Cf. I. Abrahams, *Studies in Pharisaism and the Gospels*, i, 1917, p. 36; G. F. Moore, *Judaism*, iii, 1930, pp. 109 f.; W. F. Flemington, *The New Testament Doctrine of Baptism*, 1948, p. 4; T. W. Manson, *S.J.T.*, ii, 1949, p. 392 n. Strack-Billerbeck, *Kommentar zum Neuen Testament aus Talmud und Midrasch*, i, 1922, p. 103, say that the beginnings of proselyte baptism are certainly pre-Christian. For some criticism of E. Schürer's *a priori* argument for this view (cf. *G.J.V.*, 4th ed., iii, 1909, pp. 181 ff., E. Tr., II, ii, 1890, pp. 319 ff.), endorsed by A. Plummer (in Hastings's *D.B.*, i, 1898, p. 240a) and I. Abrahams (*loc. cit.*), cf. *H.U.C.A.*, xv, 1940, pp. 315 f., where the surviving evidence is reviewed. F. Gavin, *The Jewish Antecedents of the Christian Sacraments*, 2nd ed., 1933, p. 85, says: 'The usage grew up naturally and inevitably, beginning possibly earlier but certainly by the second century B.C.'

[2] Bousset-Gressmann, *Die Religion des Judentums im späthellenistischen Zeitalter*, 3rd ed., 1926, p. 199, deny that it was a sacrament, and so Oesterley and Box, *The Religion and Worship of the Synagogue*, 1911, p. 286, while I. Abrahams, *op. cit.*, p. 42, and J. Bonsirven, *Le Judaïsme palestinien*, i, 1934, p. 30, maintain that it was. Here it is probable that the word *sacrament* has different meanings with different writers. It is not probable that the Jews thought the act of baptism conveyed grace to the convert merely *ex opere operato*, and such a view would show degeneration from the teaching of the Old Testament in relation to all rites. Nevertheless the Jews did believe that baptism could be 'the channel of supernatural grace to him whose spiritual condition made him the fit recipient of that grace' (*H.U.C.A.*, xv, 1940, p. 328), and those who hold a similar view of Christian baptism will not deny the use of the word *sacrament*. Cf. also F. Gavin, *op. cit.* where the first chapter is devoted to a defence of the thesis that Judaism had sacraments, though a sacramental doctrine was implicit, and not explicit. He says: 'The essential germinal principles of a sacramental outlook on the universe were not only tolerated by Judaism, but even lay intimately at its centre' (p. 23).

[3] Three witnesses were required (cf. T.B. *Ḳiddushin* 62b, ed. L. Goldschmidt, v, 1912, p. 915). They had to be satisfied that the motives of the convert were worthy (T.B. *Yebamoth* 47a, ed. Goldschmidt, iv, 1922, pp. 160 f.; *Gerim* i. 3, ed. M. Higger, 1930, Hebrew part, p. 69, English part, p. 48), and during the ceremony they had to recite to him some of the laws of the faith he was embracing (T.B. *Yebamoth* 47b, ed. Goldschmidt, iv, p. 161). Clearly it was regarded as essential that he should bring the spirit which made the rite the organ of his entry into Judaism. On the other hand the rite was not thought to be an empty form, but one charged with divine grace, and at its conclusion the witnesses hailed his admission into the Jewish faith, which was achieved by the act when charged with the spirit (cf. *Gerim* i, 1, ed. Higger, Hebrew part, p. 68, English part, p. 47).

While proselyte baptism is not mentioned in the Old Testament, and all our detailed information about it comes from a time later than the writing of the New Testament, it is probable that this rightly reflects the nature of the ceremony and its significance. It was therefore no formal act, but an act which had to be charged with meaning by the bringing to it of the spirit which made it the organ of the spirit of the baptized person. There were, however, some exceptions to this, at which we shall look later, for under certain circumstances children, and even unconscious children, might be baptized. Leaving these out of consideration for the moment, we observe that this ceremony marked the entry of aliens into the Covenant, and it required that they should bring to it the spirit of loyalty and acceptance of its obligations comparable with that which Israel brought to the Covenant at its first establishment under Moses.

Thirdly, there was the baptism of John. It is probable that behind this was the background of Jewish proselyte baptism, and certain that it lay behind Christian baptism. Like proselyte baptism this was administered and witnessed. It was also the symbol of a spiritual change and was performed once for all.[1] It is to be distinguished from proselyte baptism in that it was not the symbol of initiation into Judaism, but was administered to Jews. Nor was it the symbol of their conversion to another faith, for they continued to be Jews. It signified their initiation into the new age that was about to be.[2] There was an eschatological element in John's teaching. The axe was laid to the root of the

---

[1] On the differences between John's baptism and the baptism of proselytes cf. *H.U.C.A.*, xv, pp. 330 f., where reasons are given for the rejection of the common statement that John's baptism represented a moral purification, whereas proselyte baptism represented a ritual purification (so A. Plummer, in Hastings's *D.B.*, i, 1898, p. 240b; E. Schürer, *G.J.V.*, 4th ed., iii, p. 185 n., E. Tr., II, ii, p. 324 n.; J. Armitage Robinson, *E.B.*, i, 1899, col. 472; M.-J. Lagrange, *L'Evangile de Jésus-Christ*, 1936, p. 59, where it is mistakenly said that baptism preceded circumcision; J. Coppens, *S.D.B.*, i, cols. 893 f.).

[2] J. Coppens, *loc. cit.*, rightly perceived this, observing of John the Baptist that 'by the penitence of which baptism was the symbol, he prepared Israelites for the imminence of the messianic kingdom'. Cf. H. G. Marsh, *The Origin and Significance of the New Testament Baptism*, 1941, pp. 23 ff.; W. F. Flemington, *op. cit.*, p. 17; J. Schneider, *Die Taufe im Neuen Testament*, 1952, p. 23; also J. Thomas, *op. cit.*, p. 86, and A. Schweitzer, *The Mysticism of Paul the Apostle*, E. Tr. by W. Montgomery, 1931, pp. 230 ff. In the latter the eschatological significance of Christian baptism is also emphasized.

tree,[1] and the old world was passing away and a new world about to be born. That new world was the long predicted Kingdom of God, and John's first recorded word was a promise that that Kingdom was now nigh at hand.[2] By repentance men were called to prepare themselves for that Kingdom, and to signify by baptism that repentance and their readiness to be the children of the Kingdom. There is no evidence that John baptized children, and it is hard to suppose that he baptized infants.

Christian baptism has behind it the background of John's baptism, though its significance was different from that of John's. It signified admission to the Kingdom of God, indeed, but also a relation to Christ which was other than that of John's baptism. To that significance we shall come later. The New Testament records that during our Lord's ministry baptism was already practised, though He Himself did not baptize, but only His disciples.[3] We find baptism practised by the Early Church from the beginning,[4] and since John's baptism was not accepted as sufficient,[5] it is clear that Christian baptism was differentiated from it.

Not seldom Christian baptism has been linked with Jewish proselyte baptism in order to justify the baptism of infants.[6] It is undeniable that under certain circumstances children were baptized in the Jewish rite. Yet it is significant that those circumstances were entirely different from those which commonly attend infant baptism in most branches of the Christian Church which practice this rite. For according to the Jewish rule, when

[1] Matt. iii. 10; Luke iii. 9.
[2] Matt. iii. 1.
[3] Jn. iv. 1. W. F. Flemington, op. cit., p. 30, says: 'There is no other evidence in the Gospels that Jesus used the rite during his ministry. In view of the complete silence of the Synoptists, it is not surprising that some have doubted the reliability of this piece of Johannine tradition. A closer examination, however, suggests that it may well be trustworthy.' Cf. the full and careful discussion in H. G. Marsh, op. cit., pp. 109 ff.
[4] Acts ii. 41, viii. 12 f., 16, 38, ix. 18, x. 48, xvi. 15, 33, etc.
[5] Acts xix. 3 ff.
[6] So still H. G. Marsh, op. cit., p. 176; W. F. Flemington, op. cit., p. 131. J. Schneider, Die Taufe im Neuen Testament, 1952, p. 40, observes that despite formal links with proselyte baptism, Christian baptism is fundamentally so different that the argument from the one to the other is invalid.

parents were converted they and their children were given proselyte baptism,[1] but children born after the conversion did not receive baptism.[2] It was purely a conversion rite. It can therefore afford no support for the practice of baptizing the children of those who stand within the Covenant at the time of their birth, and still less for the practice of indiscriminate baptism of children,[3] which is arousing so much concern today in some paedobaptist Churches.[4]

Hence resort is commonly had to the Jewish rite of circumcision.[5] This is a totally different rite, both in its significance and its subjects, from any of the other rites at which we have looked. No Jew could possibly confuse circumcision with ordinary

---

[1] T.B. *Ketuboth* 11a, ed. Goldschmidt, iv, 1922, p. 488. The children retained the right to renounce on attaining maturity the engagements entered into on their behalf.

[2] T.B. *Yebamoth* 78a, ed. Goldschmidt, iv, 1922, p. 280.

[3] Cf. Cyprian, *Epistle* lxiv (to Fidus), 2 (*Opera omnia*, ed. W. Hartel, ii, 1871, p. 718): 'The mercy and grace of God is not to be refused to anyone born of woman' (E. Tr. by R. E. Wallis, *The Writings of Cyprian*, Ante-Nicene Christian Library, i, 1870, p. 196).

[4] Cf. J.-D. Benoit, *R.H.P.R.*, xvii, 1937, p. 457: 'Amongst the Churches which practise infant baptism the legitimacy of this rite is constantly brought into question afresh'; F. J. Leenhardt, *Le Baptême Chrétien*, 1946, p. 72: 'The baptism of infants can only be tolerated within a community of faithful believers'; N. P. Williams, *The Ideas of the Fall and of Original Sin*, 1927, p. 552: 'The indiscriminate baptism of children, with regard to whom no guarantee exists that they will be trained as Christians, is both useless and to be deprecated as a cheapening of the Sacrament'; W. F. Flemington, *op. cit.*, p. 134: 'That there are many Christians today for whom the baptizing of infants offers serious difficulties can hardly be denied. . . . The reservations about infant baptism are not confined to the Baptist communion'; E. Brunner, *The Divine-Human Encounter*, 1944, p. 132: 'The contemporary practice of infant baptism can hardly be regarded as being anything short of scandalous.'

[5] So John Calvin, *Institutes of the Christian Religion*, E. Tr. by H. Beveridge, ii, 1869, pp. 530 f.; cf. esp. p. 531: 'Everything applicable to circumcision applies also to baptism, excepting always the difference in the visible ceremony.' Cf. Benoit, *loc. cit.*, p. 461: 'These views on baptism and circumcision do not seem so conclusive to us as to Calvin.' Cf. also Leenhardt, *op. cit.*, pp. 67 f.: 'The parallel between circumcision and baptism is invoked to yield the conclusion that the new sacrament can only succeed the old if it is practised in the same manner; but Paul here *opposes* the one sacrament to the other; he shows that baptism, spiritual circumcision, does not stand on the same plane as circumcision effected by the hands of man.' Cf. also H. Windisch, *Z.N.W.*, xxviii, 1929, p. 130. K. Barth, *The Teaching of the Church regarding Baptism*, E. Tr. by E. A. Payne, 1948, p. 49, says that the reading of Calvin's chapters on baptism reveals 'where the great Calvin was sure of his subject and where he obviously was not sure, but visibly nervous, in a hopelessly confused train of thought, abusing where he ought to inform and when he wants to convince, seeking a way in the fog, which can lead him to no goal, because he has none.' On the question of baptism and circumcision cf. also H. Martin, *B.Q.*, xiv, 1952, pp. 213 ff.

lustrations, or with proselyte baptism,[1] nor could it be confused with John's baptism. It is surely one of the unsolved mysteries of Christian scholarship why the leap should be made to what is a completely different and unrelated rite.[2] Circumcision was a rite which all male Jews had to undergo, either at the time of their birth or at the time of their conversion to Judaism. It did not apply to females, and therefore could provide no analogy to the baptism of girls.[3] Judaism had no sacramental rite, within all the series at which we have looked, which applied to the infant daughters of parents who stood within the Covenant at the time of their birth, and since under such circumstances it prescribed circumcision and not baptism for boys, it offers no

[1] This confusion continues to be a stock argument in the armoury of the Paedobaptist. Cf. H. G. Marsh, *op. cit.*, p. 176; W. F. Flemington, *op. cit.*, p. 131; O. Cullmann, *op. cit.*, pp. 50 ff., E. Tr., pp. 56 ff. Cullmann neatly observes that in Judaism 'there is both infant and adult circumcision, and both adult and infant proselyte baptism' (E. Tr. p. 56), thus joining together two quite different Jewish rites to conceal the fact that neither offers any parallel to the Christian rite. It is only by invoking now one and now the other of these diverse rites that they offer specious support to the case for paedobaptism. G. H. W. Lampe, *The Seal of the Spirit*, 1951, p. 83, observes that 'Circumcision, other than the "true circumcision of the spirit" . . . is not likened to Baptism by the New Testament writers, but contrasted with it'.

[2] By the third century it is clear that there were some who regarded the baptism of infants as parallel to the circumcision of infants, for Cyprian, though he strongly supported infant baptism, objected to this analogy. He held that baptism should not be deferred till the eighth day, as the false analogy would suggest, but should take place as soon as possible. At the same time Cyprian held no doctrine of baptismal regeneration, but denied that a new-born child is unclean, saying that to kiss such a child is to kiss the hands of God. Cf. *Epistle* lxiv (to Fidus), 3, 5 (ed. W. Hartel, pp. 717 ff., E. Tr. by R. E. Wallis, pp. 196 ff.). Gregory Nazienzen, on the other hand, favoured the deferment of baptism till the age of about three, when the children would be able to understand the rudiments of the faith. He adduces circumcision on the eighth day, however, to justify earlier baptism if the children were in any danger. That this is not to equate baptism with circumcision is clear, since only exceptionally did he wish baptism to be administered without a conscious, though incipient, faith. Cf. *Oration on Holy Baptism* xxviii (P.G., xxxvi, 1885, col. 400, E. Tr. by C. G. Browne and J. E. Swallow, in *Nicene and Post-Nicene Fathers*, vii, 1894, p. 370).

[3] Cullman once more confuses the issues by speaking of the affinity of Jewish proselyte baptism with circumcision (*op. cit.*, p. 59, E. Tr., p. 65). Both significance and subjects of the two rites were different. A Jewish-born girl underwent neither rite; a Jewish-born boy was circumcised only; a female proselyte or child of a proselyte was baptized only; a male proselyte or child of a proselyte was both baptized and circumcised. Clearly the two rites had different meanings, whether for males or for females, and it is not legitimate to equate them in order to yield the conclusion that Christian baptism is rightly administered to all the four separate classes above-mentioned, including the class to which neither rite was administered. Where the premises are wrong, the conclusions are not secure, and, as has been said above, no Jew could confuse circumcision with proselyte baptism.

analogy at all for the latter rite. Further, even if circumcision were allowed to be a true analogy, it would still not justify the indiscriminate baptism of children. For the Jews only circumcised those infant boys who were born within the Covenant. The Church claims to be the New Israel, heirs of the Covenant and the promises, but it is nowhere taught that those who belong neither to the Israel according to the flesh nor to the Church stand within the Covenant. When the children of such are baptized no remote parallel can be found either in Jewish proselyte baptism or in Jewish circumcision.[1]

It is often claimed that the authority of Paul can be invoked in support of the alleged analogy. For he says: 'In whom (*i.e.* in Christ) ye were also circumcised with a circumcision not made with hands, in the putting off of the body of the flesh, in the circumcision of Christ; having been buried with him in baptism, wherein ye were also raised with him through faith in the working of God, who raised him from the dead. And you, being dead through your trespasses and the uncircumcision of your flesh, you did he quicken together with him, having forgiven us all our trespasses.'[2] Here there is no suggestion that the subjects of baptism and the subjects of circumcision are the same, or that the two rites are in any way parallel in their significance. Indeed Paul specifically mentions faith, which was not required of infants who were circumcised.[3] All he is saying is that union with Christ does away with the necessity for circumcision,[4] just as elsewhere

[1] Cf. G. H. W. Lampe, *The Seal of the Spirit*, 1951, p. 93: 'Considered individually, these rites'—*i.e.* proselyte baptism and circumcision—'are quite unlike Christian initiation. Both in their outward aspect and in their inner significance they lie poles apart from the Christian rite which springs from the Messianic Baptism of Jesus.'

[2] Col. ii. 11 ff.

[3] Similarly Justin Martyr, *First Apology* lxi (ed. B. L. Gildersleeve, 1877, p. 57: *P.G.*, vi, 1884, col. 420), says: 'As many as are persuaded and believe that what we teach and say is true, and undertake to be able to live accordingly . . . are brought by us where there is water, and are regenerated in the same manner in which we were ourselves regenerated' (E. Tr. by M. Dods, in Ante-Nicene Christian Library, 1870, p. 59).

[4] Cf. H. Martin, *Theology*, liii, 1950, p. 302: 'St. Paul tells his readers that they do not need the circumcision of the flesh, because they have received the circumcision of the heart. The bodily rite of circumcision is the type of this spiritual circumcision, this cleansing of the heart.' J. C. Fenton, *ibid.*, p. 386, claims that this passage can be used to connect baptism and circumcision as comparable rites, but neglects to show that faith was a prerequisite in circumcision, as Paul declares it to be here, or to recognize that

he says: 'Beware of the concision; for we are the circumcision, who worship by the Spirit of God, and glory in Christ Jesus, and have no confidence in the flesh.'[1]

Moreover, Paul elsewhere uses words very similar to those quoted above, though without mentioning baptism, when he says: 'And you did he quicken, when ye were dead through your trespasses and sins, wherein aforetime ye walked according to the course of this world . . . But God, being rich in mercy, for his great love wherewith he loved us, even when we were dead through our trespasses, quickened us together with Christ . . . and raised us up with him.'[2] He then goes on to speak of Jew and Gentile, circumcised and uncircumcised, being reconciled in one body in Christ. It is therefore clear that he regarded the Christian experience of Christ as something that transcended circumcision and uncircumcision, not something that was parallel to the former. This is also clear from the fact that in these passages the Apostle is thinking of grown men, who had known the lusts and sins of human life, and not of new-born babes.[3]

---

it is this false analogy which has led the Church to dispense with faith for what has become the normal Christian baptism. Martin aptly cites (p. 423) the comments on this passage of J. B. Lightfoot (*St. Paul's Epistles to the Colossians and Philemon*, 1900, p. 181) and A. S. Peake (*The Expositor's Greek Testament*, ed. by W. R. Nicoll, iii, 1912, p. 524). Peake says: 'The Apostle does not merely leave them with the statement that they have been made full in Christ, which rendered circumcision unnecessary, but adds that they have already received circumcision, not material but spiritual . . . This was their conversion, the inward circumcision of the heart, by which they entered on the blessings of the New Covenant. The outward sign of this is baptism . . . But it cannot be identified with it, for it is not made with hands.'

[1] Phil. iii. 2 f. Cf. Gal. v. 6. Cf. also Justin Martyr, *Dialogue with Trypho* xliii (*P.G.*, vi, 1884, col. 568): 'We who by Him drew near to God did not receive this circumcision according to the flesh, but one that is spiritual, which Enoch and those like him kept. But we received it by our baptism, since we had become sinners' (E. Tr. by A. Lukyn Williams, 1930, pp. 84 f.). Here there is no connecting of the baptism of infants with the circumcision of infants, but the claim that Christians have no need of circumcision, since they have received grace through the sacrament of baptism.

[2] Eph. ii. 1 ff.

[3] Speaking generally of the New Testament references to baptism, N. P. Williams says that they 'assume that its recipients are adults, and that the dispositions required in them are those of conscious and deliberate renunciation of sin and idols, and of personal faith in and allegiance to Christ' (*The Ideas of the Fall and of Original Sin*, 1927, p. 550). Cf. N. H. Snaith, *I believe in* . . ., 1949, p. 110: 'In the first days of the Christian Church . . . the significance of the rite was clear. It was baptism of believers and it was baptism by immersion. The condition for the administration of the rite was confession of faith, and it marked the recognition of the convert as a member of the Church.' J. Héring, in *Aux Sources de la Tradition Chrétienne* (Goguel Festschrift), 1950, pp. 95 ff., has recently

It must further be remembered that at the Council of Jerusalem the question whether it was necessary for Gentiles to be circumcised was discussed.[1] The question at issue was not whether baptism was a substitute for circumcision, but whether Gentiles should be required to be both circumcised and baptized. It seems to have been taken for granted that Jewish Christians would be both baptized and circumcised, as they long continued to be. The two rites were therefore clearly seen to be quite distinct in their significance and their subjects. Hence, immediately after the account of Paul's victory at the Council of Jerusalem, we read that he insisted on the circumcision of Timothy, whose mother was a Jewess.[2] No confusion between the two rites existed in his mind.[3]

It is inevitable that when the discussion of the issue is governed by a false analogy, a different significance must be attached to the sacrament from that which is given to it in the New Testament. The writer is here in the fullest agreement with Professor T. W. Manson, when he says: 'For the full understanding of most of the central things in the Christian religion we have to look first and foremost to the New Testament teaching in its setting, and that means taking account of what went before in the Old Testament and the belief and practice of Judaism, and of what came after in the belief and practice of the Church'.[4] So far as the practice of the Church is concerned, it can neither be proved nor disproved by specific references in the New Testament that the Early Church practised infant baptism,[5] and the common invoking of the

---

based on Matt. xviii. 10 an argument for infant baptism. Here it is to be observed that if the argument is valid it would apply to infants indiscriminately, since there is no evidence that the children referred to were the children of our Lord's disciples. There is no suggestion of baptism at all in the passage, however.

[1] Acts xv. 5. [2] Acts xvi. 3.

[3] Cf. F. Schleiermacher, *The Christian Faith*, E. Tr. by H. R. Mackintosh and J. S. Stewart, 1928, p. 660: 'It is going much too far to assert that baptism took the place of circumcision . . . Baptism was instituted quite independently of circumcision; moreover, circumcision was not put a stop to by baptism.'

[4] Cf. *S.J.T.*, ii, 1949, p. 392.

[5] Cf. T. W. Manson, *S.J.T.*, ii, 1949, p. 403; J.-D. Benoit, *R.H.P.R.*, xvii, 1937, p. 461. Cf. also F. Schleiermacher, *The Christian Faith*, E. Tr., p. 634: 'Every trace of infant baptism which people have professed to find in the New Testament must first be inserted there.'

Jewish idea of the solidarity of the family is completely irrelevant,[1] since in proselyte baptism, which could provide the only possible analogy for the baptism of households, subsequently born children were regarded as so completely within the solidarity of the family that they did not need to be baptized. Analogies that are not analogous prove nothing. The practice of the baptism of children born to those who stand within the Covenant is not paralleled in the case of proselyte baptism; still less is the practice of the baptism of those children who are not born within the Covenant, save when their baptism takes place at the same time as that of their parents. Yet even then account must be taken of the different theological significance of proselyte baptism and Christian baptism before the analogy could be relied on. The significance of circumcision is so completely different from the significance of Christian baptism that no analogy here could be valid anyhow, but since the practice was in no sense parallel to that which holds in paedobaptist sections of the Church there is no analogy to claim validity. A rite which was undergone only by boys born within the Covenant provides no parallel to a rite undergone by boys and girls, whether born within the Covenant or not. To turn now to circumcision and now to proselyte baptism for an analogy is even less satisfactory, when the two rites were so totally different in subjects and significance, and when neither provides any analogy for the case of children born without the Covenant, save on the occasion of the conversion of their parents. It is surely high time these misleading analogies were dismissed in the interests of clear thinking.

So far as the practice of the post-apostolic Church is concerned, it is certain that infant baptism appeared quite early, though it

---

[1] So J. V. Bartlet, in Hastings's *E.R.E.*, ii, 1909, p. 379a; H. G. Marsh, *op. cit.*, p. 176; W. F. Flemington, *op. cit.*, p. 131; O. Cullmann, *op. cit.*, p. 39, E. Tr., p. 45. Cf. H. H. Rowley, *J.T.S.*, xliv, 1943, p. 81, where it is pointed out that the doctrine of the solidarity of the family meant that children born after their mother's baptism were deemed to be included in that act and so were *not* baptized. Bartlet says that 'what we know of the Jewish practice touching proselytes—which usually regulated practice among Gentile Christians—makes it most improbable that Christianity here introduced any novel usage,' without apparently realizing that his argument would mean that there was no baptism of the children of believers.

was not unchallanged,[1] and it is well known that there was a time when ideas of baptismal regeneration [2] caused baptism to be deferred until the end of life.[3] The question cannot therefore be settled by appealing to the practice of the New Testament[4] or of the Early Church, and it is far more important to approach it in terms of Biblical thought, and of the significance which the New Testament attaches to the rite.[5] It is precisely here that the issue

[1] Cf. F. J. Leenhardt, *E.Th.R.*, xxv, 1952, p. 149: 'It is necessary to go to the third century to find incontestable evidence of the existence of paedobaptism. Remarkably enough, the first attestation is hostile to the practice, which is opposed as an innovation without justification'; also Th. Preiss, *La Vie en Christ*, 1951, p. 133: 'We should never forget that paedobaptism only became general with Constantine' (Preiss's essay 'Le Baptême des Enfants' appeared first in *Verbum Caro*, 1947, pp. 113–22, to which the present writer has had no access, and in German translation in *Th.L.Z.*, lxxiii, 1948, cols. 651 ff.). The view of Preiss is that infant baptism is valuable in a Christian family but has no meaning where there is no serious likelihood of Christian training. Nevertheless he thinks it is a good thing that there should be some Christian families which do not practise infant baptism (*op. cit.*, pp. 142 f.).

[2] G. A. Barton, *J.A.O.S.*, lvi, 1936, p. 162, traces the doctrine of baptismal regeneration to an ancient pre-Christian thought-pattern. This doctrine is still the official doctrine of the Church of England, where the priest at the end of the Baptismal Service says 'Seeing now . . . that this child is regenerate.'

[3] R. E. White, *E.T.*, li, 1949–50, p. 110, observes that 'such giants as Gregory Nazienzen, Basil, Chrysostom, Ambrose and Augustine were not baptized until they reached manhood, although all had Christian mothers'. To these Leenhardt, *E.Th.R.*, xxv, 1950, p. 149, adds Jerome, and cites the remark of F. Lovsky: 'Here indeed are facts more worthy of comment than the laborious constructions placed on enigmatic texts of Irenaeus or Clement of Alexandria' (*Foi et Vie*, March–April 1950, pp. 109 ff.; to this the present writer has had no access).

[4] Cf. F. J. Leenhardt, *Le Baptême Chrétien*, pp. 66 f., where it is agreed that Calvin's attempted demonstration that infant baptism is taught in the Bible is unconvincing, and maintained that it would be easier to conclude that infants are pure and therefore in no need of baptism. Cf. also *E.Th.R.*, xxv, 1950, p. 144, where Leenhardt says that 'Calvin professed a doctrine of the sacrament formally at variance with that which supported paedobaptism; nevertheless he retained paedobaptism. . . . Calvin avoided the contradiction, as will be shown, by emptying infant baptism of its authentic sacramental character.' Cf. *ibid.*, p. 201.

[5] The writer is here in the fullest agreement with O. Cullmann: 'It can be decided only on the ground of New Testament *doctrine*: Is infant Baptism compatible with the New Testament conception of the essence and meaning of Baptism?' (*Baptism in the New Testament*, E. Tr. by J. K. S. Reid, 1950, p. 26). The German text stands in *Die Tauflehre des Neuen Testaments*, 1948, pp. 21 f. (of this work there is also a French edition, *Le Baptême des Enfants*, translated by J.-J. von Allmen, 1948). Cf. also J.-D. Benoit, *loc. cit.*: 'We must see if, apart from precise passages, this baptism accords with the fundamental teachings of Scripture, if it agrees with the great Christian affirmations, yea more, if it is in some way postulated by them as a logical necessity.' Cf. *B.Q.*, xi, 1942–45, p. 316, where the present writer has said: 'If it could be proved conclusively that in the first century A.D. infants were baptized, that would not justify a practice that was not in accord with the New Testament teaching of the meaning of baptism; and if it could be conclusively proved that in the first century A.D. infants were not baptized,

belongs to the subject of the present lectures. Principles which have been seen to be constant throughout the Bible, though applied to a variety of situations, are found to be constant here, and cannot be abandoned without disloyalty to Biblical thought as a whole, and not merely to this or that text in the New Testament.

Professor Oscar Cullmann has recently stressed the importance of faith in relation to baptism, but more particularly the faith that follows baptism.[1] So far it is easy to agree with him, for it would be hard to find anyone who would argue that faith may be dispensed with once baptism has been administered. It is to be noted, however, that Cullmann recognized that those who have been baptized, whether in infancy or later, may not persist in the faith. He therefore argues for two quite different sorts of baptism, which he then subsumes under one by the remarkable supposition that God is capable of misleading the Church. He says that before baptism faith was demanded of those who came as adults from Judaism or from paganism, but not from those who were of Christian parentage.[2] The New Testament speaks of one baptism,[3] and it is hard to find any evidence from the New Testament that faith was not asked of those who were baptized.[4] But worse

---

that would not of itself rule out the practice, if it accorded with the New Testament teaching of its essential significance.' With this contrast N. P. Williams, *op. cit.*, p. 552, where the practice of the Church is appealed to as 'the only, but a sufficient, ground for affirming the legitimacy of Paedo-baptism'. Also W. F. Flemington, *op. cit.*, p. 135: 'New Testament statements about baptism cannot all be used in reference to infant baptism *without modification*. We must frankly recognize that much harm has been done, and a superstitious attitude to baptism too often encouraged, because New Testament language, used originally of believers' baptism, has been applied indiscriminately, as it stands, to the baptism of infants.' G. H. W. Lampe, *op. cit.*, p. 93, says: 'Despite various possible indications of the existence of infant Baptism in the New Testament, the theology of Baptism therein presented to us is concerned with the Baptism of adults alone.'

[1] Cf. *Die Tauflehre des Neuen Testaments*, pp. 43 ff., E. Tr., pp. 50 ff. Cf. F. Schleiermacher, *The Christian Faith*, E. Tr., p. 630: 'Baptism is received wrongly if it be received without faith, and it is wrongly given so.' Nevertheless, he justifies infant baptism with the proviso that 'its proper efficacy is suspended until the person baptized has really become a believer' (p. 636). Even so, he thinks the practice might be given up without harm to children since he does not think the rite makes any difference to them (p. 637). Cf. also the study of the teaching of Martin Luther by P. Althaus, *Th.L.Z.*, lxxiii, 1948, cols. 705 ff.　　　　[2] Cf. *op. cit.*, p. 46, E. Tr., p. 52.　　　　[3] Eph. iv. 5.

[4] Cf. G. H. W. Lampe, *The Seal of the Spirit*, 1951, p. 55: 'By virtue of the effective sign of Baptism, faith of course being always presupposed, the application of the Atonement to the believer implies his forgiveness; Christian Baptism therefore effects the

follows from this unscriptural view. Professor Cullmann opposes the indiscriminate baptism of children, and says: 'It runs contrary to the meaning it has pleased God to give to Baptism if the Church undertakes the Baptism of a man indiscriminately, that is, *without any divine sign suggesting the prospect of his perseverance in Baptism within the community.*'[1] It might be supposed that if the sign were genuinely a divine sign it could be relied on, but since Professor Cullmann agrees that even where what he defines as divine signs are given they cannot always be relied on,[2] it seems safer to doubt whether they are correctly so defined than to make God a deceiver. A theology of baptism which rests on such a view is certainly not Biblical, and to the writer is far from satisfying. The divine signs are said to be either faith on the part of an adult candidate for baptism or Christian parentage in the case of an infant.[3] To describe either of these as a divine sign is remarkable. For while it may be agreed that faith is only possible by the help of God, and that faith is rightly demanded before baptism, that faith can only be known to the Church by the

cleansing for which the prophets had hoped.' Leenhardt, *op. cit.*, pp. 70 f., controverts the idea that baptism should follow regeneration or conversion, and says it is the symbol of the divine will to regenerate the believer. Similarly, J. K. S. Reid, *E.T.*, lxi, 1949–50, p. 203, argues that unless baptism precedes faith it 'forfeits all claim to be a genuinely *Christian* initiation,' and maintains that the emphasis on surrender as a precondition of baptism 'assimilates the rite to the secular type of initiation ceremony'. If the rite were merely declarative, or if it operated independently of the will of the baptized, the words of E. A. Payne would seem relevant: 'It is difficult to see that (it) would not justify that indiscriminate baptism of Indian villagers with a fire hose of which Karl Barth writes so scornfully' (*S.J.T.*, iii, 1950, p. 53). It is hard to think that any would advocate such action, and Reid specifically repudiates it. He insists on the necessity for faith, but says it is altruistic faith, expressed in the assent of the sponsors. On his view this altruistic faith must apply equally in the case of adult baptism, or by his own definition there could only be secular initiation and no Christian baptism. It is surprising to be told that the Apostles and the New Testament Church did not administer Christian baptism but only a secular initiation rite. For it is undeniable that faith preceded baptism in many of the recorded cases. P.-H. Menoud, in a study of the Early Church, rightly observes: 'The Christian life is inaugurated by faith and baptism'. Cf. *La Vie de l'Église naissante*, 1952, p. 9.

[1] *Op. cit.*, p. 44, E. Tr., p. 50.

[2] *Ibid.* Cf. O. C. Quick, *The Christian Sacraments*, 1927, p. 172: 'What cannot at all be verified in experience is the supposition that Baptism in itself makes any such change in the spiritual condition of an infant as is implied by asserting that it removes once for all original sin and its hold on the soul'; p. 175: 'The spiritual and moral health of so many of the unbaptized is apparently so superior to that of so many of the baptized that it has become difficult to allege that even on the whole Baptism makes a conspicuous difference.'

[3] *Op. cit.*, p. 45, E. Tr., p. 51.

profession of the individual, and this is a human act and not a divine. The profession may be tested by the Church, but the recognition that the test may be misleading shows that this too is a human and not a divine act. The test of parentage is much more misleading, since this is one that is mechanically applied. It would be hard to establish the thesis that there is even a human presumption, let alone a divine sign, that the child of a Christian will become a genuine believer. It is to be presumed that Stalin was once baptized, since he entered a theological school, and that he added the profession of his own faith to Christian parentage. Yet so little could any divine sign of his perseverance within the community be found here that he became the leader of a militantly atheistic party.[1]

Moreover, the practice of infant baptism led to what Professor T. W. Manson calls 'the splitting of the original single rite of admission into two'.[2] This frankly recognizes that what the New Testament means by baptism is the original single rite. It is therefore quite inappropriate to attach the name of the original rite to one of the two parts into which it is split, and that the part which has the lesser association with New Testament thought on baptism. For here again the analogy is with Jewish practice and not with Christian. A Jewish boy enters potentially into the covenant at circumcision, but when he is thirteen years of age he has the *bar mitzvah* ceremony whereby he enters of his own volition into the life and faith of Israel, and is recognized as a loyal child of Judaism.[3] Of such a ceremony there is no hint in the New Testa-

[1] Cf. E. Brunner, *The Divine-Human Encounter*, 1944, p. 131: 'Most of the contemporary neopagans and also most members of atheistic societies have been baptized as infants.'

[2] Cf. *S.J.T.*, *loc. cit.*, p. 397. G. H. W. Lampe, *op. cit.*, p. 309, says that a doctrine of confirmation was developed 'to rationalize the division of the rite of initiation'. On the late development of the doctrine of confirmation, and its position in the Anglican Church, cf. Dom Gregory Dix, *The Theology of Confirmation in relation to Baptism*, 1946. Here it is shown how largely the doctrine was determined by the Forged Decretals, through Gratian and Peter Lombard (cf. pp. 23 f.), and added: 'It is an ironical fact that the *dicta* of Pseudo-Isidore . . . continue to be repeated by Reformed Divines with a quite mediaeval glibness' (p. 25). Dix recognizes that it was motives of practical convenience which caused the separation of the two halves of the primitive rite (p. 31), and thinks 'the Church can well afford Infant Baptism . . . *provided that it is never allowed to be thought of as normal*' (ibid.).

[3] This ceremony is of uncertain date, but probably quite late, in Judaism.

ment, and it is alien to its whole thought.[1] Yet it is carried over
into Christianity and confirmation is treated as the completion of
the act of baptism. The innumerable cases where the completion
never takes place in the case of those who are baptized in infancy
give something of the measure of the futility of the 'divine
sign' alleged by Professor Cullmann, and to these must be
added the further numbers of those who after confirmation
fall away. For men to invent something which has no Scriptural
warrant, and then to place on God the responsibility for its
failure by supposing that divine signs have misled them, is
unconvincing in itself and alien to the whole background of
Biblical thought.

What infant baptism is often said to guard is the profound
truth of the prevenient grace of God.[2] Here is an indubitably
Scriptural principle, which has been insisted on again and again
in the present lectures. Unhappily it does not figure in this
connection in the Bible. As Cullmann himself agrees, where an
adult is being baptized faith must precede baptism.[3] In this case,
therefore, the baptism does not declare the prevenient grace of
God, and hence a different significance must be given to baptism
according to whether it is the baptism of a believer or of an infant.
Yet the prevenient grace of God is as much a fact in the one case
as in the other.[4] That prevenient grace is manifested not in the act
of the Church in baptizing, but in the Cross of Christ. Long before
we were born God's love was there manifested, God's claim on us
was made, and the atonement for our sins was achieved. If our
heart does not respond to that love, it is improbable that it will be
moved by the fact that water was sprinkled on us when we were

---

[1] Cf. E. Brunner, *The Divine-Human Encounter*, p. 130: 'The statements of the New
Testament about baptism continued to be connected with infant baptism and yet the
bad conscience roused by this identification was soothed by completing baptism with
confirmation, which certainly does not stem from the Bible.'

[2] Cf. T. W. Manson, *loc. cit.*, pp. 401 f.; also Cullmann, *op. cit.*, p. 43, E. Tr., p. 49.
Cf. too W. F. Flemington, *op. cit.*, p. 137.

[3] *Op. cit.*, p. 49, E. Tr., p. 55.

[4] Cf. G. H. W. Lampe, *The Seal of the Spirit*, p. 57: 'Baptism, whose reception
by the believer is his visible act of trusting response to the prevenient grace of
God in Christ, is a re-presentation of Christ's own Baptism and its application to each
convert.'

unconscious.[1] If the act of God will not move us to faith, the act of man is unlikely to do so. The doctrine of the prevenient grace of God does not need infant baptism to proclaim it, for it has greater proclamation throughout the Bible.[2]

One of the profound truths which we have seen to run all through the Bible is that rites and ceremonies have no meaning so long as they are only rites and ceremonies. It is only when they are the vehicle of the spirit that they have meaning; but when they are such a vehicle, they become charged with divine power to bless and enrich. The ceremony of infant baptism cannot be the vehicle of the spirit of the babe who is baptized.[3] It may have a meaning and a value so far as the parents and the Church are concerned, since they can bring the spirit to the ceremony, but since they are not being baptized and initiated into the Church it cannot have any truly baptismal significance for them.[4]

[1] R. S. Franks, *History of the Doctrine of the Work of Christ*, i, p. 190, notes the dilemma in which Abelard was placed by the practice of infant baptism, and cites Loofs (*Leitfaden zum Studium der Dogmengeschichte*, 4th ed., 1906, p. 515) for the view that Abelard's doctrine could not be carried through without more changes than he was prepared to make. Abelard's view of the power of the Cross was that it was power to kindle love, and he was then forced to conclude that forgiveness of sins awaited baptism (cf. *P.L.*, clxxviii, 1885, col. 837). In the case of infants, however, where baptism precedes the awakening of love, he was forced to suppose that remission of sins was independent of the kindling of love (*ibid*, col. 838). Once more, therefore, it is found impossible to give a common significance to infant baptism and believers' baptism, and traditional practice triumphs over theological consistency.

[2] J. Barr, *S.J.T.*, iv, 1951, p. 274, offers the remarkable argument that the practice of believers' baptism may obscure the antecedence of Christ's work to faith. Since it can scarcely be denied that we have many instances of believers' baptism recorded in the New Testament, this implies a condemnation of apostolic practice and of New Testament teaching that is quite astonishing. When paedopaptists are driven by their efforts at rationalization to such lengths, the insecurity of their position is manifest. Moreover, it remains to be shown how anyone could suppose that his faith in the finished work of Christ today preceded that finished work.

[3] Cf. K. Barth, *The Teaching of the Church regarding Baptism*, E. Tr., p. 41: 'Neither by exegesis nor from the nature of the case can it be established that the baptized person can be a merely passive instrument. Rather it may be shown . . . that in this action the baptized is an active partner and that at whatever stage of life he may be, plainly no *infans* can be such a person.'

[4] Cf. what the writer has elsewhere written on the sacrament of Dedication, comparable to our Lord's Presentation in the Temple, *B.Q.*, xi, 1942–45, pp. 319 f. For such a rite New Testament precedent can be found in the example of our Lord; for Confirmation many years after baptism no New Testament precedent can be claimed. Cf. also N. H. Snaith, *I believe in . . .*, pp. 113 f. F. J. Leenhardt, *E.Th.R.*, xxv, 1950, p. 200, says: 'On the profit received by the parents, Calvin has something to say; but it is in respect to them alone that baptism fulfils its function of sign and produces its effects.'

Professor T. W. Manson says that the practice of believers' baptism makes the decision of the believer do all that is necessary.[1] If that were so it would deserve to be repudiated, since it would be directly contrary to teaching which we have seen to belong to the unity of the Bible. But is it really so? So far as adults are concerned Professor Cullmann asks for faith, and it is hard to suppose that Professor Manson would advocate the baptism of adults without even asking whether they believed or not. If this is really to eliminate the necessity for God, and to make the decision of the believer do all that is necessary, it is hard to see why faith should be asked in the case of adults any more than in the case of infants. When Philip said to the Ethiopian eunuch 'If thou believest with all thine heart, thou mayest (be baptized)',[2] he was not converting the eunuch's faith into the organ of salvation. It is true that there is impressive manuscript testimony in favour of regarding this verse as an addition to the text.[3] Yet since it is known to have been in existence in the second century,[4] it would still testify to the view of the Early Church that faith was necessary to baptism,[5] and even earlier we find Paul writing: 'If thou shalt confess with thy mouth Jesus as Lord, and shalt believe in thy heart that God raised him from the dead, thou shalt be saved'.[6] Similarly in the case of the Philippian gaoler faith preceded baptism.[7] Surely it is hard to suppose that these passages mean that the New Testament writers eliminated the

---

[1] Cf. *loc. cit.,* p. 399.   [2] Acts viii. 37.

[3] For the evidence cf. A. C. Clark, *The Acts of the Apostles,* 1933, *ad. loc.* Many modern editors regard it as unoriginal. So, most recently, F. F. Bruce, *The Acts of the Apostles,* 1951, p. 194. In R.V. it is relegated to the margin.

[4] Cf. Irenaeus, *Against Heresies* III, xii. 8 (*P.G.,* vii, 1882, cols. 901 f., E. Tr. by A. Roberts and W. H. Rambaut, *The Writings of Irenaeus,* Ante-Nicene Christian Library, i, 1874, p. 305; ed. W. W. Harvey, III, xii, 10, cf. *S. Irenaei Libros quinque adversus Haereses,* ii, 1857, p. 62). R. B. Rackham, *The Acts of the Apostles,* 3rd ed., 1906, p. 123, suggests that the verse stood in the original draft of the book, but that St. Luke may have drawn his pen through it when revising his work, since the profession of faith at baptism must have been familiar enough to his Christian readers.

[5] Similarly Matt. xxviii. 19, with its demand for discipleship before baptism, may be appealed to. This verse is also regarded by many scholars as secondary, in view of its use of a Trinitarian formula, but it is nevertheless valid evidence of the practice of the Church within the New Testament period. P. W. Evans, *Sacraments in the New Testament,* 1946, pp. 9 ff., argues for the probability that we have here a genuine Dominical word.   [6] Rom. x. 9.   [7] Acts xvi. 31, 33.

act of God in salvation and made the decision of the believer do all that was necessary.

In the previous chapter the necessity to distinguish between the conditions of salvation and the organ of salvation has been urged. If faith is the condition it is not to be confused with the organ. If a man wishes to travel from Manchester to London by train it is a necessary condition of his journey that he should board the train, but he would be very foolish if he supposed that his entering the train would of itself get him to London, and that he could dispense with the engine. The power that would get him to London would be the power of the engine; yet it could not succeed in getting him there if he were not on the train. Few would be so foolish as to confuse the conditions of transportation with the organ of transportation. If, then, faith is held to be necessary to baptism, it does not for one moment imply that faith is all that is necessary, and that God can be dispensed with, or that baptism is merely the act of the person who is baptized, or even of the Church and that person. In the context of Biblical thought we may say that if baptism is to be charged with meaning and power it must be both a divine and a human act.

When we approach baptism from the Bible instead of from the practice of the Church, and ask what it meant in Biblical thought instead of how we can justify later practice by false analogy and false charges of unreliability against God, we find the important passage in Romans vi, to which Baptists always appeal in justification of immersion as the mode of baptism. With that we are not concerned here. Far more important is its testimony as to the significance Paul attached to the rite. That significance is expressed in terms of death and resurrection. Immersion is an apt symbol of this, and Jewish proselyte baptism symbolized death to the old life and resurrection to the new, while the baptism of John symbolized the renunciation of the world that was and entry upon the life of the world that was to be. Here, however, we have something deeper than this. Paul says: 'Are ye ignorant that all we who were baptized into Christ Jesus were baptized into his death? We were buried therefore with him through baptism into death, that like as Christ was raised from the dead through the glory of the Father, so we also might walk in newness of life. For if we have been united with him by the likeness of his death, we shall be also by the likeness of his resurrection; knowing this, that our old man was crucified with him.'[1] Here, it is to be noted, it is not merely death to the past, or a death that could be compared with the death of Christ, but a spiritual sharing of His death.[2] Baptism is not a symbol of repentance or of belief, but of union with Christ in His death and resurrection.[3] 'Even so reckon ye also yourselves', says Paul below, 'to be dead indeed unto sin, but alive unto God through our Lord Jesus Christ.'[4]

In the previous chapter, when we were examining the significance of the Cross, we saw that in the thought of the New Testament, when seen against the background of the teaching of the Old Testament, the death of Christ must become the organ of man's approach to God that it may be the organ of divine

[1] Rom. vi. 3 ff. Cf. Cyril of Jerusalem, *Catechetical Lectures* xx. 6 (P.G., xxxiii, 1893, col. 1082, E. Tr. by E. H. Gifford, *Nicene and Post-Nicene Fathers*, vii, 1894, p. 148): 'Let no one suppose that Baptism is merely the grace of remission of sins, or . . . of adoption; . . . it purges our sins, and ministers to us the gift of the Holy Ghost, so also it is the counterpart of the sufferings of Christ.' Cyril then quotes the passage from Romans and adds: 'These words he spake to some who were disposed to think that Baptism ministers to us the remission of sins, and adoption, but has not further the fellowship also, by representation, of Christ's true sufferings.'

[2] Writing on 1 Pet. ii. 24, F. W. Beare, *The First Epistle of Peter*, 1947, p. 124, says: 'The doctrine of baptism as the sacrament through which we enter into Christ's experience of death and resurrection is again brought to remembrance. The ultimate meaning of the cross is realized in us only when we die to the old life . . . and enter, united with Christ, into the new life that God causes to spring forth.' A. Deissmann, *Paul*, E. Tr., 2nd ed., 1926, pp. 182 f., says: 'The ancient Christians were able easily to understand the mystical meaning of the several stages of baptism to the death, burial and resurrection with Christ, because having been baptised as adults, they had an indelibly vivid recollection of the ceremony performed upon them by immersion. It is by no means easy for us, brought up in the practice of infant baptism, to realise this vividness.'

[3] Cf. J. Schneider, *Die Taufe im Neuen Testament*, 1952, p. 32: 'Baptism is not the symbol of repentance, but an experience in which God gives to the penitent that which he does not yet have: the forgiveness of sins.' W. F. Flemington, E.T., lxii, 1950–51, p. 356, says that the meaning of baptism, to which Paul appeals, must have been Christian teaching generally acknowledged *circa* A.D. 58, and it shows that 'baptism means such an identification with Christ's death and resurrection that we die with Him to sin and rise with Him to newness of life.' Yet when on the following pages Flemington turns to show that infant baptism is on theological grounds congruous with the whole Christian revelation, he strangely leaves entirely out of account this acknowledged New Testament teaching. Nothing could more clearly indicate that the name baptism is being appropriated for something entirely different.

[4] Rom. vi. 11.

power unto him. The power is there, waiting to invade his life when by faith he yields his life to it. Now we see that baptism, which is the initiatory rite of the Church, is brought into relation with this first experience of the power of the Cross, lifting a man so to enter into its experience that he may be crucified with Christ and become a new creation. It cannot be even remotely suggested that an infant in the moment of baptism has an experience of the recreating power of God in Christ and of the surrender to God that makes the Cross the organ of its approach in faith to God.[1] This death with Christ means much in the thought of Paul, and he returns to it again and again. 'That I may know him and the power of his resurrection, and the fellowship of his sufferings, becoming conformed unto his death.'[2] 'I have been crucified with Christ; yet I live: and yet no longer I, but Christ liveth in me: and the life which I now live in the flesh I live in faith, the faith which is in the Son of God, who loved me and gave himself up for me.'[3] This thought he brings into relation with baptism in the passage from Romans vi quoted above, and in that other passage from Colossians, quoted earlier: 'Having been buried with him in baptism, wherein ye were also raised with him through faith

---

[1] N. P. Williams frankly acknowledges that infant baptism is something quite different from New Testament baptism in subjects and significance. He says that when we repeat the clause of the Creed 'one baptism *for the remission of sins*', 'what we affirm is our belief in baptism as anciently administered to adults . . . : we neither affirm nor deny the legitimacy of infant baptism, which is a collateral development from the original idea and institution of baptism, and which depends for its authority not upon any credal or conciliar formula, but upon the actual practice of the Church and the semi-articulate instincts of the general body of Christendom' (*op. cit.*, p. 554). In his essay in *Essays Catholic and Critical*, ed. by E. G. Selwyn, 1926, pp. 369 ff., however, he bases his argument on the Dominical institution of the sacrament, and tacitly ignores the fact that by his own admission no Dominical institution of infant baptism can be maintained. Cf. p. 373: 'If our Lord, with all His indifference to mere ceremonial, did actually "institute" the rites known as "sacraments", then those rites must be of the very highest and most central importance in the Christian life; and it is difficult to see how such an importance can be ascribed to them, unless it is the case that through them God does something for man which man cannot do for himself, that is, unless they are the means or vehicles of supernatural grace;' also p. 419: 'we are entitled to conclude that the "institution" . . . of the two original and fundamental sacraments . . . by the Founder of Christianity Himself, may be taken as proved.' It is hardly legitimate to transfer conclusions based on the Dominical institution of the sacrament to one which admittedly 'depends for its authority . . . upon the actual practice of the Church and the semi-articulate instincts of . . . Christendom.'

[2] Phil. iii. 10.

[3] Gal. ii. 20.

in the working of God.'[1] Both of these passages see in baptism an entering into the experience of Christ, and link it with the fundamental teaching of the New Testament about the death of Christ, which itself has a wider setting in the teaching of the Bible as a whole, as has been already said in the preceding chapters.

It is interesting to observe that when a paedobaptist defines the significance of baptism he ignores all of this. Thus Professor T. W. Manson says baptism signifies (a) admission to a community, (b) appropriation by Christ, and (c) the gift of the spirit.[2] The first he likens to birth into a family which does not wait until one applies for it; the second to the claim of parents upon their children, which precedes understanding or response; the third to mother-love, which is not withheld until requested. It will be noted that in this definition baptism is conceived of as a rite performed upon a wholly passive individual. It makes no demand whatever upon the one baptized in the moment of baptism. In the thought of the New Testament it signifies first and foremost union with Christ in His death and resurrection, and a newness of life which has its source in Him, and it is because of this union with Christ that it signifies admission to the community of the Church. For the Church is His body, and they who are of the Church are in Christ, and Christ in them. 'If any man hath not the Spirit of Christ, he is none of his. And if Christ is in you, the body is dead because of sin; but the spirit is life because of righteousness.'[3] Professor Manson rightly says baptism signifies appropriation by Christ, but omits to observe that it also signifies self-surrender to Him. It signifies the gift of the Spirit, indeed, because it signifies the gift of Christ. But the gift of Christ, while freely offered to all by One Whose love is as unconstrained as a mother's and whose offer precedes understanding or response, must be accepted to be possessed. If the possession of the gift were

[1] Col. ii. 12.
[2] Cf. *S.J.T.*, *loc. cit.*, p. 401. So W. G. Young, *ibid.*, v, 1952, pp. 29 ff., maintains that baptism is essentially the same whether in the case of infants or adults, and declares that in it God receives a person into the Church. Unlike Cullmann he would not appear to ask for faith before baptism in the case of either infant or adult, and would seem to dismiss the New Testament teaching that baptism is a sharing of the death and resurrection of Jesus as unworthy even of mention.   [3] Rom. viii. 9 f.

determined by the love of God alone, it would not belong only to such infants as were brought for baptism, but would belong to all men; it if were determined by the act of involuntary baptism, it would be mechanically controlled by men, and the worst superstitions that have gathered round the act of baptism would be justified.[1] It is in another atmosphere that Paul moves when he once more uses the thought of the death and resurrection of Christ in connection with the inner experience of those who are in Him. 'If the Spirit of him that raised up Jesus from the dead dwelleth in you, he that raised up Christ Jesus from the dead shall quicken also your mortal bodies through his Spirit that dwelleth in you.'[2]

Baptism is a symbol, and it is the constant teaching of the whole Bible that the symbol has no meaning without that which it symbolizes. As a mere external act it is as dead as the sacrifices which the prophets condemned.[3] Professor Cullmann allows that faith is in all cases essential to give meaning to baptism, but if that faith is something that may or may not be born in the heart many years after the baptism is administered it is useless to invest the symbol with meaning. The religious ritual that is valid, whether it be sacrifice in ancient Israel or baptism in the Church, is that which is charged with meaning in the moment of its performance, and a hollow baptism is as vain as a hollow sacrifice. The robbing of baptism of its Biblical significance leads to the creation of something else to take its place, something which is not called baptism, but to which the real meaning of New Testament baptism has to be transferred. The symbol is of less importance than that which it symbolizes. It is of importance that Baptists

---

[1] Cf. N. P. Williams, *op. cit.*, p. 551: 'It might in fact be contended, that if the epithets "magical" and "mechanical" can be applied to any parts of the traditional sacramental system at all, it is the custom of infant baptism first and foremost to which they ought to be affixed; and such a contention might be thought to derive some force from the curious stratagems employed by the Jesuit missionaries in North America to enable them to baptise dying infants amongst the heathen surreptitiously (by unobservedly flicking a few drops of water over the infant's face, and simultaneously whispering *ego te baptizo*, etc., whilst apparently engaged in conversation with the parents), for the purpose of adding as many souls as possible to the Kingdom of God.'

[2] Rom. viii. 11.

[3] Cf. N. H. Snaith, *I Believe in* . . . , p. 113: 'No rite can of itself be effective, nor can any organization make it so apart from the faith of the believer.'

no less than others should remember this. What matters most is not that a man has been voluntarily immersed, any more than that he has been baptized in infancy, but that he has truly died with Christ and been raised again to newness of life in Him, so that his life is now hid with Christ in God. The symbol is worthless without that which it symbolizes. It must be the organ of the soul's approach in faith and surrender to God before it can become the organ of God's approach in power to him.

When we turn to the other great Christian sacrament, we find an even greater diversity of view amongst Christians, and yet deeper divisions. There is no agreement even as to the name by which it is known. To some it is the Lord's Supper, to others the Holy Communion, to others the Eucharist, and to others the Mass. These various names indicate the dominant view of the character of the sacrament amongst various groups, though it should be remembered that there are few, if any, who would interpret it exclusively in terms of memorial, or communion, or thanksgiving, or sacrifice. While the primary emphasis is on this or that element, other elements are also found.

For our present purpose we must consider first of all how far this sacrament can be understood in terms of sacrifice, and this is precisely the point where the deepest cleavage is to be found. That it has been regarded as a sacrifice from the earliest times is beyond question. In the Didache we read: 'And on the Lord's day assemble yourselves together and break bread and give thanks, after confessing your transgressions, that your sacrifice may be pure. And let no man who has a difference with his fellow join your assembly till they have been reconciled, that your sacrifice be not defiled.'[1] The language of sacrifice was used of the sacrament by many of the Fathers of the Church,[2] and became firmly established until it was challenged by the reformers.

---

[1] *Didache* xiv (cf. J. B. Lightfoot, *The Apostolic Fathers*, ed. by J. R. Harmer, 1891, pp. 223 f., 234).

[2] Cf., *e.g.* Justin Martyr, *Dialogue with Trypho* xli, cxvii (*P.G.*, vi, 1884, cols. 564, 745 ff., E. Tr. by A. Lukyn Williams, 1930, pp. 81 f., 241 f.), Irenaeus, *Against Heresies* IV, xvii. f. (*P.G.*, vii, 1882, cols. 1023 f., E. Tr. by A. Roberts and W. H. Rambaut, *The Writings of Irenaeus*, i, 1874, pp. 430 f.; ed. W. W. Harvey, IV, xxix. 5, xxx., cf. *S. Irenaei Libros uinque adversus Haereses*, ii, 1857, pp. 199 f.).

Nevertheless, the sacrament was not regarded only as a sacrifice. It was also a eucharist, or service of thanksgiving, and a communion, whereby the believer was brought into union with Christ. The sacrificial aspect of the sacrament became isolated from the other elements, however, and came to be conceived to be effective apart from them,[1] and it was this development which led to the objections of the Reformers.

In this development Aquinas played an important part. Srawley observes that his teaching 'encouraged the separation of the ideas of sacrifice and communion, which had already taken place in practice, and increased the tendency to view the Mass as an *opus operatum* completed in the act of consecration.'[2] The effect of this encouragement, to use the words of Srawley again, was that 'an almost magical conception of the operation of the sacraments came to be current, which took no account of the spiritual condition of the recipients. Thus the benefits of the Mass were regarded as operating mechanically for the good of those on whose behalf it was offered.'[3]

It is to be observed that this is not merely a conceptual distinction between two aspects of the one sacrament. If the one effect could be experienced where the other was absent, they were separate and independent interpretations of the significance of the rite. This is reflected in the decrees of the Council of Trent, where the articles dealing with the Most Holy Sacrament of the Eucharist

---

[1] Cf. A. Pohle, *The Catholic Encyclopedia*, x, 1913, p. 7a: 'The simple fact that numerous heretics . . . repudiated the Mass . . . while retaining the Sacrament of the true Body and Blood of Christ, proves that the Sacrament of the Eucharist is something essentially different from the Sacrifice of the Mass.' While he holds that they are inseparable, since the consecrating and sacrificial powers of the priest coincide, he finds that one is directed to the sanctification of men and the other to the glory of God. It will be seen that the only thing which holds these two essentially separate aspects of the sacrament together here is the power of the priest, and it is implied that while neither is independent of the priest each aspect is independent of the other. Instead of the two-way traffic which has been found throughout the present study we have here two separate streams of one-way traffic, which meet only in the priest. C. Lattey, *H.J.*, xl, 1941–42, p. 187, observes that 'Catholic doctrine does not in all cases require corresponding dispositions in the recipient of the sacrament'.

[2] Cf. Hastings's *E.R.E.*, v, 1912, p. 562a. Cf. Aquinas, *Summa Theologica* III, lxxx. 12 (E. Tr. by the Fathers of the English Dominican Province, Part III, iii, 1923, p. 402): 'The perfection of this sacrament does not lie in the use of the faithful, but in the consecration of the matter.'   [3] *Loc. cit.*

and with the Sacrifice of the Mass are quite separate, the former being drawn up in 1551 and the latter not until eleven years later.[1] It is also reflected in the teaching of Bellarmine, who distinguished between the Eucharist, which could only benefit the recipient, and the Mass, which benefited those for whom it was offered by the mere fact of its being offered.[2]

That this latter view, when separated from the other, should lead to magical, or quasi-magical, views of the sacrament was inevitable. For it rested on a purely *ex opere operato* view of the rite, similar to the popular view of the potency of ritual that the pre-exilic prophets had condemned. Against such a view the protest of the Reformers was both natural and necessary, though this does not mean that it took the right form. It would have been wiser to return to the view that bound the various aspects of the sacrament indissolubly together, rather than to reject wholly the sacrificial view because of this separate development it had had. The Roman view of the Mass, as defined by the Council of Trent, declares: 'If anyone shall say that in the Mass a true and proper sacrifice is not offered unto God, or that what is offered is none other than that Christ is given to us to eat, let him be anathema.'[3] As against such a position, so early as 1523 Zwingli had defended the thesis that 'Christ, who offered Himself once for all on the Cross, is for ever the effectual sacrifice and victim for the sins of all the faithful. From this it follows that the Mass is not a sacrifice but a commemoration of the sacrifice once for all offered on the Cross, and as it were a seal of the redemption afforded in Christ.'[4] So far as the first part of this thesis is concerned, many who yet

[1] The Eucharist was dealt with on Oct. 11th, 1551, in the thirteenth session, and the Sacrifice of the Mass on Sept. 17th, 1562, in the twenty-second session. Cf. F. Kattenbusch, in *P.R.E.*, 3rd ed., xii, 1903, p. 690. Similarly in the *Dictionnaire de Théologie Catholique* the sacrament of the Eucharist and the sacrifice of the Mass are dealt with in two separate articles.

[2] Cf. *De Eucharistia* III, xxii (*Disputationes de controversiis Christianae fidei*, iii, 1613, cols. 570 ff.) and *De Missa* I, xix (*ibid.*, col. 774).

[3] Cf. Twenty-second Session, Canon I (cf. G. D. Mansi, *Sacrorum Conciliorum nova et amplissima collectio*, xxxiii, 1902, col. 131).

[4] Cf. Darwell Stone, *History of the Doctrine of the Holy Eucharist*, ii, 1909, p. 38; S. M. Jackson, *Huldreich Zwingli*, 1901, p. 183. The Latin text is given in B. J. Kidd, *Documents illustrative of the Continental Reformation*, 1911, p. 412.

regarded the sacrament as a sacrifice would have agreed. Chrysostom said: 'It is not another sacrifice . . . but we offer always the
same; or rather we perform a remembrance of a sacrifice',[1] and
Duns Scotus in the later Middle Ages 'shows . . . anxiety to
defend the unique character of the sacrifice of the Cross, and
maintains that the sacrifice of the Mass has not the same value as
the Passion of Christ, and that in it Christ does not offer immediately by an act of His own will, though He is offered as being
contained in the sacrifice.'[2]

Nevertheless, the Reformers rejected the whole sacrificial
interpretation of the sacrament. Calvin declares the belief that
the Mass was a sacrifice for obtaining the remission of sins 'a most
pestilential error',[3] and the thirty-first Article of the Church of
England, as contained in the Book of Common Prayer, reads:
'The offering of Christ once made is that perfect redemption,
propitiation, and satisfaction, for all the sins of the whole world,
both original and actual; and there is none other satisfaction
for sin, but that alone. Wherefore the sacrifices of Masses, in
which it was commonly said that the priest did offer Christ for
the quick and the dead, to have remission of pain or guilt,
were blasphemous fables, and dangerous deceits.'

In the thesis of Zwingli, quoted above, it is declared that the
Mass is not a sacrifice but a memorial service, as though these
were mutually exclusive. The memorial significance has been
greatly emphasized by the Reformed Churches, and it may
rightly be found there. It is true that the words 'This do in remembrance of Me' are found only in Luke[4] and Paul[5] and not in the

[1] Cf. *Homilies on Hebrews* xvii. 3 (*P.G.*, lxiii, 1862, col. 131, E. Tr. by F. Gardiner,
Nicene and Post-Nicene Fathers, xiv, 1890, p. 449a). Cf. also Cyprian, *Epistle* lxiii (to
Caecilius), 14, 17 (ed. W. Hartel, ii, p. 714, E. Tr. by R. E. Wallis, i, pp. 218 f.).

[2] Cf. J. H. Srawley, in Hastings's *E.R.E.*, v, 1912, p. 562b. Cf. *Quaestiones quodlibetales*
xx (Duns Scotus, *Opera omnia*, xxvi, 1895, pp. 298 ff.).

[3] Cf. *Institutes*, E. Tr. by H. Beveridge, ii, 1869, p. 607. For a study of the Calvinist
doctrine of the sacrament, cf. J. Cadier, *E.Th.R.*, xxvi, 1951, pp. 5–156.

[4] Lk. xxii. 19. In the R.S.V. these words are removed to the margin, along with the
rest of verses 19b, 20, as not belonging to the original text of the Gospel. For the textual
evidence cf. M.-J. Lagrange, *Évangile selon St. Luc*, 7th ed., 1948, pp. 545 ff. F. C. Grant,
An Introduction to New Testament Thought, p. 283, says: 'The "longer reading" (vss.
19b–20) closely resembles the narrative found in First Corinthians and probably represents
an early attempt to complete what must have looked like a fragmentary and incomplete
account of the institution of the Supper.'   [5] 1 Cor. xi. 24 f.

other three Gospels, and their authenticity has accordingly been challenged,[1] but if any repetition of the Last Supper is observed at all, a memorial element inevitably belongs to it. Of itself, it must recall that night, and if when bread and wine are taken our Lord's words 'This is my body'[2] and 'This is my blood of the covenant'[3] are repeated, His death on Calvary must be remembered. A memorial significance is integral to the sacrament.

Beyond this, we may rightly find varied significance in the rite. None of His people can think of their Lord's death without thanksgiving for the redemption which He wrought, and a eucharistic element must therefore be present. Nor can it be supposed that this is in any way exceptionable. Moreover, the sacrament is a present experience. 'Take, eat' and 'Drink ye' are found to refer not merely to the symbols, but to Him Whom they represent, Who may be received into our hearts to order our lives. The element of communion is therefore to be found here—communion with Christ and communion with the Church, which, no less than the bread, though in a different way, is the Body of Christ. It is by no accident that the Fourth Gospel gives the discourse on the True Vine in its account of the Last Supper in the Upper Room,[4] where Jesus calls for a oneness with Himself as intimate as the union of the branch and the tree. Moreover, since this is no individual feast, its social significance for the fellowship of the Church of Christ, which must draw all its life from Him and which must therefore know a profound unity of spirit when it is truly in Him, cannot be overlooked or forgotten. Further, this rite is a sacrament, not merely in the sense of something sacred and ministering grace to the believer, but in the sense that the word *sacramentum* acquired in Latin, viz. a vow of loyalty.[5] 'This is my blood of the *covenant*',[6] or 'This cup is the

---

[1] On this cf. N. P. Williams, in *Essays Catholic and Critical*, ed. by E. G. Selwyn, 1926, p. 382; J. Jeremias, *Die Abendmahlsworte Jesu*, 2nd ed., 1949, pp. 81 f.; A. J. B. Higgins, *The Lord's Supper in the New Testament*, 1952, pp. 38 f.

[2] Mk. xiv. 22.   [3] Mk. xiv. 24.   [4] Jn. xv.

[5] It should be remembered that baptism also was a *sacramentum*, and it is hard to see how this term could be applied to infant baptism. Cf. E. G. Selwyn, *The First Epistle of St. Peter*, 1946, p. 205: 'The idea that baptism was a seal of contract given by a good conscience towards God is not far removed from that which led to the application of the word *sacramentum*, "military oath", to Baptism and the Eucharist.'   [6] Mk. xiv. 24.

new *covenant* in my blood',[1] reminds us that here as ever we deal with something that is two-sided. We receive enrichment, but we also bring loyalty. We remember the establishment of the covenant that we may renew the covenant by bringing afresh the spirit of our consecration.[2]

All of this is in close accord with New Testament thought, and also with Old Testament teaching, and much of it with the thought of the Old Testament on sacrifice.[3] The Passover, with which the Last Supper was associated by reason of the time when it took place, was a memorial, but a memorial which was designed to awaken gratitude and renewed consecration. In this and in other sacrifices the offerer ate part of the sacrificed animal, and it is well known that one theory of the primary meaning of sacrifice is that it was designed to bring about communion with the deity. While it is questionable if we can rightly isolate a single element and label it the primary element, it is certain that this element of communion entered into some sacrifices. Into many of the sacrificial meals the social element entered, just as it enters into the Christian sacrament which we are considering. It has been sufficiently insisted through all the present lectures that in the teaching of the Old Testament sacrifice can only mediate blessing when it is the organ of the offerer's approach to God and renewal of right spiritual relations with Him.

In one respect, however, we frequently find the contrast with the Old Testament emphasized. It is often pointed out that whereas Jesus said 'Drink ye . . . this is my blood',[4] and whereas in the Fourth Gospel we read 'he that eateth my flesh and drinketh my blood abideth in me and I in him',[5] this is alien to the whole thought and teaching of the Old Testament, where the blood is

[1] Lk. xxii. 20.
[2] Cf. Martin Bucer: 'Three things are bestowed and received, the symbols of bread and wine, the body and blood of the Lord, and the ratification of the new covenant and of the remission of sins' (cf. Darwell Stone, *op. cit.*, ii, 1909, p. 47; the Latin text, abbreviated in Stone's rendering, stands in M. Bucer, *Scripta Anglicana*, 1577, pp. 544 f.).
[3] Cf. the writer's article 'Sacrament and Sacrifice', *H.J.*, xl, 1941–42, pp. 181 ff.
[4] Matt. xxvi. 27 f.
[5] Jn. vi. 56.

forbidden on any account to be consumed.[1] It is to be observed that in the law of the Old Testament the blood was not to be consumed because it was too sacred to be consumed. The blood was the life.[2] While in the Lord's Supper actual blood was not drunk, but only a symbol of that blood, what is here affirmed is in harmony with Old Testament thought. Christ was giving His life, that which was supremely sacred, not merely on behalf of men but to them, to be the source of their life. 'I live; and yet no longer I, but Christ liveth in me'.[3] The wine was a symbol of the blood which is the life, and the life of Christ may flow into the life of His people, as the life of the vine flows into its branches. Sacred indeed was the blood of Christ, and sacred too His life. But the life that was taken was not destroyed, and He Who died lives and lives to give Himself to His people. The wine is therefore not alone a symbol of the blood that was shed, but of the life that still is, and he who rightly drinks of the wine drinks not alone in remembrance but in enrichment; for he receives anew of the life of His Redeemer and Lord, Who is present in the sacrament, and present to bless.

While, therefore, as a memorial this rite might point—and certainly does point—to the sacrifice of the Cross, which was offered once for all and needs not to be repeated, other elements of its significance have sacrificial associations though they are not primarily memorial, but have reference to the actual experience

---

[1] Cf. C. G. Montefiore, *The Synoptic Gospels*, i, 1909, p. 326: 'I would also venture to suggest how difficult it is for us to believe that a Palestinian or Galilean Jew could have suggested that in drinking wine his disciples were, even symbolically, drinking blood. For the horror with which the drinking of blood was regarded by the Jews is well known'; J. Klausner, *Jesus of Nazareth*, E. Tr. by H. Danby, 2nd ed., p. 329: 'It is quite impossible to admit that Jesus would have said to his disciples that they should eat of his body and drink of his blood'; H. Loewe, in *A Rabbinic Anthology*, 1938, p. 647: 'Jews shudder at certain passages in Hebrews and Romans, and the Gospel verses describing the institution of the Eucharist are painfully repugnant to them. This is due to the blood element which is so prominent and, indeed, essential.' Since there can be little doubt that Hebrews and Romans were written by Jews, it is hard to see why Jesus could not have uttered the words of institution. A first-century Jew, who had been trained in Palestine, when he wrote 1 Cor. xi. 24 ff., found no difficulty in supposing that Jesus spoke these words, and he was better acquainted with the contemporary Jewish mind than any modern writer can be. If a Pharisaically trained Jew of that age did not find the words abhorrent, where is the evidence that Jesus must have found them abhorrent?

[2] Lev. xvii. 11.   [3] Gal. ii. 20.

of the partaker. That the sacrifice of Calvary is a single historical event, which cannot be repeated, is agreed by all. The thesis of Zwingli, already quoted, would seem to imply that Roman Catholics held that the sacrifice of the Cross had exhausted its power and needed to be renewed.[1] This does less than justice to their thought. Rupert of Deutz, who held that Christ was indeed present on the altar, declares that this 'was not that He may again suffer, but that to faith, to which all past things are present, His passion may be represented by way of a memory',[2] while Thomas Aquinas declares that the sacrament is a representative image of the Passion of Christ.[3] Describing the views of William of Auvergne,[4] Srawley says: 'By his one oblation of the Cross, Christ has reconciled and sanctified the world. The sacrifice of the Mass is the application by the will of Christ of the benefits which accrue from the sacrifice of the Cross'.[5] A modern Romanist writer, protesting against the Protestant misunderstanding of the Roman Catholic positions, says: 'The sacrifice once offered on the Cross filled the infinite reservoirs to overflowing with healing waters: but those who thirst after justice must come with their chalices and draw out what they need to quench their thirst.'[6] While the metaphor here is not really

[1] Cf. J. Calvin, *Institutes*, E. Tr. by H. Beveridge, ii, p. 609: 'To such a sacrifice'—*i.e.* Christ's sacrifice on the Cross—' . . . shall we, as if it were imperfect, presume daily to append innumerable sacrifices?' Calvin goes on to dismiss the view that the one sacrifice is repeated as an imposture by which the father of lies is wont to cloak his fraud, and as smoke easily dispersed.

[2] *De Trinitate et operibus suis: in Genesim* VI, xxxii (*P.L.*, clxvii, 1893, col. 431). Cf. Darwell Stone, *op. cit.*, i, 1909, p. 292.

[3] *Summa Theologica* III, lxxxiii. 1 (E. Tr., Part III, iii, 1923, p. 434). Cf. C. H. Dodd, in Manson's *Companion to the Bible*, 1939, p. 386: 'In speaking of the broken bread as His body, and associating the cup with His blood, He was effecting in a symbol that sacrifice of Himself which He was about to accomplish in fact. In giving to His disciples the bread to eat and the cup to drink, He was associating them with Him in that sacrifice and its consequences.'

[4] *De sacramento encharistiae* (*Opera Omnia*, 1591, pp. 410 f.).

[5] Cf. Hastings's *E.R.E.*, v, 1912, p. 561b. Cf. E. Masure, *The Christian Sacrifice*, E. Tr. by Dom Illtyd Trethowan, 1944, p. 237: 'If the Church is . . . to offer a sacrifice herself, this cannot be other than that of Christ and the Cross, since we already know that only this is acceptable to the Father for all time. In short, the Church must offer in all ages and in every place a sacrifice which is at the same time hers and Christ's, enabling the faithful to participate by communicating with the victim in all the fruits, otherwise unobtainable, whi were won on Calvary.'

[6] Cf. J. Pohle, *The Catholic Encyclopedia*, x, 1913, p. 13b.

sacrificial, and it suggests that the action in the sacrament is merely the action of the worshipper, this passage is relevant as showing that there is full recognition of the once-for-allness of Calvary.

It is to be observed that the very Epistle in the New Testament which speaks of the once-for-allness of the Cross speaks also of 'crucifying afresh the Son of God'.[1] Here is a warning that we must not be the slaves of language, and that thought is more elusive than words. As an event of history the Cross is unique; yet there is a sense in which it may be repeated.[2] Pohle, who has been quoted above, draws a distinction between objective and subjective redemption.[3] This is in harmony with what has been said in the previous chapter, where it was argued that the sacrifice of the Cross becomes effective for a man in the moment when he makes the Cross the organ of his approach to God in surrender. As an objective sacrifice it took place once for all under Pontius Pilate; yet for us it is a present sacrifice in the moment of our obedience and submission. The New Testament knows two attitudes to the Cross of Christ, and two only. They who reject Him and His way, and cast Him out of their hearts, crucify Him afresh and are numbered with His crucifiers; they who make His Cross the organ of their approach to God are crucified with Him.[4] They die and are born anew, because they die with Him and rise to newness of life in Him.

It may now be observed that Paul brings similar language into relation with the sacrament of the Lord's Supper. He says: 'Whosoever shall eat the bread or drink the cup of the Lord unworthily shall be guilty of the body and the blood of the Lord,'[5] What Paul clearly means is the same as is meant in the other passage by crucifying afresh the Son of God. The agony of Christ is renewed when men reject Him, or when they make the sacrament of the Lord's Supper a hollow formality, like the sacrifices the prophets denounced. If to those who come unworthily the Supper is in any sense a renewal of the Crucifixion

[1] Heb. vi. 6.

[2] Cf. O. C. Quick, *The Christian Sacraments*, 1927, pp. 199 f.: 'Christ died once in time, but He offers Himself eternally. In the Eucharist we make a memorial of Christ's death; but we make before God an offering of Himself.'

[3] *Loc. cit.*   [4] Rom. vi. 5 ff., Gal. ii. 20.   [5] I Cor. xi. 27.

in judgement, to those who come worthily it may be a renewal of the power of the Cross in blessing.

Here is a sacrificial view of the Lord's Supper which is in the fullest accord with Biblical thought as a whole and with New Testament thought in particular. It does not isolate the sacrificial significance and make it operative for those who do not make the sacrament the organ of their approach to God, but recognizes that as all valid sacrifice must bear a two-way traffic, so this must bear a two-way traffic.[1] Paul's insistence on the spirit of the partaker, and on the necessity to eat worthily, makes this clear. The same act may be the organ of judgement or of blessing. For the effect of the act is not independent of the spirit of him who partakes. William of Auvergne maintained that 'the first and chief sacrifice is that of ourselves, without the offering of which nothing that we present to God is pleasing or acceptable to Him.'[2] Sacrament and sacrifice cannot be separated from one another, but must coalesce. The whole mediates grace to a man's heart, provided it is also an offering which he brings to God. So often we think of sacrifice merely as man's offering to God, and not also as the bearer of divine blessing to man, or as a quasi-magical means of bringing blessing to him without regard to his spirit. One of the fundamental notes running through the Bible is that separated these things are futile and vain, but that together they become rich and full of blessing.

In so far as it is a sacrifice, what is offered to God is not the self-surrender to which reference has so often been made. The Reformers held it to be preposterous that a man should suppose that he could bring to God any gift that was worthy.[3] This

---

[1] Cf. the definition of sacrifice offered by E. Masure, *op. cit.*, E. Tr., p. 78: 'Sacrifice is a sensible sign (or rite) in which under the symbols (or species) of a victim, man, to pay his dues to God and so to realize his end, bears witness that he renounces sin which is his evil (immolation), and that he turns to God who is his good (oblation)—hoping that the divine acceptance, sanctifying his offering, will win for him the heavenly alliance at which he aims and that the victim will bring him by communion the guarantee of it.'

[2] Cf. J. H. Srawley, in Hastings's *E.R.E.*, v, 1912, p. 561b; also Darwell Stone, *op. cit.*, i, 1909, pp. 317 f.

[3] Cf. J. Calvin, *Institutes*, E. Tr. by H. Beveridge, ii, p. 612: 'The sacrifice of the mass pretends to give a price to God to be received as satisfaction. . . . When the liberality of the divine goodness ought to have been recognized, and thanks returned, he makes God to be his debtor.'

would indeed be preposterous if he came with any gift which derived from himself. In speaking of the initial act of surrender to Christ in the preceding chapter we said that a man must so yield himself that the old man is crucified with Christ and dies. What he brings to God is the sacrifice of Christ, and he becomes united with Christ, so that he offers to God the obedience of Christ, with Whom he is now one.[1] His surrender is the condition of his salvation, and not its organ—the condition of his approach to God and not its channel. He dies that he may live, and in the same moment he is lifted on the obedience of Christ into the presence of God and receives from Him the new self which derives its life from Christ.[2]

What, then, is the relation of the sacrament of the Lord's Supper to baptism? In so far as it has sacrificial significance, is it not closely similar to the significance we have found in baptism? If baptism is a dying unto Christ and rising anew in Him, how can the experience symbolized in the Lord's Supper also be a dying with Christ and a rising anew in Him? Here we are brought, as so often, into the paradox of truth and experience.

Let it be noted, first, however, that in the Early Church the two sacraments of baptism and the Lord's Supper were brought into close association.[3] The newly baptized were admitted immedi-

---

[1] Cf. W. Spens, in *Essays Catholic and Critical*, ed. by E. G. Selwyn, 1926, p. 436: 'The Last Supper and the Eucharist are not separate sacrifices from that of Calvary, but supply a necessary element in the sacrifice of Calvary, by expressly investing our Lord's death before God and man with its sacrificial significance.' Cf. O. C. Quick, *The Christian Sacraments*, 1927, p. 199: 'Christian people may rightly offer Christ as an oblation apart from themselves, only in so far as they honestly intend that through their action the Christ, Whom they offer, may draw them into His own self-offering.'

[2] P. Melanchthon protested that 'we do not offer Christ to God, but He offered Himself once for all' (cf. B. J. Kidd, *Documents illustrative of the Continental Reformation*, 1911, p. 93). With this the present writer is in full agreement. But, as is clear from what has been said in the preceding and the present chapters, it is here maintained that Christ's sacrifice on the Cross becomes our sacrifice when it is the organ of our approach to God, and it then becomes the organ of God's approach to us in power. As an objective sacrifice it cannot be repeated, but as our sacrifice it may be renewed—not by a priestly act, but by our approach in the spirit which makes possible the two-way traffic.

[3] Cf. E. G. Selwyn, *The First Epistle of St. Peter*, 1946, pp. 297 f.: 'The context of 1 Pet. ii. 1–10 is baptismal as well as Eucharistic; and this should be borne in mind when we speak of the passage as sacramental. The custom of keeping the two sacraments together, in time as well as in thought, which was characteristic of the Church in the early centuries may well have had its origin in Apostolic times.'

ately to the Lord's table. This was before the baptismal rite had been torn asunder into two. It was a single ceremony, and it and the first communion belonged intimately together. But with the growth of infant baptism this led to infant communion. Cyprian refers to children who at the outset of their lives were brought to the Lord's table,[1] and Augustine teaches that since John vi. 53 shows that this sacrament is as essential to salvation as baptism, infants need this as much as the other.[2] This practice continued for many centuries and is still found in the Greek Orthodox Church. In the Roman Church it continued down to the twelfth or thirteenth century, but then disappeared,[3] and the Council of Trent decreed that children below the age of reason were bound by no necessity to observe this sacrament.[4] Here, therefore, the two sacraments that were seen to belong together were torn apart, and the Churches which have split the rites of baptism into two rites give the name of baptism to that which has no Scriptural baptismal significance and link the first communion with the other which has no Scriptural warrant. It is further interesting to observe that the belief in baptismal regeneration has persisted, while the belief in the necessity for the sacrament of the Lord's Supper has been abandoned, despite the clearer Scriptural warrant for the latter than for the former. 'Except ye eat the flesh of the Son of Man and drink his blood ye have not life in yourselves. He that eateth my flesh and drinketh my blood hath eternal life; and I will raise him up at the last day.'[5]

To return to the relation between the two sacraments, we may observe that in New Testament thought both are related to the Cross of Christ, the great central fact of our faith. That is an act of history which cannot be repeated and which needs not to be repeated. There the sacrifice which transcended any Temple

---

[1] Cf. *On the Lapsed* 9 (ed. W. Hartel, i, 1868, p. 43, E. Tr. by R. E. Wallis, i, 1870, p. 357).

[2] Cf. *De peccatorum meritis et remissione* xx (*P.L.*, xliv, 1865, col. 123).

[3] Cf. G. Rietschel, in *P.R.E.*, 3rd ed., x, 1901, p. 290, where it is stated that it is doubtful if it survived in Germany after the twelfth century, while the Council of Bordeaux in 1255 pronounced against it.

[4] Twenty-first Session, Canon IV (Mansi, *op. cit.*, xxxiii. col. 123).

[5] Jn. vi. 53 f.

sacrifice was offered. That sacrifice becomes effective for men of every generation in the moment when by surrender and faith they make the Cross the organ of their approach to God. Baptism symbolizes the initial experience of death and resurrection, of union with Christ and rebirth in Him, of the forgiveness of sins and the cleansing of the heart. It is only appropriate to mark that experience, and not to anticipate it by many years. It is meaningless without that which it symbolizes, but it may be a channel of blessing to those who know the experience which it symbolizes. It marks the time when the historical death of Christ enters anew into history in their individual experience, and gives an objectivity to their covenant with their Lord. This is an experience which does not need to be repeated, and hence baptism is a sacrament which needs to be administered but once.

The sacrament of the Lord's Supper as a memorial continues to remind the believer of the Cross. It also continues to lift him into the life of Christ, so that he may feed on Him and receive of His Spirit into the heart, and calls forth his glad thanksgiving. It continues to bind him in the fellowship of the Church, and to hold him in the corporate Body of Christ. But as a sacrifice, is it not meaningless? He has entered into the sacrifice of the Cross once, and it has become for him a sacrifice that cannot be repeated. Nevertheless, there is a sense in which that which cannot be repeated may yet be repeated. In the story of the washing of the disciples' feet, Jesus said to Peter: 'If I wash thee not, thou hast no part with me.' Peter answered: 'Lord, not my feet only, but also my hands and my head.' Jesus replied: 'He that is bathed needeth not save to wash his feet, but is clean every whit.'[1] The metaphor is not perfect, yet the meaning is clear. The washing of the feet symbolizes the renewed cleansing of the whole body. He who is born anew in Christ is reborn but once; nevertheless he needs to be continually reborn in Him. The initial experience is unrepeatable; yet in a sense it has to be repeated. The Cross of Christ continues to have meaning and also power for him. The sacrament of the Lord's Supper reminds him of the dying of his

[1] Jn. xiii. 8 ff.

Lord that the work of the Cross may be renewed in him. In the sacred experience of this sacrament the Cross becomes anew his sacrifice unto God, that the power of God may be renewed in his heart. His covenant with God, the covenant which first becomes real for him in the moment of his first dying with Christ, is renewed as he presents himself anew unto God in Christ. Instead of repeating the crucifixion of Christ for his own judgement by eating unworthily, he repeats the sacrifice of Christ and of himself in Christ.[1]

Here, as everywhere, the symbol is worthless without that which is symbolized. Biblical religion everywhere makes that which is symbolized more important than the symbol, and finds peril in a symbol which becomes an end in itself. Yet it does not despise symbols when they are charged with meaning. The Lord's Supper is a symbol which represents the constant renewal of our surrender to Christ and the renewal of His work in us— the washing of the feet of those who are bathed—which revalidates for us His sacrifice on our behalf by calling forth anew from us the spirit He must ask. If it represents this it has meaning when it marks the experience of that renewal, but is futile and worse if it but replaces the experience.

Here we must leave the large theme which has engaged our attention. Only a few of its aspects have been dealt with, and these have been but lightly touched. The threads of unity which run through both Testaments are many, and we have traced but a few of these, noting some of the correspondences between the Old and New Testaments which bind them securely together, and above all noting the fundamental conception of the nature of religion which belongs to the whole Bible. Everywhere it is man's response to the achieved work of God, his yielding to the constraint of grace, his fellowship with God and obedience to Him, his reflection of the Spirit of God in every aspect of his life, and the lifting of his life into the purpose of God. It does not despise symbols, though many of the symbols of the Old Testament are transcended in the New. It demands, however, that the

[1] Cf. *The Rediscovery of the Old Testament*, 1946, p. 170.

symbols shall be invested with reality by being made the vehicles of the spirit. If Christ is the fulfilment of the hope of the Old Testament, He is also the satisfaction of the need of every man. It is in union with Him that man, who was made in the image of God, can reflect that image, for in union with Him he is lifted into the life of God, without Whose fellowship he cannot walk in God's way.

ADDITIONAL NOTE

While the present work has been in the Press, the work of P. Ch. Marcel, *The Biblical Doctrine of Infant Baptism* (E. Tr. by P. E. Hughes), 1953, has been published. It was impossible to take account of its arguments in the text or footnotes, and it is impossible here to traverse them at length. Marcel agrees with the present writer that the theological significance of baptism in the light of the teaching of both Testaments is of more importance than the argument from the absence of mention of infant baptism in the New Testament, or the reading of infant baptism into New Testament texts (cf. Marcel, pp. 15 f., 187 and pp. 161 f. n. in the present work). Like so many writers he makes the appeal to circumcision in justification of infant baptism, and cites Calvin with approval for the view that the fact that circumcision was not applied to females is of no significance, since they are not by nature fitted for it (p. 158). This ignores the fact that circumcision of both sexes has been practised among some peoples. Of greater importance is Marcel's admission (p. 19): 'At the present moment the cause of pedobaptism is *theologically* lost, and its advocates, deprived of *theological* arguments, attempt to find a precarious refuge in facts and notions which cannot afford the least bit of genuine justification, such as the testimony of history, the tradition of the ancient Church or Reformed tradition, inscriptions, mosaics, sculptures, pieces of money, citations from the fathers, and so on—what have they not tried to seize upon!' Here, again, he is in agreement with the present writer as against many of the advocates of paedobaptism dealt with in the present work. Marcel's own attempt to provide a theological justification of infant baptism is, however, no more successful, since in relation to the baptism of adults he draws on the New Testament and declares it to be the sign and seal of regeneration, and holds that it can only be administered on evidence of repentance and faith (pp. 144, 183), whereas in relation to the baptism of infants he turns to the Old Testament and to infant circumcision and declares that baptism testifies to their salvation by sealing and confirming the covenant of God upon them (p. 201). While he rightly declares in one place: 'A sacrament received without faith confers nothing more than the Word heard without faith' (p. 49), he is reduced to the necessity of denying this elsewhere in the case of infants who are baptized, and to except them from the theological principles on which he bases his study. He says: 'Even as the Word is efficacious only for him who receives it with faith, similarly the sacraments, *as far as they concern adults*, are only efficacious as means of grace for those who receive them with faith' (p. 44). There is a fundamental difference between a sacrament which is efficacious only when received in faith and one which is efficacious when it is not received in faith, and it is doubtful if Marcel can have convinced himself when he protested that the basis of baptism is the same in the two cases. The theological significance of the two baptisms cannot be the same, when they are so differently conditioned.

As to the alleged efficacy of infant baptism, Marcel makes a most damaging admission which can only embarrass the cause he seeks to serve. For he says (p. 169), in dealing with the time of the efficacy of baptism, that the sacraments become effective when one receives them with faith, but that 'this reception by faith of the sacrament of baptism is not bound to a precise moment dependent on external circumstances', but that 'it depends on the state of soul of the believer, for whom his baptism bears fruit *on each occasion on which he refers back to it with faith*', but confesses on the same page that 'in the Reformed Church the great majority of Christians never refer back to their baptism'. The time of the efficacy for this great majority is thus defined as never, and to the present writer it seems futile to seek a theological justification of a rite that is admitted to be hollow and inefficacious in the majority of cases.

It will be noted that in the passage quoted above from p. 44 Marcel refers to 'the sacraments, as far as they concern adults'. This would seem to imply that he would advocate the administering of both sacraments to infants, and this would follow from his argument elsewhere. For he says (p. 123) that children are members of the visible

Church, and (p. 190) that 'Scripture assigns to the children of believers the enjoyment of the same privileges as are experienced by those who are of an age to confess their faith'. If his argument is valid for baptism it is valid also for the Lord's Supper. It remains to be seen how many paedobaptists will endorse his arguments and will seek to restore infant communion to Western Churches. Throughout, Marcel is concerned only with the children of believers, as in the passage just cited, and he offers no support whatever to the practice of indiscriminate baptism which is still so widely practised.

INDEX

(a) SUBJECTS

(b) AUTHORS